THE ECONOMIC CRISIS AND
AMERICAN SOCIETY

MANUEL CASTELLS

The Economic Crisis and American Society

PRINCETON UNIVERSITY PRESS

To Virginia Rogers
    and to my friends in
    Madison, without whose work and help
    this book would not exist.

CONTENTS

■■

LIST OF TABLES

LIST OF FIGURES

ACKNOWLEDGMENTS

■■■

The analyses presented here have been made possible only because a number of American friends guided me to the right sources, provided me with crucial information, stimulated me with their discussions, and, finally, commented extensively on the first draft of this manuscript, leading toward a substantial rectification of the original argument of the book.

I am particularly grateful to Maurice Zeitlin, Erik Wright, James Cockcroft, Michael Reich, Vicente Navarro, David Harvey, Michael Aiken, Robert Alford, Bill Tabb, Jim O'Connor, Glenn Yago, Janice Perlman, Nancy DiTomaso, Stephen Cohen, John Mollenkopf, Roger Friedland, Frances Piven, Bob Cohen, Marvin Surkin, Ron Lawson, Allan Wolfe, Lourdes Beneria, Mike Miller, Frank Riesman, Martin Rein, John Friedman, Adam Przeworski, Joan Przeworski, Ira Katznelson, Gerald Marwell, Bill Sewell, Howard Erlanger, Bill Friedland, Pamela Roby, Peter Marcuse, and Bill Domhoff, among many others.

In Paris I had very thorough and fruitful criticism from Christian Sautter, Jacques Attali, Jean-Pierre Delilez, Philippe Guillemard, Bruno Theret, and Nicos Poulantzas.

Thanks to all these contributions, some of my overstatements have been toned down and misinterpretations straightened out.

I have to acknowledge also the very important material and intellectual help received from the Department of Sociology at the University of Wisconsin at Madison, where the book was conceived and written in 1975 and 1977. Faculty, staff, and students were very supportive, friendly, and stimulating, creating the intellectual and personal milieu that was necessary to carry on this research.

Additional help came from the Department of Sociology of the University of California at Santa Cruz where I taught in the fall of 1975, as well as from other institutions who invited me for shorter periods: MIT, the Graduate Center at CUNY, the University of Chicago (Political Science Department), The Johns Hopkins University, Boston University, and Columbia University. Visits and discussions with "experts" and militants during my trips to San Francisco, Los Angeles, Boston, New York, Baltimore, Washington, D.C., and Chicago, were certainly decisive in my understanding of the United States. Finally, as the reader will be able to verify, the analyses presented here rely heavily on research carried on during the 1970s by the different groups of the Union of Radical Political Economists.

Therefore, although I assume the entire responsibility for the book, I want to emphasize the collective character of the production of the analysis presented in the following pages.

THE ECONOMIC CRISIS AND
AMERICAN SOCIETY

INTRODUCTION

■■■

T HE SHADOW OF the crisis spreads over the world. Beyond the effects of temporary variations of the business cycle, the daily life of people in most countries is being shaped by the economic crisis of the 1970s and its lasting effects on the world capitalist system.

Closed factories, empty offices, millions of unemployed, days of hunger, declining cities, crowded hospitals, ailing administrations, explosions of violence, ideologies of austerity, fatuous discourses, popular revolts, new political strategies, old political conflicts, hopes, fears, promises, threats, manipulation, mobilization, repression, fearful stock markets, militant labor unions, disturbed computers, nervous policemen, stunned economists, subtle politicians, rampaging prophets, suffering people—so many images that we have been told were gone forever, gone with the wind of post-industrial capitalism. And now they are back again, brought by the wind of capitalist crises.

These images raise some basic questions—about work and pleasure, about jobs and cities, about repression and beliefs, about women and men, about history, about politics. Suddenly, the cultural patterns that have been grounded on continued economic growth are shaken. Our jobs can be lost, our house mortgages foreclosed, our children out of school, our institutions unstable, our peace bombed. We realize that life is not an endless cute commercial advertisement. Thirty years of sustained economic growth have been called into question in a few months. To be sure, economic recovery is announced at regular intervals and, from time to time, business activity does pick up. It also goes down. There were still 16 million unemployed people in the OECD countries at the end of 1977. And several important capitalist countries (Britain, France, Italy, Spain) still had double-digit inflation. The United States still had 8 million unemployed and was under continuous threat of inflationary spurts.

The problem is not only the economy. Since the end of 1973, a number of economic, political, and ideological factors, which had previously been isolated, came together to form a whole, which led to a potential calling into question of the economic and social organization of advanced capitalism. The inflationary process that had followed a continuous upswing since the 1940s reached a peak that deeply affected the financial markets and excessively raised the interest rates. The international monetary system became increasingly unstable as a consequence of the changing patterns of world capital flows and international trade, leading to the crisis of the dollar. Profits were being squeezed because of an overheated economy, tightened financial markets, and militant labor demands. Public expenditures and state involvement in the economy have reached a breaking point for a market economy. Under these conditions, the sudden increase in the oil prices by the OPEC countries, the subsequent speculative maneuvers by the oil companies, and the general rise in the price of energy constituted accelerating factors that triggered the crisis. Worldwide inflation led to worldwide recession, mostly because of corporate and state policies purposely designed to discipline labor, stabilize financial markets, and reorganize public services. The crisis thus became visible. Because of the widespread impact of the oil-price increase the capitalist governments decided this was a good moment to announce that the crisis had been provoked by "the Arab sheiks." But, in fact, the crisis had been latent for a long time (at least since 1967). The purpose of this initiative was to provide a cause absolutely external to the logic of capitalism—a historical accident was responsible for the crisis. By this device the capitalist governments could try to make people accept austerity policies without blaming the system for their hard times.

Nevertheless, the crisis was deeper than anybody could imagine. If the business cycle needed a recession to restore the rate of profit, it soon became very clear that inflation and stagnation were linked in such a way that correcting one process triggered the other. Economic policies were increasingly ineffectual since the fine tuning, between stimulating the economy and controlling inflation, became more and more impossible. This "stop-and-go" process seems to have become a permanent feature of the leading capitalist economies. The consequences of such a trend are ever more disruptive.

Furthermore, for the first time since the Great Depression,

business cycles became synchronized all over the world. In fact, this is a sign of the formation of a world economy. In periods of expansion, the cycles between different countries are complementary, as capital shifts its investments according to the variations in investment opportunities. But when there is a crisis, the interpenetration of production and distribution of commodities and the circulation of capital flows determine a general pattern of recession. Consequently, it is much more difficult to restart the economy because it requires a simultaneous, or at least complementary, upswing in several major countries. This is extremely unlikely to happen because the evolution of each national economy will depend upon social and political processes largely specific to each society. Therefore, the crisis is deepened by its world dimension and by the contradiction of interests between the international economy and national states, which remain the primary policymakers.

Still worse for the stability of advanced capitalism, the crisis is not only economic but also *political and ideological*. And it is the linkage among these three dimensions that characterizes it as a structural crisis in the historical expansion of the capitalist mode of production.

Actually, we are not living in the midst of social disruption caused by the economic crisis. On the contrary, *we are living in an economic crisis caused by a general process of social disruption in most advanced capitalist societies, which has called into question the structure of social relationships underlying the pattern of capital accumulation.* The crisis came because, on the one hand, there was a breakdown of the prevailing social order that triggered the structural tendencies toward a falling rate of profit; on the other hand, there were influences from some contingent precipitating factors (such as the increase in the price of oil and raw materials brought about by changes in international social relationships of dominance).

During the decade 1967-1977, most of the advanced capitalist societies went through a period of turmoil, social innovation, and political conflict. In the United States the social movements of the 1960s profoundly affected the consciences of millions of Americans. Civil rights movements, black protest, student revolts, antiwar activities, community and social welfare demands, public workers' struggles, increased union organizing, wildcat strikes, women's liberation—all of these movements undermined the social hegemony of the corporate elite, notwithstanding the political innocence of the participants (which prevented them from becoming a revolutionary challenge in the short term).

In different forms all the major capitalist societies* experienced very important social movements that eventually produced decisive changes in their model of economic growth and political systems. The May 1968 movement in France was the beginning of a process of social struggle that led to the crisis of Gaullism and the resurgence of the Left. In Italy, the student revolt of 1968 and, particularly, the *autunno caldo* in the factories in 1969 gave rise to a powerful multidimensional social movement, to the crisis of hegemony of the Italian bourgeoisie, and to the early steps of the historical compromise with the Communists. In Britain, the increasing radicalization of the trade unions brought the Labour party into the government and formed within it a solid left wing that developed a mass-based socialist strategy in the old bastion of conservative capitalism. Fascism was wiped out in Europe after the collapse of the dictatorships in Portugal, Greece, and Spain, as a result of the combined pressure of social struggles and the internal crises of state apparatuses.

Even more, these social upheavals came at a time when the world system was being challenged by the greatest defeat of imperialism in history: the final stages of the Indochina War, leading to the liberation of Vietnam, Laos, and Cambodia.

These domestic and international social conflicts seriously hurt the political domination of the ruling classes in Western capitalism. The stability of the institutions themselves was threatened, and there followed dramatic changes of political personnel and sudden crises of legitimacy. Watergate was not an "accident." It was, as we try to show, the consequence of political contradictions within the ruling class in the aftermath of the social movements of the 1960s, of the weakening of U.S. imperialist hegemony, and of the first symptoms of the economic crisis. In any case, there were too many similar events in the

* As well as some socialist countries, *significantly enough*. Remember the Chinese Cultural Revolution (1966), the Czechoslovakian Spring Revolution (1968), the Polish popular revolts (1971).

same period to think of them all as "accidents": the fall of De Gaulle, and the increasing instability of the French ruling class; the forced dismissal of Kakuei Tanaka after a "scandal"; the forced dismissal of Willy Brandt after another "scandal"; the world "scandal" of Lockheed briberies, with its serious impact, particularly on Holland; the increasing internal controversy of Italian Christian Democrats; the unexpected and sudden retirement of Harold Wilson, after he was supposedly involved indirectly in a "scandal"; and so on.

At the same time, a major ideological crisis was progressively undermining the traditional capitalist values of the work ethic, family life, commodity production, and consumption. Ecological consciousness questioned the naive belief in the benefits of scientific progress in spite of backward and oppressive social relationships. The trends toward a new hedonism, communal life, individual pleasure, self-integrity, and self-management challenged the prevailing patterns of production, consumption, and authority. Of course, most of these revolts were powerless and utopian self-affirmations rather than alternative political blueprints. But this is, in fact, the historical experience for all fundamental processes of social transformation. Social movements lay the groundwork for a new society in their practice before they are able to be translated into effective political strategies adequate to overcome the resistance to historical change represented by the dominant interests vested in the economic and political institutions. If women do not do housework any more (at least no more than their husbands), this fact does not change capitalist social relationships of production, but it does fundamentally shake the family's authority, the basic channel of social integration into the dominant values. If young workers stay in the sun outside the factory three days a week, this does not put into practice a Marxist-Leninist principle, but it does break down the primary structure required for capital to exploit labor, namely, labor considering itself as labor. If "Black is beautiful," if "La Raza Unida jamás será vencida," the neutron bomb can still be deployed, but the silent majority of American minorities will start moving toward principles of equality that decisively undermine the segmentation of the labor market and the split within the working class, thereby shaking the domination of the military-industrial complex. If people mobilize for solar energy and attack nuclear power, they will not destroy the energy-producing monopoly corporations (which are still likely to control whatever source of energy is developed), but they are protecting humankind; they are supporting a form of energy allowing decentralized management (in opposition to the necessarily centralized and authoritarian management of nuclear power), and they are deciding what to do with knowledge themselves. This kind of activity is objectively subversive for a system based on the appropriation of science by corporate capital.

It is true that all of these trends will not by themselves lead to a general collapse of the system because as long as there is no *political challenge and alternative* corresponding to the ideals and contradictions expressed by the social movements, the prevailing forces will be able to survive, by cooptation, repression, and manipulation. Nevertheless, if these interrelated factors do not lead to a general breakdown of the system, they do lead to a crisis: the crisis of world capitalism in the 1970s.

It is in this sense that we can speak of a structural crisis of the capitalist system. This is not to say that capitalism is going to crumble by itself at a given historical moment. Such a catastrophic vision of an economic crisis has more to do with messianic beliefs than with social research. Capitalism has developed very powerful mechanisms of social control and economic regulation that prevent major transformations of the system *as long as the political factors remain unmodified*. Nevertheless, the contradictions of the system at different levels could require a fundamental transformation of the functioning of the system, either within the framework of capitalism or outside its prevailing logic, depending upon the balance between social classes and political forces. But, in either case, *what defines a situation of structural crisis is that it becomes impossible to expand or reproduce the system without a transformation or reorganization of the basic characteristics of production, distribution, and management, and their expression in terms of social organization*. This is the main hypothesis of our analysis and the social purpose of this book: to view the world capitalist crisis of the 1970s as the threshold of a new world and to explore what possibilities exist. Just as we can see the Great Depression of the thirties as a period of transition to new historical forms of capitalism as well as the root of the development of postcapitalist modes of production in a large part of the world, so we can look at the crisis of the seventies and ask ourselves *what are the underlying causes and what are the foreseeable consequences of the economic crisis on the structure and evolution of advanced capitalism.*

Naturally, given the acuteness of the crisis, numerous attempts to answer these questions have already been made, with the goal of understanding the phenomenon in order to prepare "solutions" to it. But the "solutions" actually command interpretations that are mainly rationalizations of different political stands. Most of these interpretations proceed by extrapolation of tendencies from the observations of a few facts taken in isolation. Now, even if the majority of the cited trends are true, it remains to be proven that they are the cause, and not the effect of the crisis. Because it is so difficult to grasp the complexity of a worldwide network of systemic interactions, one can understand the success of simple ideological arguments aimed at deducing all observed effects from a fundamental cause as the primary source of all contradictions. It is in this manner that the previously cited interpretation of the crisis as an "energy crisis" proceeds. Inflation would be due to the sudden increase in the price of oil by OPEC countries, and recession is the product of the corresponding decline in the profit rate and the restriction of demand due to controls on credit. In an even more mechanistic explanation, which is used for influencing public opinion, one is led to believe that there is a shortage of energy and raw materials. We are also led to believe that "petrodollars" are responsible for upsetting the international monetary system, that "Arab sheiks" will soon buy up everything, with a serious risk to us of becoming colonized.

The object of this book is not to polemicize against the ideologies of the crisis, however, but to advance a rigorous treatment of its structural causes. We shall therefore not stop to analyze such arguments, but for the sake of clarity, let us recall the following facts.

There is no shortage of energy in general or of oil in particular (see Table 1). There is a potential shortage in certain areas of the

TABLE 1. GROWTH OF OIL RESERVES AND OIL EXTRACTION BY SELECTED AREAS (1950 = 100)

	World		U.S.A.		U.S.S.R.		Middle East	
Year	Reserves	Extraction	Reserves	Extraction	Reserves	Extraction	Reserves	Extraction
1960	380	200	136	128	650	390	555	303
1965	475	286	140	141	680	643	648	482
1970	795	445	142	196	1250	933	1040	810
1972	860	495	151	196	1760	1040	1120	1050
1950[a]	11,004	525	3,521	271	614	38	4,679[a]	88

[a] Absolute value in millions of tons.
Source: U. N. Statistical Yearbook, various years.

world (United States and Western Europe), and there is a deterioration in relationships of power between countries producing oil and countries consuming oil. Other sources of energy could be widely developed. Coal, for example, was abandoned for reasons tied more to the interest of large companies than to productivity. Now liquid coal is being produced. Most important is the technological progress made in the development of nuclear power and the potential use of other energy sources, particularly solar energy.

The crisis of energy is not a crisis of supply. It is a question of *the price of energy*, in the wake of a sudden increase in the price of oil, which was the result of five circumstances. First, the relationship of international forces in the Middle East shifted to the advantage of the oil-producing countries. Second, the rise in prices was used for their own profit by the large oil companies, which benefited incredibly by the revaluation of their stock and by subsequent speculative maneuvers. Third, the price increase in oil only partially remedied a completely abnormal situation, even in capitalist terms, in which the price of an essential product was stably maintained during a period of world inflation by imperialist ties of power over the oil-producing countries. Fourth, the price increase imposed by the producing countries represented only a very small part of the price increase passed on to the consumer. The exact proportion varied for different countries, according to the profits of the company, the expenses of distribution, the taxes collected by the state, and the large speculative operations carried on by the oil trusts. Finally, in any case, the increased price of petroleum accounted for only a small part (about one-fifth) of the general price increases in 1973-1974, even when taking into account its multiplicative effects.

Thus, although the increase in oil prices was a very important factor in precipitating preexisting inflationary trends, it can by no means be considered the cause of the crisis.

There is no energy crisis. Is it then a question of a "crisis of civilization"? Indeed, certain social philosophers believe that the present convulsions are the consequences of a major change in the cultural values of Western societies. According to them, we may be passing from a "production society" to a "leisure society," with the value of work being brought into fundamental doubt. This interpretation represents a profoundly idealistic strain, which recognizes a real trend without being able to identify its structural historical sources. It is symptomatic rather than analytic. If there is a transformation of social practices, ideological currents, and social organization, it is not because of a sudden awareness of some collective anguish; it is a function of the present modifications in class relationships.

To some extent the cultural interpretations of the crisis are a renewed form of a type of idealistic social thought common in the nineteenth century, which analyzes historical processes in terms of "civilization." Such a perspective dissolves social relations into the "spirit of the age." In fact, a certain "Marxist" interpretation of the crisis is closer to the statements of a "crisis of civilization" than to class analysis, for when it is said that the crisis is "the crisis of capitalism," without giving any specific explanation, capitalism is equated with "civilization," and nothing is explained about the historically determined causes of the crisis. Indeed, for thirty years capitalism has not had a general crisis, and the present one does not manifest any historical ineluctability. One of the dangers we must watch out for in understanding the problem of the "crisis" is the return to a certain social naturalism which, clothed in Marxist language, refers to the immutable essence of capitalism and to the necessary nature of its crisis, which in one way or another is always the same. Now, if the capitalist mode of production develops in a contradictory manner through crisis, then the nature of these crises is a historical process that must be analyzed as such and recognized in its specificity. That is why it does not suffice to replace the Arabs with capitalism in order to find a "leftist" explanation of the historical moments in which we are living.

A truly social analysis of the present crisis must be undertaken. Is it an economic crisis? No! It is a crisis of the mode of production and, therefore, a crisis in class relationships defined first of all (but not only) by the process of production. We must avoid in our work the final theoretical trap that is the most subtle and dangerous one—*economicism*. A structural economic crisis is not explained by the economy but by society, because the economy is not a "mechanism" but a social process continuously shaped and recast by the changing relationships of humankind to the productive forces and by the class struggle defining humankind in a historically specific manner. This theoretical hypothesis and this social purpose explain the characteristics and the organization of the analysis undertaken in this book.

To understand the structural crisis of a worldwide system as it is in advanced capitalism, we must start by understanding the development of this crisis in the system's core, namely, the United States. But the United States is not only the center of the process of world capital accumulation; it is also a *society*, historically formed and continuously reshaped by class struggles, ideological patterns, and political conflicts even though the unique way these are manifested in American society tends to obscure their true nature. Therefore, after studying the U.S. economy, we have to consider the roots of the crisis in the American class structure as well as its effects on the different dimensions of such class structure. On the basis of our knowledge of the impact of a socially produced economic crisis in an economically determined society, we will be able to understand the interests and positions of different classes, fractions, and social groups.

The mediation of this pattern of contradictory interests by the political process will provide an explanation of the policies dealing with the crisis, of their different chances of success, and of the consequences of their development for the capitalist model of accumulation and social organization.

To understand the new world in process of formation, we have to know what the process of development of the economic crisis in the United States was, what the underlying social conditions of this process were, what the impact of the crisis on the American class structure is, how it is expressed in the political process, nationally and internationally, and what the policies are that could come out of such a process to reshape the capitalist system.

Before proceeding with the various steps of this analysis, we must examine the theoretical tools our intellectual adventure demands, fashioned from already existing research into the theory of economic crises as well as from a specific approach to the problem. We need a new theory to understand a new world.

1

■■

Toward a Social Theory of Economic
Crises in Advanced Capitalism

THE CRISIS shaking the capitalist world in the 1970s is multi-dimensional, political and ideological as well as economic. Consequently, the only useful explanatory framework is one able to integrate these different levels of social reality within the perspective of a contradictory historical development. The Marxist tradition is, to our knowledge, the only one that even attempts to put together the movement of capital and the process of social change as jointly determined by class struggles over production, consumption, power, and cultural values. Therefore, we will rely on this tradition to construct a tentative theoretical scheme capable of providing us with an understanding of current historical trends. But our reliance on it will not be unqualified: we reject any dogmatic position that tries to preserve the whole theory in its original form in spite of later historical experience. Accordingly, we will suggest modifications of the conceptual apparatus when required, and we will consider the Marxist tradition as a whole and not just as a particular fragment of *Capital* by Marx. We must embrace social reality in its entirety and treat the dynamics of class struggle in all its ramifications, which obviously include the contradictions of capital accumulation, but without reducing society to the narrowest expression of its dominant pole.

The Marxist theory of economic crises is usually associated with the Marxian theory of the *tendency of the falling rate of profit*. In fact, as we shall see, this theory summarizes an overall historical trend. But, as it has been presented in its simplest form, in rather plain economistic terms and within a context of religious belief in the inevitability of a general and sudden breakdown of capitalism, this tradition had led both to the repetition of unsustainable dogmatic statements and to the dismissal of the explanatory value of the Marxist theory of crises. Both positions leave us without a valuable tool to understand and transform our world, since most critics are unable to propose any alternative beyond ad hoc interpretations of specific situations. While this pragmatism certainly represents a safe way of avoiding intellectual pitfalls, it has a negative effect on the value of theory as a tool of social change because it means that we are only able to explain social events after they have happened instead of being able to predict tendencies and act on them in order to *change the trend*.

That is why we would rather risk exposing ourselves to criticism by trying to use and develop the Marxist theory of crises than use its obvious weaknesses as a pretext to withdraw from any attempt at explanation. Since the production of knowledge is a collective process, our proposition will be just one element in it, finding its fruitfulness through the necessary rectification that will emerge from other theoretical efforts as well as from future historical experience.

We will start with a summary of the Marxian theory of crisis both because the theory of the falling rate of profit has a strong tradition and because it contains some structural elements crucial to understanding capitalist crises. We will then proceed to a brief examination of the debate surrounding this theory in the recent literature. We will examine both its theoretical coherence and its empirical adequacy. Next we will discuss the meaning of the few empirical tests that have been made on the theory and the hypothetical interpretations that can be supported by these data. Turning then to a revision of the theoretical framework, we will propose an alternative scheme, which, while relying on the general Marxist theory and incorporating some elements of the law of the falling rate of profit, will try to provide additional theoretical tools to explain both the new social trends appearing in advanced capitalism and the forces that have led to the current structural crisis.

1. THE THEORY OF THE FALLING RATE OF PROFIT AND ITS CRITICS

The theory of the falling rate of profit as originally proposed by Marx in Volume III of *Capital*[1] is presented in the form of an apparent paradox: the more capitalism develops, the more the average rate of profit for capital declines. Falling profit rates result in a surplus of capital because the increasing mass of capital accumulated by the growing extraction of surplus value finds fewer and fewer possibilities for investment with an adequate return. There follows a decline in productive investment, which leads to a decline in employment and to a concomitant reduction of wages paid by capital. As wages decline, demand shrinks in a parallel way, provoking a crisis in the selling of the already stocked commodities. Thus, a crisis of overproduction occurs because even the restricted productive capacity cannot be absorbed by the existing solvent demand since demand in turn has been reduced by falling investments. The inability to realize its commodities induces capital to halt production, increasing unemployment and depressing markets. Because capitalism is organized on a world scale the crisis spreads throughout many nations in a highly interconnected spiraling process. Since capitalist production is interested in creating use value only as a support for exchange value, the economy can only be restarted when mass unemployment allows very low wages, when the bankruptcy of many firms has devaluated fixed capital, creating demand for new means of production, and when the state intervenes or there is a sudden event (such as a war) that increases substantially the outlets for profitable capital investment.

This mechanism of crisis production is widely accepted by most non-Marxist economic theorists, particularly Keynesians. What is specific to Marxian thought is the relationship between the falling rate of profit and the dynamics of capitalist accumulation. Why *must* the average rate of profit decrease in the long term? Because, Marx says, an increasing organic composition of capital is the result of the process of capital accumulation. The organic composition of capital is the relationship between the *value* (the amount of social labor) used in the production of means of production, raw materials, and other work objects (*constant capital*) and the *value* used in the reproduction of the labor power put into work in the process of production (*variable capital*). Marx often refers to the organic composition as the relationship of "dead labor" (machines, buildings, raw materials, etc.) to "living labor" (workers). But it is important to keep in mind that this relationship is a relationship of *values* and should be entirely differentiated from the *technical composition of capital*, which is the relationship between the material means of production and the mass of workers organized in the process of capital production or, more precisely, the relationship between fixed capital and labor.

The tendency of the organic composition to rise with the process of capital accumulation leads to a tendency for the rate of profit to fall because "living labor," *the only source of value*, tends to be replaced by "dead labor," which is able to transmit into the commodities only the same amount of value already embodied in the means of production. Therefore, in spite of an increasing mass of surplus value produced by capitalism, the relationship between the value invested and the surplus value will be less and less favorable to the latter. Since the rate of profit depends ultimately on the rate of surplus value, profit rates will tend to fall in the long run. Using the traditional Marxian presentation of the relationship between the different elements of the process of production of surplus value and profit, we have:[2]

$$Q = \frac{c}{v} \qquad e = \frac{s}{v} \qquad p' = \frac{s}{c + v}$$

where Q: organic composition of capital
  c: constant capital
  v: variable capital
  s: surplus value
  e: rate of surplus value
  p': rate of profit

If we divide both terms by v,

$$p' = \frac{s/v}{\dfrac{c}{v} + \dfrac{v}{v}} = \frac{e}{\dfrac{c}{v} + 1}$$

Therefore, p' is a direct function of e and an inverse function of c/v. So, *for a given e*, p' will vary according to the evolution of c/v: the greater Q is, the more p' decreases.

But why does the organic composition of capital increase with the development of the capitalist mode of production? It is not a question here of a natural mechanism but of a historical process, which as Marx unveils it is marked by the development of class struggle and is therefore not inexorable. It is a result of the combined effect of three phenomena:

1. *Intercapitalist competition* leads each capitalist to try to surpass his rivals by introducing more technologically advanced means of production that allow him to reduce production costs and raise profits. Nevertheless, while replacing "living labor" with "dead labor" increases the profit for individual capitalists, it reduces the total rate of surplus value appropriated at the global level. Moreover, the competition leads little by little to the concentration and formation of monopolies. Even then, however, competition is not suppressed. It simply changes scale and becomes intermonopolistic competition on a world scale. Economic political decisions made by large firms are primary factors in their strategy to dominate the markets because in order to develop they must invest in large administrative apparatuses and in other operations that are not productive. Monopoly corporations push toward a fast growth of investments in constant capital, and owing to their interrelations and uninterrupted penetration into all sectors of the economy, they are able to dissolve the outmoded sectors with a low organic composition in order to replace them with units of a higher organic composition.

2. *The development of productive forces* demands direct as well as indirect investments that are more and more costly. Because this development accelerates the process of obsolescence of fixed capital, the rate of turnover of constant capital also accelerates. Then, as a consequence, its relative importance in relation to variable capital increases by the same amount over the long run.

3. The fundamental element of this tendency toward the rise in the organic composition of capital is nevertheless the predisposition of the capitalist to save the greatest amount of variable capital and to replace it progressively with constant capital. And this is due essentially to the *development of the labor movement*, to the emphasis on class struggle, to the deterioration of capital's power vis-à-vis labor.

Although this third structural cause is not explicitly laid out in Volume III of *Capital*, it is a clear consequence of the whole analysis developed by Marx in Volume I. This is a crucial point, and we will return to it in the final presentation of our general framework.

Now, at the same time that Marx presented the law of the tendency of the rate of profit to fall as a consequence of the secular trend toward a rising of organic composition of capital, he also referred to the existence of *countertendencies* that would stop or even reverse the structural tendency. These tendencies are: the increasing intensity of exploitation; the depression of wages below the value of labor power; the cheapening of elements of constant capital; relative overpopulation; foreign trade; the increase of stock capital. *No specific prediction about the domination of the tendency or of the countertendencies over time is included as an essential part of the theory*. Why, then, is the falling rate of profit called the tendency and the opposite forces the countertendencies? The terminology is certainly not arbitrary. The reason stems from the theoretical hierarchy of the elements of the explanation and *not* the historical sequence. This will become clearer at the end of our analysis.

To summarize, the Marxian theory of the economic crisis in the process of capital accumulation caused by the falling rate of profit can be presented as follows:

1. Capitalist accumulation leads to an increasing organic composition of capital (namely, replacement of "living labor" by "dead labor" in the process of production). This happens as a consequence of intercapitalist competition, the development of productive forces, and workers' resistance to exploitation.

2. The increasing organic composition of capital necessarily produces a falling rate of profit for a given rate of surplus value.

3. Falling rates of profit lead to declining investment, provoking overaccumulation of capital, overproduction of commodities, and massive restriction of demand.

4. The tendency of the organic composition of capital to rise in the process of accumulation can be halted by counteracting influences.

5. The tendency of the rate of profit to fall can be reversed, in spite of the increasing organic composition, if the rate of exploitation rises faster than the organic composition.

This formulation of the theory is not a made-up version of it but is, we believe, consistent with the original Marxian writings. We do not want to enter into a Marxological discussion here, particularly because, as we shall see, a reorganization of the theory is required in order to be able to understand the crises in advanced capitalism. The point of presenting the argument in this way is to emphasize that most of the criticism addressed to the theory of the falling rate of profit refers, in fact, to the rather simplistic and mechanistic version circulated during the thirties by some "theoreticians" of the Third International. These formulations presented both tendencies (the rise in the organic composition and the fall in the rate of profit) as necessary and almost natural trends intrinsic to capitalist accumulation. The counteracting influences, for these messianic believers, did not more than delay the process that would necessarily lead to a catastrophic breakdown of the capitalist economy. The obvious practical lesson that could be drawn from this view was that a revolutionary coup had to be prepared in order to duplicate the assault on the Winter Palace in the aftermath of a general collapse similar to that in Czarist Russia.

This political background explains most of the violence of the current controversy over the theory of the falling rate of profit. In fact, what many of the critics of the theory are actually attacking is intellectual dogmatism and political Stalinism. In this sense, the debate represents a healthy reaction against the remnants of a pseudo-Marxist interpretation of human history that sees it as subject to some kind of natural or technological determinism.

While we certainly agree with most of the intellectual and political meaning of the current reaction, it is important to consider the relevance of the theory itself purged of the connotations generated by its historical use.

Viewed in this way, the intellectual trends in France are certainly very different from those in the Anglo-Saxon world. In France the overwhelming majority of Marxist economists (from Paul Boccara[3] and the Communist group of *Economie et Politique*[4] to the pro-Fourth International group of *Critiques de l'économie politique*[5]) rely to a great degree on the theory of the falling rate of profit as presented previously, even though different groups have totally contradictory approaches to the relationship of this tendency to the class struggle and the role of the state.

In the United States and Great Britain there is, on the contrary, a very powerful trend toward dismissing this theory as inadequate for interpreting the crisis under the conditions of

monopoly capitalism. This has been brought about partly because of the major criticism developed by the most respected and
most respectable of American Marxist economists, Paul Baran
and Paul Sweezy. For Sweezy, "it is an absurdly untenable notion that the capital accumulation process necessarily implies a
runaway organic composition of capital increasing without as-
signable limit and much more rapidly than the rate of surplus
value."[6]

This is in opposition to authors like Mattick, Cogoy, and Yaffe
who have tried to present a more rigorous and up-to-date formulation of the theory.[7] For some of the critics, like Hodgson, author
of a well-known article on the subject,[8] the abandonment of this
theory is a precondition for rebuilding a revolutionary Marxist
thought. Even the well-balanced and multicausal explanation of
the capitalist crisis by Ernest Mandel in his major work, *Late
Capitalism*,[9] has been assailed on the grounds that he uses the
theory of the falling rate of profit as one of the main structural
trends underlying the current crisis.[10]

Instead of discussing in detail each author's criticism, let us
consider the main arguments that are repeatedly presented
against the theory in the different versions. At the theoretical
level, criticism focuses primarily on three points: the decisive
changes in the organic composition of capital produced by the
increasing productivity of labor as a consequence of technological progress; the crucial role played by the circulation of capital
in triggering the crisis; and the naturalistic assumptions of the
theory that underestimate the process of class struggle as the determinant element in the formation of the rate of profit. We will
briefly examine the debate along these three different, although
interrelated, lines.

The first argument concerns the key distinction between the
technical composition and the organic composition of capital.
There is general agreement on the covariation between capital
accumulation and the increase in technical composition, but the
evolution of the organic composition could be entirely different
because of the changing value of constant and variable capital. If
technological progress allows the production of cheaper means of
production and raw materials and *at the same time* increases the
productivity of labor, the same amount of capital spent in wages

could mobilize a higher proportion of value embodied in the form of "living labor," while the same amount of capital invested in "dead labor" would represent a smaller value if measured in labor time required to produce the means of production and raw materials. Therefore, the effect of increasing productivity does not raise the organic composition of capital but, on the contrary, decreases it. Indeed, with the increasing technical composition of capital, capital per worker, in terms of value, tends to fall, and the rate of profit tends to rise! Although this may be true in some situations in the process of technological innovation, the argument is much more dubious in its general formulation. Mandel has made a particularly strong point in his discussion of this basic argument of the theory's critics:

> According to Marx, technical progress is induced under the constraint of competition, by the constant pressure to economise on production costs, whose macro-economic outcome cannot be different from its micro-economic results. Cost economies without an increase in the organic composition of capital would presuppose either that living labour could profitably replace more and more complex machinery, or that Department I, [sector producing the means of production] could produce modern machinery which saves labour and value without an increase in the intrinsic value of such machine complexes, or a decrease in the value of new materials greater than the decrease in the value of wage-goods. This, however, would necessitate a more rapid growth in the productivity of labour in Department I than in the economy as a whole. Since new equipment must be constructed with pre-existent machinery and pre-given techniques, and *its own value* is thus determined by present labour productivity, and not by the future productivity it helps to increase; and since this equipment cannot be mass-produced in the initial stages, such an assumption is unrealistic over the long-run. Consequently, economies in unit costs will have a long-term tendency towards economies in labour-costs. . . . Economy in costs will thus always be accompanied in the long-run by a relative decrease in the share of wage costs in the value of the commodity, and hence also by the relative decline of the variable component of total capital.[11]

In any case, what cannot be assumed as a systematic tendency is the proposition symmetrically opposed to the theory of the falling rate of profit, namely, that increases in productivity *by definition* tend to depress the value of c and increase the value of v. The social investment required to boost labor productivity can demand such costly new means of production, not to mention the costs of the general conditions of production required (scientific research, for instance), that the value devoted by society as a whole (if not by monopoly capital) to the productivity increases is considerably higher. Because of the disagreement over the value effects of different technological innovations, it seems that *no general law can be assumed at an a priori level on the relationship between technology, productivity, and value distribution among the elements of capital investment.*

The second argument concerns the necessity of linking the processes of production and circulation in the explanation of capitalist crises. In a very well-structured article relying on Marx's *Grundrisse*, Michael Lebowitz argues that the time of circulation has a critical effect on the rate of profit because of the rigidity of capital when fixed in inventories. And time of circulation is dependent upon the consumption capacity of the society. Since there is an increasing gap between the productive power and the consuming power of the society, there is a rising circulation time that reflects this gap.

> Increasing circulation time produces involuntary inventory investment and reduced cash flows, i.e. increased capital tied up in circulation and reduced turnover of surplus value, both characteristics of the falling rate of profit. What follows are pressures on the money market and, ultimately, restrictions of production; it is the crisis of "overproduction," the forcible assertion of "the unity of the two phases that have become independent of each other." It is the increase in circulation time which leads to the crisis: "the crisis occurs not only because the commodity is unsalable, but because it is not salable within a particular period of time."[12]

In order for capital to overcome the barrier represented by the realization problem, an increasing proportion of capital has to be transferred from the productive process to the selling effort. Then, as more capital is required to put in motion the same productive labor, the rate of profit tends to fall. Even more, in order to expand consumption, capital stimulates the needs of the workers.

> The effect of the creation of new needs for workers is to raise the value of labour-power. And the effect where workers are organized in trade unions leads to demands for higher wages. Thus the contradiction of the capitalist mode of production emerges in a different form. On the one hand, each capital attempts to restrict wages to a minimum, and this restricts the ability of the workers to buy commodities. On the other hand, each capital attempts to generate new needs for workers, and this leads to increased wage demands. The result of the effort to widen the sphere of circulation is therefore a tendency to reduce the rate of surplus value. Accordingly, the result of effort to suppress the barrier of the falling rate of profit produces the tendency for a falling rate of profit.[13]

This argument has some similarity to Baran and Sweezy's explanation of crises,[14] which actually does not contradict the theory of the falling rate of profit except in its most mechanistic version. The theory of the falling rate of profit can account for the development of the crisis at the level of circulation because increasingly substituting "dead labor" for "living labor" results in a tendency toward relative surplus population that leads, at the same time, to the overaccumulation of capital (because of the falling rate of profit), to the overproduction of commodities (because of the necessary valorization of fixed capital without corresponding outlets), and to underconsumption by workers (because of the increasing proportion of idle labor). But *while the falling rate of profit explains the crisis of realization at the structural level, the increasing circulation time does not explain the fall of the rate of profit otherwise than in terms of the business cycle.* If it is true that the theory of the crisis must link the processes of production and circulation as two equally important factors in the formation of the rate of profit, only the contradictions appearing in the process of production seem to be structurally related to the characteristics of capitalist accumulation because profit, while realized in circulation, ultimately depends on the extraction of surplus value in the process of production. Nevertheless, what this argument underlines is the necessity of considering the value required to put labor into the process of creation of value in its totality. The socially necessary unproductive expenses are more and more an element of constant capital. This is a decisive hint that transforms the whole structure of capital and that we will discuss in detail in a further step of our analysis.

Last but not least is the argument objecting to the technological determinism of the theory on the grounds that *the rate of profit depends primarily on the rate of exploitation*, that is, on the characteristics of class struggle. There are two different versions of this position. One position, which is represented mainly by Radford Boddy and James Crotty in the United States,[15] relies primarily on the effects of the business cycle on the rate of profit. When an expansionary phase occurs, the labor market becomes tight, the union's bargaining power is increased, and capital has to transfer a share of the surplus value to wages so the rate of profit falls. Another version is expressed in the influential study on the profit squeeze in Britain by Andrew Glynn and Bob Sutcliffe,[16] who treat the decreasing share of profits in the national product as the effect of the class struggle in the overall political context. Two qualifications are required to evaluate the fruitfulness of this perspective. The first is, as Peter Bell has pointed out,[17] that it is important not to remain at the level of the relationships of distribution between social groups but to consider the overall social process of struggle between classes as historically defined. The second is that the effects of the class struggle on the rate of profit are not undetermined but structured by the specific logic of capitalist accumulation in each historical stage. In this sense, *we do not see the theory of class struggle and the theory of the falling rate of profit as contradictory but as complementary*. This is because the first explains the effects of society on capital and the second the effects of capital on society. By considering capital as a social relationship and not as a mass of money or material means of production, this theory then takes a decisive step in the analysis of crises as a historical process. But if it is formulated at a highly general level, it loses its explanatory capacity because it does not provide any understanding of the *differential effects* of the antagonisms between capital and labor in the functioning of capital. One of our main propositions is that a theory of economic crises must show the specific link between the process of exploitation (defining class struggle) and the process of accumulation of capital (defining the logic of the dominant pole in a capitalist society).

Actually, the main trend emerging from our brief overview of the current debate on the theory of the falling rate of profit is the broad indeterminacy of the arguments discussed at this level of generality. This is not an artifact produced by our manner of presenting the debate. Rather, it is an effect of the almost theological tenor of this battle over the classicial writings of Marx (and sometimes Ricardo). In fact, most of the arguments are an introduction to the so-called decisive criticism of the theory of the falling rate of profit: the empirical evidence. Mainstream economists and Marxist detractors of the theory converge toward consensus on a major point, namely, that historical experience contradicts the prediction—there is no secular trend toward a rising organic composition of capital, and the rate of profit has a purely cyclical variation. Obviously, the consequences drawn from this "factual evidence" are different. For the mainstream economists, the Marxist theory is a pure ideological device; for the neo-Marxists, it demonstrates an urgent need to revise the theory to make it able to explain the later stages of capitalism. While this is clearly a fruitful and indeed very Marxian position, we must first learn what the new trends are.

Let us examine, then, the controversy on the empirical value of the theory of the falling rate of profit in the light of historical experience.

2. DID THE ORGANIC COMPOSITION RISE?
   DID THE RATE OF PROFIT FALL?
   FROM THE CONTROVERSY TO THE HISTORY
   OF CAPITALIST ACCUMULATION

The main argument presented to dismiss the theory of the falling rate of profit is its inadequacy as an explanation of the actual trends of capitalist accumulation in the last fifty years. What is denied most specifically is the fact that capitalist development has led to an increase in the organic composition of capital. Consequently, the cyclical variations of the rate of profit are attributed to different factors, according to competing theories, largely external to the evolution of the composition of capital.

The obvious problem in trying to verify or reject the theory in regard to the empirical observations is the lack of fit between the existing statistical data and the Marxist concepts: the theory argues about *value* while the statistics show the evolution of *prices* or of physical measures or of both because the calculations necessary to translate different elements of capital into "average labor time" are difficult to do. In fact, this controversy is a good example of the vicious circle that exists in the social sciences. Owing to the social dominance of some specific theoretical approaches (neoclassical economics, for instance), the data are collected by institutions following a logic that can hardly be compatible with the assumptions of alternative theories. It is extremely hard for Marxists to bridge the gap between the two codes because of the amount of work involved in such an operation and the lack of institutional support for this type of research.

The failure to present convincing empirical evidence is used by the detractors of Marxist theory as proof of the ideological bias and erroneous character of such a theory. Therefore, data collection continues to be undertaken on the basis of existing categories. In this way research in economics reproduces the social conditions that demonstrate the superior ability of neoclassical or Keynesian theories to provide adequate information to support their hypotheses.

And when the failure of established theories to explain a given historical process (like the current crisis) requires the use of an alternative theoretical framework, the socially determined underdevelopment of Marxist oriented empirical research results in inevitable errors. Investigators are forced to try to understand the real world on the basis of information largely inadequate for answering the questions a Marxist theory must ask. This social background accounts for much of the confusion that exists over the empirical trends observed in the evolution of the organic composition of capital.

The data used to support the absence of any secular tendency for the organic composition to rise come mainly from the statistics on the capital-output ratios developed for the United States (1869-1955) by Simon Kuznets.[18] Actually, these figures show a fairly stable ratio for the whole net capital stock and a convergence between the different economic sectors. But Mandel cites a number of sources for the United States and Germany that support the hypothesis of the rise of the organic composition, particularly since 1945.[19] He argues that Kuznets's measures are statistically inadequate because they include surplus value (in addition to fixed capital and variable capital) in factor costs and exclude the value of circulating constant capital. In his review of Mandel's *Late Capitalism*, Rowthorn strongly criticizes Mandel's use of these studies and presents other data on the evolution of the capital-output ratio in advanced capitalist countries to show the stability or decrease of these ratios in the manufacturing sectors of eight out of eleven countries between 1950-1960 and 1960-1969. However, Rowthorn does not discuss the main empirical reference cited by Mandel in support of his argument about the increasing substitution of "dead labor" for "living labor" in the United States: the very important study by Anne Carter using input-output coefficients to measure the structural changes of the American economy between 1939 and 1961.[20] When closely examined, this research does show an increase in the capital-to-labor ratio in the great majority of economic sectors: "Direct labor saving is the most striking feature of structural change. Labor coefficients are very large compared to those for most other inputs specified; they decrease over time in virtually all sectors." Moreover, this labor-saving tendency of American capitalism does not come from its effect on productivity. Actually, "labor-to-output ratios vary only slightly with final demand composition, and the aggregate national productivity measures are not changed appreciably by changing final demand weights. However, changing final demand proportions *do tend to reduce changes over time in the aggregate capital-to-output ratio*." And, as Carter says, this finding confirms the tendency shown by Bert Hickman in his study.[21] Why, then, is there a strong capitalist predilection to save labor costs? Carter gives two reasons:

> The clear-cut tendency for direct labor costs to dominate structural change stems from two broad and related developments

in the American economy. The first: labor is a large element of cost. With rising living standards (and higher training requirements), its price tends to rise dramatically relative to the price of most capital goods, and, to a lesser extent, relative to intermediate inputs. Thus, efforts are concentrated on economizing labor, and labor coefficients fall in relation to other input coefficients. Decisions to substitute one intermediate input for another—to use techniques favoring a particular intermediate input—require the anticipation of developments in other sections of the economy. . . . Because such decisions are, in principle, interdependent, they are potentially more complex than decisions to economize direct labor.

In short, the labor-saving trend is the dominant factor in the patterns of change in the American economy between 1939 and 1961. It is, in fact, the response of capital to the historical development of workers' needs and demands.

If we now turn to the process of capitalist accumulation in France, some recent studies by INSEE (the government bureau of statistics) show a very interesting pattern, summarized in Figures 1 and 2.[22]

What we observe is that, in the postwar period, the fixed capital-to-labor ratio grew considerably. But this growth resulted in a decreasing rate of productivity of capital investment and a very rapidly increasing productivity of labor. On the other hand, the rate of profit grew until 1969 in spite of the decreasing productivity of capital, because of the counteracting effects of the increasing ratio of profit to wages and the increasing prices of commodities. Nevertheless, the rate of profit stabilized and later fell in 1969 when the ratio of profits to wages deteriorated in the aftermath of the social movements of 1968. Therefore, these studies clearly show that there was an increasing ratio of the stock of fixed capital to employed labor; that there was a decrease in the productivity of capital; that the decrease in the productivity of capital was not reflected in a falling rate of profit because of the increase in the rate of exploitation at the levels of production and consumption; and, finally, that the counteracting tendencies were very fragile because they depended directly on the relationship of power between capital and labor.

Again, despite the tendencies revealed by these different con-

Figure 1

Productivity of Labor and Capital and Capital-Labor Ratio,
France, 1950-1972

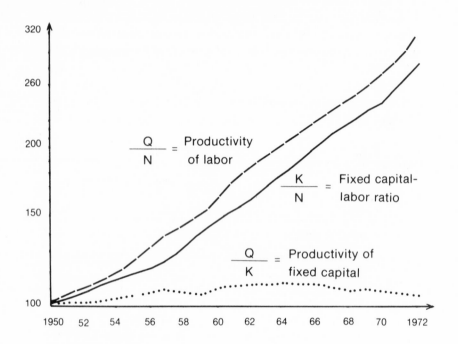

Q = Net output;
N = Employed labor:
K = Fixed capital stock

Source: Institut National de la Statistique et des Etudes Economiques, *Fresque historique du systeme productif français,* Paris, 1974.

flicting statistical observations, a major problem remains un-solved—the lack of fit between the data presented and the theoretical categories. Under these circumstances, most of the data provided are *illustrations* supporting the arguments devel-oped in the debate, tentative and loose indicators that do not allow any scientifically grounded conclusion on a matter of such great importance.

The discussion could be improved if we had at our disposal a series of empirical studies that would, on the explicit basis of the Marxist theory of the falling rate of profit, attempt to convert the

Figure 2

The Profitability of Capital and Its Components,
France, 1959-1972

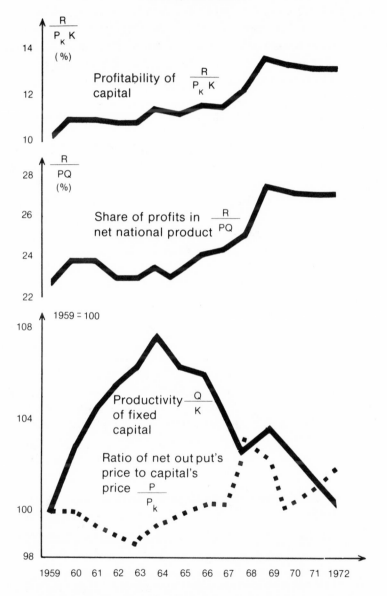

Source: Michel Bénard, "Rendement économique et productivité du capital
fixe de 1959 à 1972," *Economie et Statistique* 60, Oct. 1976, pp. 7-17.

existing statistical data into categories adequate to observe the relationship between the historical process of capital accumulation and the theoretical framework under debate. To our knowledge, only two such empirical studies exist, both on the United States. They are the pioneer research done by Joseph Gillman[23] and the unpublished Ph.D. dissertation of S. H. Mage.[24]

While the statistical methods used in both studies have been criticized, they remain, nevertheless, the only empirical hint we have so far about the adequacy of the theory to explain the historical evolution of a national economy. Since we are interested in comparing their findings on a common statistical basis, we have accepted Hodgson's recalculation of the data, done to make both studies equivalent on the basis of his own formula for the organic composition of capital,[25] while relying on our own examination of Gillman's and Mage's work. We have found it useful to present the data in the form elaborated by Hodgson because his formula tends to reduce the actual rate of growth of the organic composition of capital (as compared to Marx's original formula). Besides, as one of the strongest critics of the theory, he cannot be suspected of using biased empirical treatment to support the Marxian hypothesis. Thus, any argument in favor of the theory of a falling rate of profit is enhanced by the empirical base we have chosen. Let us examine closely both series because, as we will see, the picture they present is clearly different from that leading to the usually accepted conclusion that the theory should be rejected on empirical grounds.

Gillman studied the evolution of the organic composition of capital, the rate of surplus value, and the rate of profit in the U.S. manufacturing sector between 1880 and 1952. Figure 3 presents this evolution. (Remember, there is a difference in the form of calculating the data between Figure 3, reproduced from Gill-

TABLE 2. THE ORGANIC COMPOSITION OF CAPITAL IN THE U.S. ECONOMY, ACCORDING TO MAGE

Year	1900	1905	1910	1915	1920	1925	1930
q	3.67	3.16	3.13	3.51	3.65	3.95	4.47
Year	1935	1940	1945	1950	1955	1960	
q	4.92	4.09	2.64	3.45	3.64	4.20	

Source: S. H . Mage, "The Law of the Falling Tendency of the Rate of Profit," Ph.D. diss., Columbia University, 1963, pp. 208-209.

TABLE 3. THE ORGANIC COMPOSITION OF CAPITAL IN THE
MANUFACTURING SECTOR OF THE U.S. ECONOMY, ACCORDING
TO GILLMAN

Year	1880	1890	1900	1912	1919	1921	1923
q	0.41	0.52	0.72	0.95	1.40	2.04	1.34
Year	1925	1927	1929	1931	1933	1935	1937
q	1.30	1.30	1.19	1.79	1.95	1.47	1.18
Year	1939	1947	1949	1950	1951	1952	
q	1.20	1.04	1.23	1.11	1.10	1.11	

Source: Joseph M. Gillman, *The Falling Rate of Profit*, London. Dennis Dobson,
1957, p. 100, adapted by Geoff Hodgson, "The Theory of the Falling Rate of
Profit," *New Left Review*, no. 84, 1974, p. 72.

man's book, and Table 3, reorganized by Hodgson.) Gillman
found that *the law was verified for the period between 1880 and
1919*: the organic composition did rise, and the rate of profit did
fall. After 1919 the organic composition oscillated, with the exception of a break during the Depression of the thirties. This finding is easily explained. In a deep depression there is a huge stock
of idle fixed capital and a significantly reduced number of
employed workers.

The data provided by Mage present a totally different pattern.
What should be emphasized is the fact that they cover the whole
U.S. economy (whereas Gillman's data cover only the manufacturing sector) for the period 1900-1960. According to Mage, the
organic composition of capital in the U.S. economy was quite
stable between 1900 and 1920. *It rose steadily between 1920 and
1930*. It continued to rise during the Depression, following the
pattern observed by Gillman, which is explained by the mechanisms we have already discussed. It started to decrease in the late
thirties, probably because of the effect of the employment programs launched by the New Deal. It fell dramatically during the
war. This wartime decline is also an ad hoc effect explained by a
very simple mechanism: wartime employment meant full employment and high wages, which considerably raised the value of
variable capital, without any significant increase in the stock of
fixed capital that was put to work after being idle during the Depression. Thus, the organic composition of capital reached its
lowest level in 1945. But *from 1945 to 1960 the organic composition of capital rose steadily at an almost constant rate*. Surpris-
ingly enough, the Mage study has generally been considered as a

Figure 3

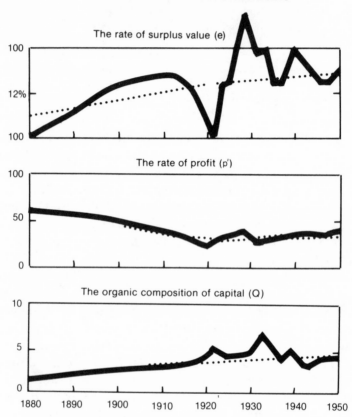

The Marxist Ratios: Stock Basis

The rate of surplus value (e)

The rate of profit (p')

The organic composition of capital (Q)

Source: Joseph M. Gillman, *The Falling Rate of Profit,*
London: Dennis Dobson, 1957, p. 57.

rebuttal of the assumption of a rising organic composition of capital! Although it is certainly true that we cannot observe a secular
trend, we do find a tendency of the organic composition to increase between 1945 and 1960, that is, during the period of expansion that preceded the economic crisis triggered in the late
sixties. But we cannot yet draw any conclusion from this.

Let us consider now the discrepancies between the two series
of observations. Obviously, they could be the consequence of

statistical errors. But let us assume that the calculations are correct and that the standardization provided by Hodgson is correct. Why are the patterns of evolution so different? In order to make the argument simpler, we will not consider the two exceptional periods. They are the Depression of the thirties and World War II, which was its aftermath. (This is not a distorting assumption, since the difference between the two series does not apply to the period 1930-1945.) Taking Gillman's data as an indicator of the evolution of the organic composition in the manufacturing sector and Mage's as the same indicator for the whole economy, we have the following pattern of evolution:

Period	Trend of the organic composition of capital in the manufacturing sector	Trend of the organic composition of capital in the whole economy
1880/1900-1920	constant increase	stable fluctuations
1920-1930	rapid constant decrease	rapid constant increase
1945-1952/1960	stable	constant increase

Instead of jumping to conclusions about the inconsistency of these two empirical studies, we should try to understand the different patterns of evolution as an interrelated process showing the transformation of the industrial sector within the framework of the whole economy. For this purpose we need to rely on a general interpretation of the historical evolution of American capitalism. It is obviously a difficult task to introduce such a comprehensive view in the discussion of a specific theoretical issue that we are using merely as a starting point. Fortunately, there exists an excellent work, not well known in the United States, which we consider to be the best Marxist analysis of the process of capital accumulation in America. It is Michel Aglietta's study of regulation and crises in U.S. capitalism.[26] Following his analysis we can provide, on a very broad level, an explanation of the observed pattern in the evolution of the organic composition of capital. In the first period (1880-1920) capitalist industry grew very rapidly through a process of investment in constant capital in an environment largely dominated by a small-commodity mode of production. The organic composition was high in industry, increasingly capitalistic, and low in the overall economy, still based essentially on the availability of immigrant labor. The rate of profit in manufacturing tended to decline. As a reaction to this tendency, technological innovation was massively and suddenly introduced into manufacturing not only in the means of production but also in the labor process (Taylor's "scientific management"). At the same time, oil exploitation began on a large scale, reducing the cost of energy. The dramatic increase in the productivity of labor and the lower costs of the elements of constant capital led to a decrease in the organic composition of capital and to an increase in the rate of profit. But this trend in the manufacturing sector was made possible by the concomitant transformation of the social environment. Banking, management, advertising, and commercial activities developed simultaneously with an upward trend in the social service sector. These elements were crucial in the social and technological background for the increase in industrial productivity. The whole society was embraced in the fully capitalist social relationships of production, distribution, and management. The concentration and centralization of surplus value provoked a capital-intensive development of most nonmanufacturing sectors. As the organic composition of capital decreased in industry, it increased at the level of society.

Nevertheless, this process of accumulation had a barrier. This was the consumption capacity of the society. The working class was not yet prepared to absorb the products of the rapidly developing industry of consumer goods, while the new professions still represented a very narrow market. Thus, the 1929 crisis was primarily a crisis of realization. And this pattern of accumulation was only able to recover because of the war. The production of means of destruction created a huge outlet, and after the war the reconstruction of an almost totally destroyed Europe created additional outlets. After World War II, through the combined efforts of capital and state, policies were developed to unblock the bottlenecks existing in solvent demand. The mainstream of the working class was transformed into a profitable market by increasing its standard of living. This was made possible through the development of collective bargaining with monopoly capital and the socialization of the cost of reproduction of labor power by means of state intervention in the organization and financing of a new urban infrastructure and a system of social services. This new process of accumulation, which began in 1945, initiated again the tendency of the organic composition of capital to rise at the level of the whole economy, increasing the substitution of capital for labor, as shown by Carter's study. Nevertheless, this process was not fully reflected in the manufacturing sector because of two continuing factors: the increased productivity of labor (increase in the relative surplus value) in the monopoly sector and, in the competitive sector, an increase in labor-intensive development and in the rate of absolute surplus value, possible because of the fragmentation of the labor market resulting especially from the immigration of black agricultural laborers from the rural South to work in northern industries. Still, the increasing organic composition of capital at the level of the whole economy, combined with militant action by labor unions and the shrinking demand caused by the growing surplus population, meant that the ratio of corporate profit to the gross national product declined. These were the conditions that eventually caused the structural economic crisis.

While this interpretation is only a tentative blueprint, it does rely on the idea of a complementary relationship between the characteristics of accumulation of capital in industry and in the whole economy, which is certainly the type of explanation put forward by Gillman himself on the basis of his data. *Gillman did not reject the theory of the falling rate of profit*. He proposed a theoretical reformulation to take into consideration his empirical findings. He attributed the success of accumulation during the twenties to the growth of a very sophisticated system of capital management that was made possible only by a massive increase in unproductive but necessary expenses.

With the increase in the size and complexity of industrial enterprise, however—with mergers, integrations, and concentrations of industry—the capitalist is no longer, can no longer be, the sole or even the principal operator of his business. In fact, the individual capitalist of the Marxist formula largely disappears and the collective capitalist, the corporation, takes his place. Now the "capitalist" hires his administration, and the surplus-value which formerly was all his own, except for what he paid out of it as rent and interest, he now shares with a host of administrative functionaries. p no longer equals s; it now equals s, minus the cost of these new functions and minus the expanded costs of government. But this is not all.

With the new administrative functions goes a variety of expenditures which have been growing with the growing integration and monopolization of industry. Sales, advertising, promotion and a whole congeries of administrative expenses have risen in the past several decades to eat into the capitalist's surplus-value. . . . They are, therefore, "unproductive" expenditures, in the Marxist sense. That is, they are unproductive of surplus-value. They are as unproductive of surplus-value when incurred inside the factory gate as, according to Marx, are the expenses of marketing which are incurred outside the factory gate.

. . . Since 1919 fifty per cent and more of the surplus-value realized at the factory gate has been going, in the large, to meet these and similar unproductive expenses, including (indirect) business taxes. The s in our formula, therefore, is gross, not net as far as the industrial capitalist and his profit rate are concerned. . . . Taking the economy as whole, these growing "unproductive" expenditures eat into the surplus-value produced and tend to effect a decline in the rate of the net surplus-value realized and, so, of the net profits realized. . . . The formula as we have used it so far cannot reveal these net results.[27]

He considered these expenses (u) as a part of *constant capital* since they were as necessary as machines to enable labor to produce value. Under these new conditions he recalculated the data gathered and obtained the statistical results shown in Table 4. When unproductive expenses are added to constant capital, *the organic composition tends to rise slightly (between 1919 and 1939) and the rate of profit tends to fall*. This extraordinary insight into the changing conditions of capitalist accumulation (and the corresponding reformulation of the Marxian law) opens up a whole new field of discussion, which we will consider within a broader theoretical framework.[28]

TABLE 4. THE ORGANIC COMPOSITION OF CAPITAL IN THE
MANUFACTURING SECTOR OF THE U.S. ECONOMY, WHEN
UNPRODUCTIVE NECESSARY EXPENSES ARE ADDED TO
CONSTANT CAPITAL (AUGMENTED C FLOW BASIS),
ACCORDING TO GILLMAN

Year	O.C.C.	p' percent
1919	4.6	12.0
1920	4.1	8.0
1921	4.5	2.1
1922	4.3	9.8
1923	4.3	9.8
1924	4.4	8.3
1925	4.6	8.8
1926	4.6	9.4
1927	4.6	8.0
1928	4.7	9.3
1929	4.7	9.6
1930	4.9	4.9
1931	4.9	1.2
1932	5.2	—
1933	5.0	3.8
1934	4.7	5.6
1935	4.8	7.2
1936	5.0	8.6
1937	4.6	7.9
1938	5.1	4.7
1939	4.7	8.2

Source: Joseph M. Gillman, *The Falling Rate of Profit*, London. Dennis Dobson,
1957, p. 99. Reprinted by permission of Dennis Dobson Publishers.

However suggestive the preceding discussion may have been,
it is impossible to consider it as a trustworthy analysis of the
process of capital accumulation in the United States because of
the unreliability of the empirical basis used in the analysis. Our
purpose in presenting it was to show that the so-called empirical
evidence existing against the theory of the falling rate of profit is
partly irrelevant, partly contradictory, and partly supportive of the
main propositions of the theory.

A further discussion of the empirical proof of the law is useless
because of some basic epistemological obstacles to any such an
attempt at verification. The first one refers to the unit of observation of capital accumulation. It has been demonstrated that this
process is worldwide.[29] Most Marxist economists agree with this

proposition, but very few of them see the practical consequences it has for research. Any tendency related to the dynamics of the mode of production can only be observed through the process of interaction among the elements of the whole system. Historically, if there is a secular tendency of the organic composition of capital to increase and the rate of profit to decrease, this can only be proved by studying, in terms of value, the process of accumulation at the world level. No study of the United States, Britain, or France alone can provide the empirical answer we are seeking. Therefore, most of the debate under consideration is apologetic, formal, and shaped by academic rituals.

Furthermore, the theory postulates that it is not necessary for the organic composition to rise; in fact, a complex set of tendencies and countertendencies produces a process of contradictory historical development. That we are not able to find a long-term secular trend for the organic composition to increase and the rate of profit to decrease does not contradict the theory; an intrinsic part of the theory is that reality is the result of conflicting forces. Actually, the most intelligent critics of the Marxian theory openly accept such an epistemological principle. Sweezy refers to "the notion of the rate of exploitation and the organic composition as 'empirically verifiable relations from which the analysis can begin,'" and says: "Those of us who question the universal (for capitalism) validity of the law of the falling tendency of the rate of profit obviously entertain no such ridiculous idea."[30]

Of what use, then, is a theory that cannot be observed at work in its historical development? Is the Marxist theory of crises a new form of metaphysics, a question of belief, a matter of taste? Certainly not. A theory is a tool for understanding reality. And an appropriate social theory is one that is able to explain historical experience in a more comprehensive and adequate way than any alternative explanation. But a theory explains the observed process through a series of intellectual mediations, not by direct or simplistic observations of a reality adjusting mechanically to the formal relationships defined by the theory.

The theory of the falling rate of profit and all other theories of crises must be judged on the grounds of their capacity to provide an understanding of historical experience through laws of long-term development. But this understanding will not come about because of a point-to-point correspondence between theory and empirical observations. Rather, it will result from the application of a theoretical construct to a given reality that becomes meaningful on the basis of the proposed scheme of interpretation.[31] By what criteria do we decide on the adequacy of a particular theory? *All the observations under analysis must be explained by the theory, and none of the observed relationships should contradict any of its major assumptions.* It should be comprehensive and logically consistent. Of the theories that meet these criteria, the one that is simplest in form will be preferred. These fundamental methodological principles commit us to change the approach used until now in our search for a theoretical starting point to understand the crisis. On the basis of the preceding discussions, we will reverse the order of our thinking to provide an explanatory hypothetical framework for the social study of the economic crises in advanced capitalism. As we shall see, there are several crucial arguments that still use the basic structure of the theory of the falling rate of profit. But this theory must be developed to take into consideration the historical experience that occurred after its initial formulation. Our interest in reorganizing the theory does not refer to any reflex of religious loyalty to the holy books. It comes from the conviction that, as Erik Wright says, the theory of the falling rate of profit is the only one linking a theory of crisis with an explanation of the determinants of the rate of accumulation.[32] It is the only *general theory* of capitalist development that has tried to explain the historical contradictions of the system. But it must be used with a double qualification. The naturalistic and mechanistic elements must be separated from the theory, and the theory must be more explicitly related to the basic theory of the class struggle.

The analysis of the social process of economic crisis in American society in the following chapters of the book will provide the measure of the usefulness of the proposed theory at its current stage of development.

3. ELEMENTS FOR A THEORY OF ECONOMIC CRISES IN ADVANCED CAPITALISM

Our examination of the empirical arguments in support of the alternative explanations of the capitalist crises does not lead to any specific conclusion. We must, in fact, begin from a theoretical framework that is able to provide some meaning to the observations of the historical process. Unfortunately, most of the available analytical models are inadequate to this task or allow only piecemeal interpretations.[33] For instance, the underconsumption theory is incapable of explaining the characteristics of the process of accumulation; the profit-squeeze theory remains almost entirely at the level of distribution without coming to grips with the contradictions in the overall process of production and circulation; and the "capital-state" theory, centered on the growing contradictions of the expansion of the public sector, deals mostly with a particular trend (albeit the most fundamental one) of capitalist accumulation. Although the falling-rate-of-profit theory appears to be the most comprehensive, in its usual formulation it has a strong mechanistic bias and needs more explicit connections to the determinants of historical class practices. Under these conditions should we renounce the attempt to develop any general theory of the crisis?

In this context, Erik Wright's position seems at first very reasonable. After pointing out the weaknesses of each specific theory, he proposes applying each of them to a particular historical period of capital accumulation. Thus, if the falling-rate-of-profit theory was fruitful for the last phase of competitive capitalism, the crisis in monopoly capitalism may be better explained by the underconsumption perspective, and the theory of state monopoly capitalism is most useful for understanding developments after World War II. While this position establishes the crucial link between historical experience and the transformation of theory, it poses more problems than it solves. A theory, unlike an ad hoc interpretation, must be built by developing and rectifying its elements, instead of replacing the overall framework when something new occurs. If we need a *total* reformulation, this is a sign that the theory was not an adequate conceptual tool in the first place. So, if new elements appear to be decisive in the process of capitalist crises (such as realization problems or state intervention), then we must include these elements in a coherent and meaningful way. If some of the arguments or propositions of the preexisting theory (like the inevitability of the rising organic composition of capital) are challenged by historical experience, we have to modify the theory in the same sense. That is what we will attempt to do now by presenting a systematic theoretical framework linking the basic assumptions of Marxist theory with the specific hypotheses leading to capitalist economic crises and with the main lines of the historical process that caused the current crisis.

3.1. THE MARXIST THEORY OF CONTRADICTORY HISTORICAL DEVELOPMENT OF THE MODES OF PRODUCTION*

Societies are produced, structured, shaped, and transformed by historically defined processes of class struggle. Class struggle stems from the contradictory relationships existing in all processes of production in historical societies, especially the contradiction that arises between producers and organizers of production. The latter appropriate a substantial share of the product through their social domination, enforced politically, ideologically, and militarily. The specific mechanisms through which this appropriation of the product by the nonproducers is accomplished define a mode of production. A capitalist mode of production is defined by the social separation between the producers and their means of production. Because the means of production are owned and controlled by the nonproducers, they are able to organize production and to appropriate the surplus value. Capital is a social relationship. It is the structural social position that perpetuates and expands itself by expropriating from the producers their means of production, by appropriating their labor power as the precondition for allowing them to produce and reproduce themselves, by organizing the production process, by appropriating the new value created in the process of production, and by transforming this value into capital through the process of exchange of commodities. It thus transforms all possible goods and services into commodities and enforces this social organization of production, consumption, and exchange through the state and through ideological apparatuses adequate

---

* It is obviously impossible to present a summary here of the general framework of Marxist theory (or our interpretation of it), as it appears in the writings (and practices) of Marx, Engels, Lenin, Mao, Gramsci, and so many others. We have been content to select a few basic propositions that allow us to develop the specific theory of the crises of accumulation in advanced capitalism.

to shape people's consciousness (family, education, religion, mass media, everyday life institutions, etc.).

Because capital is a contradictory relationship, its expansion is at the same time the expansion of labor. Wherever there are expropriators, there are also the expropriated. The rise of the bourgeoisie as a historical actor born from the capitalist social relationship has also brought the upsurge of the proletariat as the living flesh of exploited labor. The main contradiction in a capitalist society, and therefore in the process of capital accumulation, is the contradiction between capital and labor. Societies are much more complex, as we shall see in this book. There are many relatively autonomous historical mediations that have to be considered in order to understand actual societies. But remembering this basic contradiction is the key to explaining our world. In spite of all the ideological propaganda that proclaims over and over the end of the class struggle between the bourgeoisie and the workers, this is still the cornerstone of any analysis of the process of social change.

This basic contradiction has very concrete manifestations. Capital tends to perpetuate these social relationships and to appropriate as much value as possible from the value-producing process of production; labor tends to keep for its consumption as much as possible of the value produced and tries to win control over the process of production, and ultimately, over the means of production itself. The extent, the intensity, and the level of these manifestations depend on historical conditions. But it is the contradictions that explain conditions and not the opposite. The contradiction between capital and labor is not a contradiction expressed only in the process of production, namely, in the workplace. It is a contradiction in the social relationships of production and is expressed at the level of the overall society, in political and ideological dimensions as well as at the economic level. The decisive issue is not what the distribution of surplus value is but how it is decided. We must make a very clear differentiation between a class-struggle analysis and its interpretation in terms of the differential bargaining power for the sharing of income between capital and labor within the framework of capitalist social relationships.

It follows that the main contradiction in the process of capital accumulation centers on the appropriation of the value produced. The rate of surplus value (absolute or relative) will be the crucial element in determining the rate of accumulation. The rate of surplus value will depend on the conditions and forms of exploitation that capital will try to enforce and labor will try to resist. The process of production, the process of circulation, and social organization will be determined by the specific forms and rhythms of this contradiction.

Nevertheless, if a society is capitalist, capital is the dominant element in the contradiction structuring social relationships and historical processes. Therefore, capital's internal structure must be taken into consideration as the main determinant of the expansion of the mode of production as a whole, even though its expansion is significantly shaped (and ultimately reversed?) by labor's challenge to structural domination.

Capital exists primarily because of its exploitation of labor and its appropriation of labor (we will call this relationship 1). But it also relates to itself (relationship 2) and, through the process of human labor production that it organizes, to the appropriation and transformation of nature (relationship 3). We can name these basic relationships according to the Marxist tradition:

1. The relationship of *exploitation* or appropriation of surplus value.
2. The relationship of *intercapitalist competition*, which is the struggle for the appropriation of surplus value (produced by labor) between different *units* of capital. Under the conditions of monopoly capital the competition between units of capital changes but does not disappear. On the contrary, it tends to become much more acute and to be used in exerting social power in addition to trying to control the market.
3. The *development of productive forces*, that is, the relationship between labor and nature through the means of production in a general social relationship organized by capital. The development of productive forces means the capacity of human labor to transform nature (and to transform itself)

by the combination of *energy* and *information* in a process of transformation of matter.[34]

The basic proposition of the theory is that there is *a hierarchy of structural determination*, schematically represented thus:

$$1 \longrightarrow 2 \longrightarrow 3$$

We can introduce feedback, and interaction effects can be assumed, but these are merely refinements of the theory that rely on the basic hypothesis of these essential relationships defining the dynamics of a capitalist society. This hierarchy is what we call social organization (relationship 4).

The *social organization* is a set of cultural values, ideological apparatuses, and political institutions that are produced by the process of social contradictions and tend to reproduce the relationships of production, distribution, and management. It is expressed primarily through the state and the ideological apparatuses:

So, we have

$$1 \to \quad 2 \to \quad 3$$
$$\text{or}$$
$$(C > L) \to \quad (C >< C) \to \quad (L > N)$$
$$\text{and}$$
$$4 = \{ 1 \to \quad 2 \to \quad 3 \}$$
$$\text{or}$$
$$CMP = \{ (C > L) \to (C >< C) \to (L > N) \}$$

where C = capital $>$ = domination-appropriation
      L = labor $><$ = competition-domination
      N = nature $\to$ = determination
      CMP = capitalist mode of production

        1 is at the same time: production
                             consumption
                             distribution
        2 is at the same time: production
                             circulation
                             realization
        3 is expanded reproduction of the elements of the process of production
        4 is expanded reproduction of the social relation-

ships of production, consumption, circulation, and distribution

Since 1 is a *contradictory relationship* (defined by the bipolar antagonistic relationship between capital and labor), so are 2, 3, and 4. Society is not a system of structural self-reproduction but an unstable contradictory structure of asymmetrical multidimensional relationships.

Historically, the capitalist mode of production expands in articulation (unevenly structured) with other preceding modes of production. We call this composite historical structure a *social formation*. A social formation is always under the domination of a particular stage of a given mode of production. Historically, the development of the capitalist mode of production has always been a worldwide process.

On the basis of these theoretical premises we can now present a tentative explanatory framework for understanding the crises in the process of capitalist accumulation.

3.2. Tendencies toward Crisis in the Process of Capitalist Accumulation

Every mode of production expands under the logic intrinsic to its dominant pole, but is increasingly shaped by the contradictory logic opposed to it in the process of class struggle.

The expansion of the capitalist mode of production is realized through the process of accumulation. Accumulation of capital is the social process of conversion of capital into surplus value and of surplus value into capital on an expanded scale.* However, there are several characteristics that should be remembered. The process presupposes the dominance of the capitalist social relationships in the class struggle and is, by itself, a realization of this dominant capitalist logic. The conversion into new capital follows the distinction between constant and variable capital. The process is organized at the level of social capital, which means taking into consideration the economy as a whole. The driving force of this process of accumulation is the profit of capital, that is, the surplus value that can be appropriated by capital after reproduc-

---

* When surplus value is converted into less capital, there is a process of disaccumulation.

ing constant and variable capital and after using the value required for the reproduction of social relationships of production (taxes to the state, funding of nonprofit ideological apparatuses, etc.).

The only limit to this process of capitalist accumulation comes from the general crisis of the social relationships on which the process is based. As this limit is a political limit, it will depend ultimately on the power relationships generated in the overall process of class struggle.

Although there may be no economic limits, there are many important barriers capital must overcome in order to develop its logic.[35] *The effects produced by these structural barriers to the capitalist logic in the process of accumulation of capital are the roots of the so-called structural economic crises* (to be differentiated from the cyclical crises that are a normal part of the business cycle). What is specific about a structural crisis is that the process of accumulation cannot continue until the barriers are removed or counteracted. This solution usually means that there will be a basic transformation in the relationships between classes, between fractions of capital, and between capital and the productive forces.

The main structural barrier existing in capitalist production and circulation is the worker's resistance to exploitation. Since an increase in the rate of surplus value is the basic element required for the accumulation of capital, the struggle over the relative social amount of paid and unpaid labor is the first determinant of the rate of exploitation and, therefore, of the rate of profit and the speed and shape of the accumulation process. This is not an undetermined factor. Historically, labor's resistance tends to increase, and capital is increasingly unable to appropriate the same amount of labor in absolute terms.

The tendency is for "the expropriators to be expropriated." This is the central proposition of the Marxist theory of crisis, and this has been the dominant element of historical experience in the long term and at the world level since the beginning of capitalism. *There is a secular structural* * *tendency for the rate of*

* Why structural? Because the struggle over surplus value is the basic structural feature of the capitalist system and because it is also structural that wherever there is exploitation there is also resistance to it. The exploitation inherent in the system causes the development of this resistance.

absolute surplus value to decrease and, therefore, a tendency for the rate of profit to fall.

Capital, being unable to expand by increasing the rate of absolute surplus value, is then forced to broaden its basis of accumulation through a higher rate of relative surplus value; that is, it must increase the productivity of labor to create more value in the same amount of time. This is done by developing the productive forces along whatever lines tend to be most profitable for capital. In such a process the physical proportion of the mass of the means of production used in the production process will increase in relationship to the amount of human labor. As a consequence of the first tendency, the development of the class struggle leads to a decreasing rate of absolute surplus value, and *there is a second secular tendency, which is to increase the technical composition of capital, in order to increase the rate of relative surplus value.* To say this is not to say that the organic composition of capital tends to increase. As several economists have emphasized, we cannot say anything about changes in the ratio c/v caused by an increase in the technical composition of capital as long as we do not express such a tendency in value terms. It is possible that the development of productive forces may reduce the value of c and increase the value of v in spite of the higher proportion of fixed capital per worker. On the other hand, we have argued that we do not have any empirical basis to sustain this argument. In fact, the organic composition of capital could have a tendency to rise at the world level. But here we are not discussing the problem of the actual existence of the tendency; what we are trying to identify is what emerges from the structural logic and from the historical experience of the mode of production. On these grounds, we do not equate the tendency of the technical composition of capital to rise with increasing organic composition. Must we then hold that the evolution of the organic composition is undetermined? Not at all, for reasons we shall clarify in the following steps.

Now, that the technical composition of capital cannot be equated to the evolution of the organic composition does not mean that the former is a secondary trend in the process leading to capitalist crises. To consider this trend a secondary one is a common misunderstanding in existing analyses. In fact, *the increasing technical composition of capital changes in depth the re-*

lationship between capital, labor, and the productive forces and creates new conditions and provokes new barriers in the process of accumulation. Improvements in the productivity of labor are possible because of the concentration and centralization of capital as well as because of the investment of accumulated surplus value, which is coordinated by management. The increases in productivity are structurally linked to the formation of a monopoly sector.* Since the reason for the improvement in productivity (development of productive forces) is labor's resistance to capitalist exploitation, it will be an uneven process of accumulation, primarily determined by the class struggle.

At the same time that a monopoly sector is developing, based to a very great degree on the increase of relative surplus value, another sector (competitive) is expanding on the basis of a constant (or increased) rate of absolute surplus value. However, the advantage in productivity is generally not used by the monopoly sector to eliminate the "competitive" sector. On the contrary, it will tend to preserve the competitive sector, but impose on it a lower rate of profit. The monopoly sector will appropriate an increasing share of the surplus value produced in the competitive sector, which it can do because of the relationship of domination between competitive capital and monopoly capital. Therefore, more and more value is centralized in the highly productive monopoly sector, which employs (proportionally) less and less labor. The implications are obvious. There is an increasing gap between the productive power and consuming power of the society, which leads to a relative population surplus.

The development of productive forces also requires a transformation of the labor process and of human labor that demands social and technological conditions incompatible with capitalist logic. For instance, the development of scientific research requires a massive investment in education which is only profitable in the long term. So too the introduction of information as a productive force in the process of work requires a great deal of autonomy in decisionmaking and produces a situation that is al-

---

* What this relationship does not imply is that monopoly capital favors productivity. As we shall see (and *this* is the contradiction), monopoly can be a structural obstacle. Rather, the development of productive forces implies a central allocation of surplus value that, under capitalism, takes the form of monopoly corporations.

most entirely contradictory to the discipline capital imposes on workers.

Finally, the tendency to increase the rate of relative surplus value through the development of the productivity of labor could lead ultimately to total automation of the productive process—to capital-reproducing machines. This is obviously contradictory to the existence of capital itself. Therefore, it is a limit and not an actual historical process. Yet it is important to remember that if in the process of accumulation we cannot equate the technical and organic composition of capital (because of the effects of interaction between productivity of labor and the value ratio between c and v), the tendency to increase the technical composition also has a limit. This limit is the total elimination of human labor from the process of productive work. Certainly, productive human labor will not totally disappear even with automation. But a general diffusion of automation would substantially decrease the proportion of push-button productive workers in respect to the value produced, thereby altering completely the relationship between producers and the whole social organization. Capital relies on the private appropriation of productive human labor. Therefore, the tendencies toward automation introduce a fundamental contradiction into a system that cannot replace workers with machines yet is pushed toward making this substitution because of the increasing pressure from workers. This is the real meaning of the Marxian proposition about the tendency of capitalism to eliminate living labor, thereby causing its own destruction.

Accumulation through the increase in the rate of relative surplus value also has some fundamental consequences for the structure of capitalism that could give us a new perspective on the logic of its development. As Gillman has suggested, in order to improve the productivity of labor, monopoly capital has to make massive investments to create conditions that will more effectively use the value appropriated. The centralization and allocation of surplus value for long-term normalization of the rate of profit requires the expansion of organizations and people to work in them in order to be able to deal with new conditions in the process of production and circulation. Note that we are not referring here to the growth of the public sector, which is required to reproduce the social conditions of capitalism or to act as a countertendency to the falling rate of profit. We refer, as Gillman did, to the expenses incurred by capital itself in order to adapt its management to the requirements of the process of accumulation based on increasing relative surplus value and expanding and controlling the market. Since these expenses are necessary to create new markets for capital itself, they are mostly caused by new functions of management and control. What is the status of these expenses? They are capitalist expenses; they are part of the surplus value appropriated by capital. They are unproductive but necessary expenses, and they are required to organize the process of production and circulation in the new forms of increased productivity. But they do not create value; they only transfer to the product the value they embodied. Therefore, it can be argued that they are a part of constant capital, and because they must be continuously increased to support capital accumulation, they will tend to raise the organic composition of capital. If we express ourselves in terms of value and no longer identify constant capital with machines, we may speak in terms of the ratio between "capitalist appropriated dead labor" and "capitalist appropriated living labor" in the process of production. *Thus, the organic composition of capital might actually tend to rise, undermining in the same way the structural basis for the formation of the rate of profit.* We would then be in the paradoxical situation of saying that an increasing number of people are employed as "dead labor." This is theoretically coherent, and it could produce a very crucial hint in our understanding of the crisis in the so-called service sector.* As we saw, Gillman's calculations, using this hypothesis, reversed the historically observed trend and showed a rise in the organic composition, which was defined by adding u (unproductive necessary capitalist expenses) to constant capital. Although theoretical research on this point is too provisional to be conclusive, it nevertheless invites us to think about the classical law of the falling rate of profit in new terms provided by the changing reality of capitalism.

---

* Obviously, it does not follow that the clerks in the monopoly corporations are "capitalists." We are speaking here in terms of value from the point of view of capital. The class analysis of these positions must introduce the concept of collective worker as well as political and ideological elements.

The third barrier is a consequence of the relationship of capital to itself, that is, the conditions of intercapitalist competition. The law of a capital unit is that it expands not only by appropriating and consuming human labor but also by appropriating and destroying other capital units. Competition is the rule. The best ones will win while other units go bankrupt or are absorbed. The process of capital accumulation is also a process of capital concentration and centralization. Under the conditions of monopoly capitalism as well, intercapitalist competition is a major structural law of the system. What changes is the form of competition. It is basically realized by the appropriation of technology and information, control over specific markets, access to financial resources, and influence on sectors of the state apparatus. It is a giant's struggle, although it is a struggle with pacts, reciprocal concessions, and bargaining. Competition will continue because it is structurally unthinkable to have a unified social capital: it would destroy the basis for the rule of allowing the disposition of surplus value to the *private* ownership (control) of the means of production.*

Competition means being able to improve one's position relative to others. Traditionally, competition has meant reducing prices and attracting consumers at the cost of other competing units. Monopoly competition is based not only on control of the market but on the capacity to create the most favorable conditions for capital investment: attracting knowledge, increasing the profit of banking capital, and mobilizing resources to influence the political system and the mass media. In whatever way monopoly capital is used, there is always present the implication that it is able to devote an increasing share of the value produced to the creation of an advantageous situation vis-à-vis other units. Since the advantage must be gained without reducing the rate of profit, and the methods used, like cutting prices or developing new research, are nonprofitable in the short term, these expenditures must come from savings in constant or variable capital.

* "Capitalist-like" social relationships in societies entirely controlled by state apparatuses are, in fact, elements of a more complex reality that correspond to postcapitalist modes of production.

Savings in variable capital in absolute terms are usually impossible because of the workers' resistance to absolute exploitation. So these funds are obtained by increasing productivity by putting pressure on the means of production to intensify the productivity of labor. Savings in constant capital require the introduction of new machines that cheapen the means of production, reduce operating costs, and allow capital to take advantage of this innovative capital unit without infringing on the rate of profit. Thus, *intercapitalist competition leads to accelerated investment in fixed capital, raising the technical composition of capital*.

At this point, we will go on to an additional step in the analysis of structural tendencies. Because of the particular form of this increase in the technical composition—that is, because this investment in fixed capital comes from the dynamics of intercapitalist competition—it has a corresponding effect on the organic composition of capital, increasing it also. Why? If we are unable to equate the technical composition and the organic composition of capital in the long term, how can they be equated in the short term?

To increase productivity, new machines are introduced. These machines are more productive than the old ones, so in the long term they increase labor productivity and pay for themselves. However, in the short term, at the time that capitalists introduce the machines into the process of production in order to become more competitive, the machines represent the value that was consumed in producing them. Since they are new machines (because by definition they represent an innovation), they will *normally* represent a higher value than the machines they replace. And normally also, they tend to eliminate productive labor. So, before starting to function, before creating more value through the higher productivity of the remaining labor, they raise c and lower v: in the short term the organic composition of capital rises at the social level. Now, since the process of intercapitalist competition is a continuous one and technological innovation is introduced through this mechanism, the long-term trend would be understood, viewed as a tendency, as a succession of short-term trends. New machines are introduced over and over again to achieve a better position before the counteracting effects of increasing labor productivity have been fully integrated. Therefore, *there is a structural tendency for the organic composition of capital to rise*, as part of the logic of capitalist accumulation. But this tendency does not come from the development of productive forces, which, on the contrary, could reduce the organic composition. It comes from the combined effect of class struggle pushing capital into labor-saving investments and intercapitalist competition. Intercapitalist competition makes it impossible to plan technological improvements of productivity that would allow the value of new investments to be reduced by creating conditions permitting cheaper replacement for the new machines. We can see now why Marx so stressed the importance of intercapitalist competition in determining the falling rate of profit.

The third basic barrier to the process of accumulation, then, is *the rising organic composition of capital (leading to a tendency of the rate of profit to fall) as a consequence of the development of social productivity under the conditions of intercapitalist competition.*

When we established the relationship between the introduction of the new machines and the rising organic composition, we added the adverb "normally." This qualification is important because under some conditions it is possible to transform the process of production to increase labor productivity without increasing the value of constant capital. This could happen where there is a continuing discontinuous technological revolution, such as the introduction into the productive process of new discoveries that had not previously had costly processes of production or innovation. Actually, there is some historical experience that confirms this possibility. For instance, the sudden introduction of computerized systems into management functions produced a dramatic cheapening of necessary unproductive expenses of capital. Other examples are the introduction of electricity in industry, the discovery of oil resources, and the application of chemical research to food production.

Thus, to some extent, the capitalist system, unable to raise the absolute rate of surplus value and suffering from the contradictory effect of intercapitalist competition, has to develop the productive forces, has to further technological innovation, in order to appropriate more and more value from increasingly productive human labor. But this development of productive forces has to be done in a profitable manner, in order to produce commodities that can be sold in a structurally shrinking market (relative to productive capacity). This fundamental development of productive forces under capitalism triggers new contradictions that represent the fourth major barrier to the accumulation of capital.

For the short term there is a complex mechanism that we must analyze carefully. Because of the expansion of productive forces in the form of fixed capital investments, the mass of value embodied in the means of production is increasingly higher even though we accept the idea that the organic composition does not rise. This mass of value has to be realized in commodities in order for capital to accumulate. Because of the increasing mass of value and the increasing productivity of labor, the amount of value transferred from the means of production to every unit of the product is smaller.* Then there is a very long turnover of fixed capital. In other words, it takes more and more time for fixed capital to be "productively consumed" in the process of production and circulation. Or we can say that capital needs more time to recover through production and circulation the investments that it made in fixed capital in order to develop productivity.

The race of capital to avoid raising the organic composition of capital by introducing continuous technological innovations provokes a process of accelerated obsolescence of the means of production. This means that capital devalues its own means of production by increasing productivity at a rate that forces the replacement of the existing means of production before they have transferred their embodied value to commodities.

This is a basic contradiction. Capital needs more and more time to realize the value invested in fixed capital but allows itself less and less time to do so. It creates obsolescence by continuously innovating to escape from the double pressure of mounting

---

* This is *not* we insist, an argument about organic composition. The value in the product could be high because of the high productivity of labor without intervention of fixed capital.

labor costs and the tendency for the organic composition of capital to increase.

The final result is a process of continuously devaluating fixed capital that tends to cut the share of surplus value appropriated by capital. This is one of the major structural sources of state intervention to assume the cost of socially devalued capital.

The long-term contradiction that comes from the need of capital to develop the productive forces is a more fundamental one. It concerns the social conditions of scientific research and technological innovation. Scientific research and technological innovation require massive investments that are only profitable in the long term. They also require a great deal of autonomy in decisionmaking in relation to the requirements of particular units of capital. In other words, the process of technological innovation can only be effective under conditions of production that evade capitalist logic. A continuing high rate of innovation can only exist in a society where human creativity is favored by the type of social organization and the characteristics of the work process. It requires a very highly developed system of education, not just professional training and ideological manipulation. It demands an increasing noncapitalist sector of social services able to provide information to the workers as well as improving their initiative. It implies, primarily, that there must be a great deal of initiative in the process of production, which basically contradicts the model of authority in the organization of a capitalist firm. Many of these social functions are necessary for the development of the productive forces, but they are incompatible with capitalist logic. Therefore, they are assumed by the state.

The final contradiction, then, is that *in order to expand and avoid the barriers existing in the process of accumulation, capital grows by generating, in an increasing proportion, a sector of activities, rules, and apparatuses that denies its own logic.* Capital pursues its accumulation by increasing reliance on the state. But this tendency points toward the historical limit of the system.

Let us summarize the argument. Capitalist accumulation relies primarily on the rate of exploitation. Therefore, the process of class struggle at the level of the overall society defines the basic characteristics of the process of accumulation. Because of the historical tendency of workers to increase their own power, the basis for the formation of capitalist profit structurally shrinks. Capital responds by developing productive forces and increasing labor productivity. However, because it is not a unified planned effort but a process of internal struggle, through intercapitalist competition, the increase in productivity tends to be accomplished through increases in the organic composition of capital that could eventually lead to a falling rate of profit. To overcome this barrier, capital triggers a process of technological revolution that, despite improving productivity, devalues its fixed capital investments and relies more and more on the expansion of social and institutional conditions contradictory to the capitalist logic. Capital must develop productive forces in order to continue its accumulation. But the social conditions necessary for the development of productive forces are increasingly contradictory to capitalist social relationships. Since capital shapes society, the state is used more and more as a basic mechanism to absorb, smooth, and regulate the contradictions that emerge in the process of accumulation. However, the state is not a purely regulatory capitalist apparatus. It expresses the contradictions of society and must also fulfill the functions of legitimating the dominant interests and integrating the dominated class into the system. The growing state intervention to support the capitalist logic in all spheres of economic and social life undermines the basis for its legitimacy as the representative of the general interest.[36]

This vulnerability of the state comes at a time when mounting social mobilization and political challenges in advanced capitalism are being expressed at many levels and in many sectors of the state apparatus.[37] By expanding itself through the state, capital denies its own logic and undermines its hegemony over civilian society. The crisis of accumulation of capital and the crisis of the capitalist state are increasingly linked. To prevent the rate of profit from falling, capital tends to create the social conditions leading to its historical limit: the transformation of labor power into the power of labor.

3.3. COUNTERTENDENCIES TO THE CRISIS OF CAPITALIST ACCUMULATION

If we consider the enormous development of the productive forces of social labor in the last thirty years alone as compared with all preceding periods; if we consider, in particular, the enormous mass of fixed capital, aside from the actual machinery, which goes into the process of social production as a whole, then the difficulty which has hitherto troubled the economist, namely to explain the falling rate of profit, gives place to its opposite, namely to explain why this fall is not greater and more rapid. There must be some counteracting influences at work, which cross and annul the effect of the general law, and which give it merely the characteristic of a tendency, for which reason we have referred to the fall of the general rate of profit as a tendency to fall.

This sounds like a neo-Marxist statement trying to adapt the classical theory of the falling rate of profit to the recent contradictory historical experience. And yet it is the opening paragraph of Marx's Chapter 14 of Volume III of *Capital*, where he introduces dialectical reasoning about the reciprocal effect of tendencies and countertendencies to explain the actual process of capitalist accumulation. This methodological approach is the fundamental starting point of any adequate explanation of economic crises.

Why do we call them countertendencies? Why is the falling rate of profit a tendency? Are we opposing the logic of the system to some mechanisms of rectification that are merely historical events or secondary trends of the capitalist mode of production? In fact, many critics of the Marxist theory use the semantic difference in labeling between "tendencies" and "countertendencies" as proof of the mechanistic assumptions of the Marxist theory, which is later "adapted" to experience by introducing some ad hoc explanations. It is true that because societies are shaped by social conflicts and political decisions, the classes (and particularly the bourgeoisie) can consciously act to modify the tendencies toward crisis within the limits of capitalist social relationships. But we are not referring only to these historical practices when we speak of countertendencies. We are showing trends of the process of accumulation that are as structural as those leading to the falling rate of profit at a given stage in the mode of production. Both tendencies and countertendencies are structural and intrinsic to capitalist logic. That is why the process of accumulation is a contradictory one. Not only does it tend toward a crisis, but it also tends at the same time to prevent the crisis, triggering new contradictions that lead to new forms of crisis in a process that is economically endless, socially disruptive, and politically limited within a historical perspective.

This is not just our interpretation of the theory; it is certainly Marx's thought also. We offer as proof that the first "counteracting influence" explained by Marx is "increasing intensity of exploitation." How can the process of exploitation be considered a secondary trend, a "countertendency" of the capitalist system? The process of exploitation is the center and the main determinant of the process of accumulation. This is clear from the beginning of *Capital*. It is a central tendency of the capitalist mode of production, but it can be a countertendency to the crisis of capitalist accumulation.* And this is the explanation for the terms being used. We do not talk about tendencies of the mode of production but about structural tendencies toward a crisis of accumulation and structural countertendencies to this crisis. Both tendencies and countertendencies are structural features of the mode of production, but these features tend to produce contradictory effects on the falling rate of profit.

Let us try now to analyze these countertendencies under the conditions of advanced capitalism. We shall see that they generally lead to inflation. The major hypothesis of our analysis is that *the joint development and the coexistence of stagnation and inflation are the result of the contradictory development of the two major axes of advanced capitalism: the tendency of the rate of profit to fall, which leads to stagnation, and the opposing set of countertendencies, which cause structural inflation.***

One by one we will examine the principal countertendencies that have formed the base of the policies of capital since the great crisis of 1929. For the sake of clarity we are going to analyze the countertendencies separately even though they are obviously interdependent.

---

* It can also be a major tendency toward crisis, since it depends on the relationship of power between classes.

** Our analysis refers here to the main structural tendencies of the capitalist mode of production after World War II. While the United States is the center of the system, the discussion below is not restricted to American capitalism.

3.3.1. *The Increase in the Rate of Exploitation of Labor*

The reinforcement of exploitation is the most direct counteracting trend to the tendency of the rate of profit to fall. It is a question of obtaining, with the same organic composition, a greater rate of surplus value through several complementary mechanisms, which include: 1) increasing the workload of labor; 2) not reducing labor time in proportion to the development of productive forces; 3) putting pressure on wages and on the global cost of reproduction of labor power, aimed at lowering this cost in an absolute or relative manner, in relation to the historical growth of human needs; and 4) raising the efficiency and skills of the labor force without an equivalent raise in wages, thereby allowing capital to appropriate an additional mass of new surplus value resulting from the increased productivity of labor (relative surplus value).

These tendencies of capital to reinforce exploitation are opposed by the struggle of the workers and the growing power of the labor movement on the level of economic bargaining as well as on the political scene. These particular power relationships created in the advanced capitalist countries have forced the bourgeoisie to act on the rate of surplus value by ways other than direct confrontation with the labor movement because on that level the situation for capital has been continuously deteriorating over the long term.

New ways of reinforcing exploitation have therefore developed on two distinct levels. One occurs in the processes of consumption and the other in the exploitation of specific groups of workers.

Capital takes out a larger share of the surplus value distributed in the form of revenue by three principal means: 1) by increased emphasis on "indirect wages," or collective services essential for the reproduction of the labor force (housing, social equipment, health, education) with less and less of their cost directly assumed by capital; 2) by forced savings, which workers are compelled to accept in order to be assured of the social benefits they have secured through great struggle (such as social security and unemployment insurance); and 3) by the action of capital on the prices of consumer products, which recovers with one hand at the level of consumption what it loses from the other at the level of wages paid out to producers.

It must be pointed out that this "compensation mechanism" is not automatic, and it rests on two previous and fundamental conditions.

First, control over prices by capital is made possible by monopolistic concentration, which, through partial control of markets, allows prices to be maintained in spite of the reduction of production costs obtained by gains in productivity.[38] In order to understand "creeping inflation" it is necessary to understand the relationship between monopolies and prices that are above the work value in production. This action of monopolies must be seen as reflecting the structural necessity of raising their levy on surplus value outside the direct process of production where they are increasingly challenged by workers' demands.

Second, if capital is able to obtain through the level of consumption and indirect wages what the workers' struggle has forbidden it in direct wages, it is because of the organizational and political weakness of the demands of workers as consumers. Out of this will come recognition of the necessity for workers gradually to "socialize their struggle" and to extend the range of demands they make to encompass their living conditions and, generally, situations outside their place of work. The upsurge of consumer movements and of urban movements in most advanced capitalist societies creates yet another obstacle to capitalist exploitation in the consumption process.[39]

Capital enhances its position in the sphere of production also by creating new conditions of exploitation. To do so, it creates a relative surplus of labor on the world level by incorporating into the labor market categories of workers who, because of their political and ideological weakness, can be overexploited by capital. This explains the massive influx of immigrant workers into the advanced capitalist countries.

These workers are politically vulnerable because they have the legal status of foreigners and are ideologically isolated from the mass of workers. The bourgeoisie is able to impose on them working and living conditions greatly inferior to those obtained by the labor movement in industrialized countries. Capital's dream is to put into operation twenty-first-century technology with a nineteenth-century proletariat.[40]

A similar situation exists for ethnic minorities within nations (for example, the blacks in the United States). Overexploitation can also result in situations marked by traditional ideological prejudices and social discrimination. That is why women are being increasingly employed in the expanding service activities. However, this continuous splitting up of the working class by constantly changing its internal composition does gradually reunify the categories that were considered marginal because these previously marginal workers find they have a common interest—they are all being exploited. In this way, the headlong rush of capital to get around its contradictions ends up by broadening the struggle. For example, German and French capital, faced with the growing difficulty of imposing substandard working conditions on immigrant workers who were threatening the "social peace" by becoming more militant in the labor unions, are beginning to transfer more and more of their investments to the Third World countries. Instead of importing immigrant workers, they will simply try to take advantage of political repression and reproduce the conditions of overexploitation in the dominated countries. But exploitation leads to struggle, which forces changes in the conditions of exploitation. We can now foresee that the development of an industrial proletariat in the dominated countries will be a decisive element in sharpening class contradictions in a situation that is much more explosive than in the dominating countries. Through this process the political and ideological conditions that allow this overexploitation will be further jeopardized, and capital will once again be faced with its basic contradiction, but on a much greater scale and under much more unfavorable conditions.

That is why, if it is true that the reinforcement of exploitation is the fundamental countertendency introduced by monopoly capital to overcome its crisis, it will never suffice or even slow down the coming of the crisis. Therefore, the decisionmaking bodies of capital have reinforced this countertendency with other economic and political initiatives.

The attempt of capital to recover at the level of consumption a share of the value that it has to shift from profits to wages is the basis of the famous wage-price spiral. Because markets are controlled largely by monopoly capital, corporations are able to impose the prices they want. The increasing cost of living triggers workers' demands for more wages at the level of production. The wages obtained through struggle and bargaining will be added by monopoly capital to the prices charged for commodities. This does not mean that workers' demands are the cause of inflation, as capitalist propaganda argues. What it does mean is that one of the causes of inflation is that corporations find it increasingly difficult to raise their profits through direct exploitation and therefore raise prices for the whole society in order to preserve their privileges. This practice produces widespread inflation damaging to the process of circulation. Why does inflation result from this mechanism? It does because the increase in prices does not correspond to an increase in production, but only to a purely monetary raise brought about by collective bargaining.

3.3.2. Monopolistic Accumulation, Technological Progress, and Financing

One of the countertendencies indicated by Marx in Volume III of Capital is what he called "the cheapening of the elements of constant capital," which allows acting on the productivity of labor by acting on the constant capital without altering the organic composition in any way. Indeed, given the rise in the value of labor power and the reduction in the value of the means of production (through technological progress), fewer workers and more machines can be used with a similar organic composition. The overall significance of this countertendency for the development of the mode of production must be established. For it implies the formation of management units of capital that are capable by themselves of integrating the reduction of costs of constant capital—that is, they are capable of generating and managing an acceleration of technological progress. This is made possible by monopolistic concentration, with large production and management units having the capacity to be self-financing. In this way, as capitalist development proceeds through private monopoly control of scientific and technological revolutions, large capitalist financial units are formed joining industrial and banking capital.

But this trend is related to the basic contradiction between the increase in fixed capital and the acceleration of its obsolescence. What this implies is that there is a continuous devaluation of fixed capital that has to be considered by the corporations as a permanent factor in the process of accumulation.

As Aglietta emphasizes, "when obsolescence becomes a permanent and general process, it can be foreseen statistically. This trend takes, then, the monetary form of an insurance fund derived from the global profit. This fund is added to the amortizing fund: these are merged. And it is incorporated a priori in the price of production costs. Therefore, intensifying the rate of obsolescence leads to a very important growth of the financial share of the global cash-flow, which proportionally decreases the net profit."[41] This trend accounts for the increasing dependency of corporations upon borrowing capital from financial markets. Actually, the debt of large corporations has increased dramatically since 1945. It is a self-sustaining process. More and more capital is needed not only to replace obsolete fixed capital but also to pay the interests on the increasing proportion of capital that is borrowed. Such a demand for capital tightens the financial markets and raises the rates of interest, making the whole process more expensive. The banks themselves have to borrow capital from each other to meet this level of demand. This process is going on at an accelerated rate all over the world. Without immediate state action, any major default could lead to a general financial breakdown.

The relationship between the conditions for enhancing productivity and the firms' cash-flow (one of the more complex and yet most decisive aspects of the functioning of monopoly capital) has some very serious unstabilizing effects because it takes place within a new context of intercapitalist competition. Monopoly competition occurs through a power struggle among monopoly corporations that attempt to control technology, markets, raw material, and social influence. In this struggle the maximum short-term rate of profit is less important than the normalization of a relatively high rate of profit over the long term. This means that a considerable amount of capital has to be made available in the short term in order for each firm to be able to match its competitors' maneuvers, which might given them a decisive advantage over itself.

The corporations' cash-flow (global profit + amortizing fund + fixed capital replacement funds) increases because it is necessary to compensate for the continuous devaluation of capital. It is essential that this cash-flow exist in liquid form or in short-term payments so that there are enough resources available at all times to deal effectively with intercapitalist monopoly competition.

Let us summarize the argument. The cheapening of the elements of constant capital requires massive technological innovation, which can only be financed by very large corporations. However, the continuous devaluation of fixed capital and new conditions of intercapitalist competition demand so much capital that it greatly exceeds the ability of the corporations to generate it from their own process of accumulation. Therefore, the general level of debt of the society increases dramatically. There is a growing gap between the value produced and the amount of money in circulation. This is a cause of inflation.

Because of the pressure on the financial markets, interest rates become higher, increasing the price of capital in the production process. This is also a cause of inflation, as well as of recession.

Finally, the necessity for corporations to maintain large cash reserves for short-term emergencies encourages speculative investments and increases the monetary value of capital without contributing to the process of accumulation through production. The result is a higher amount of nominal capital for a given total output, reinforcing tendencies toward structural inflation.

Thus, the process of technological innovation under monopoly capital triggers several major contradictions that lead to inflation.

3.3.3. The Expansion of Outlets

The crises of accumulation could be partially prevented if the crises of realization that are the consequence of overaccumulation of capital could be avoided or shortened. In order to counteract this tendency, which produces an increasing gap between the productive capacity and the consuming capacity of the system, new outlets must be created that do not interfere with the distribution of income among consumers. There are two decisive factors in the expansion of outlets in advanced capitalism that are part of two crucial structural trends that redefine the whole process of accumulation: increasing state intervention, which creates public demand; and the internationalization of capital, which includes the formation of a world market.

There is an additional mechanism introduced by a conscious capitalist policy in the aftermath of World War II that really helped stimulate consumption by expanding outlets—sales effort.[42] It has three important aspects.

First is the "scientific management" of the market through marketing techniques and monopoly control over prices, quality, and other characteristics of the products. One could say that we have moved from a market economy to a marketing society.

Second is the conditioning and stimulation of consumption through massive advertising. Commercial advertising has become one of the most sophisticated, expensive, and powerful ideological apparatuses in history. Although it is not completely able to shape people's minds, it does have a great deal of influence on the production of cultural values and human behavior patterns in advanced capitalism.

Third, in a capitalist economy it is not enough for people to consume. It is also necessary to maintain a solvent demand, that is, to have people with money to pay for consumer goods. One of the basic features of capitalist accumulation in the last thirty years has been the massive expansion of consumer demand through credit. This represents an increasing debt for families and accelerates the amount of the means of payment at a higher rate than the amount of production. The permanent use of credit is one of the main mechanisms used to stimulate demand. It has led to a widening of the gap between the production and the circulation of capital that favors inflation, as we shall see in our study of the so-called debt economy in the United States.

3.3.4. The Devaluation of a Fraction of Social Capital

The fall of the rate of profit on the level of global social capital will not disturb the drive of capitalist growth as long as particular fractions of hegemonic capital continue to be remunerated at a rate equal or superior to the previous one.

Yet, it seems that our recent historical experience fits within this analysis. That is, if one can observe a fall in the global rate of accumulation of advanced capitalist societies, there is at the same time a fluctuation in the profit rate of the large monopoly sectors. In order for such a differential evolution to happen, it is necessary that an important fraction of the capital accumulated at the level of society be *devalued*—that is, that it cease to function as capital (becoming, for example, public spending functioning at a loss) or that it be remunerated at a profit rate lower than the average one. Some capital will continue to be invested in certain areas even though the profit rate is low.

This trend is not a purely economic mechanism. Such a situation implies the nonfunctioning of the law of equalization of the rate of profit, which was established by Marx and is one of the bases for the releasing of crises. The relative rigidity of capital at the monopolistic stage produces economies that could be characterized in some ways as "dualist," that is, economies in which the monopolistic sector and the small and medium capital sector follow different rules of economic behavior.[43]

The monopolistic sector *imposes* these conditions. Instead of completely absorbing the backward sectors, it uses them as a kind of cushion for absorbing crises, as a reservoir of labor power, and as a means of devaluating capital. By forcing them to function at a profit rate lower than average, it raises its own profit by as much. For, on the one hand, it lowers its own costs; and, on the other hand, it lines up its prices with those of the backward sectors, which are necessarily higher because their lower productivity increases the cost of production.

Such an economic "dualism" establishes in a structural manner the growing distortion in the relations between the cost of production and the exchange of products. With backward sectors maintained and prices aligned accordingly, all the profits generated by the productivity of labor are put back into the hands of the monopolies. The social lowering of production costs made possible by technological progress is therefore appropriated by monopoly capital on the basis of its domination over a large sector of the economy functioning with devalued capital.

Nevertheless, the essential part of the process of devaluation of capital occurs by means of the growing deductions that the state takes out of the accumulated surplus value. The systematic intervention of the state into the economy constitutes the principal countertendency to overcome crises. The state thereby becomes the main factor of structural change in advanced capitalism.

3.3.5. *Capitalist Accumulation and State Intervention*

After the great crisis of 1929, the theory and practice of advanced capitalism saw a systematic intervention of the state into the whole of the economy gradually take place.[44] At first, and in agreement with Keynesian analyses, the intervention had limited objectives, such as renewing demand by unbonded, short-term public investments and establishing procedures capable of regulating and programming the fluctuations of the capitalist economy in ways that would prevent crisis. However, state intervention has now become an essential part of advanced capitalist economies in all countries regardless of what the principal modality of that intervention might be, running from nationalization (as in France or Italy) to massive public spending (as in the United States).[45] Through a diversity of forms, this intervention assumes five principal functions, each of which is essential to the survival of the system.*

1. *The state assumes a fundamental role in the devaluation of a fraction of the social capital*, which allows monopolies to raise the profit rate by transforming a part of the accumulated surplus value into public expenditures without any direct reference to profit (while yet not excluding the search for productivity through budgetary rationalization). This practice shifts to the state the costs of unprofitable economic activities. But we must insist that it is not a question of a "service" rendered to any particular capitalist; rather, it is a permanent act of devaluation aimed at fighting the effect on particular profit rates of the global tendency of the rate of profit to fall. In much the same way, the American government years ago burned a part of the wheat harvest to maintain world prices. What crises of accumulation were

---

* Beyond the traditional functions of the state as a political and ideological apparatus that is shaped mostly by the dominating classes (which functions nevertheless also play an economic role related to unproductive expenditures that generate demand and are useful in the management operations of capital).

doing to fixed capital investments until World War II is now being done permanently to prevent those crises, mostly through state action.

2. *The state subsidizes private capital directly and indirectly*, particularly the hegemonic fractions of monopoly capital. It does so directly through fiscal measures such as loans and credits with advantageous conditions, as well as by means of tying public funds to economic ventures under the direction of the corporations. It does so indirectly by furnishing indispensable equipment and services to monopoly firms—industrial infrastructure, energy, transportation, etc. In this way, the devalued capital contributes to the valuation of private monopoly capital following the pattern of power among the different fractions of capital.

3. *The state assumes more and more of the social costs of private capital*. In fact, most of the costs of the reproduction of labor power, at the historically defined level of their needs, are provided by the state. In most advanced capitalist countries the state assumes a major part of the costs of scientific research. This support is essential for technological progress and includes education and training of the labor power. These expenses are fundamental to the development of the productivity of social labor, but they are very expensive for capital. Therefore, the state's taking over these expenses is equivalent to a global increase in the value produced by the same variable capital. There is a lowering of the organic composition of capital, without particular capitalists having to increase their own expenses in variable capital or in technological research.

4. *The state contributes to the continuous expansion of outlets* in order to counteract monopolistic overaccumulation and prevent a crisis of overproduction. This expansion is achieved by continuously developing unproductive activities that generate a very important demand. Huge military expenditures, for example, represent a major means of state support of monopolistic accumulation. Next to military expenditures one can place the expanding omnipresent, useless administrative bureaucracy (as in Spain or Italy) or the persistence of sumptuary expenses that represent a significant part of the budget of numerous states. Also, by absorbing surplus population and reducing the tendency toward unemployment through increasing the proportion of

salaried civil servants, the state maintains the consuming capacity of the society.

Without such a mass of unproductive expenditures, there would be no outlets for the level of accumulation reached by monopolies. The intervention of the state in this domain, then, is essential.[46]

5. Finally, in advanced capitalism *the state plays a growing role in the reproduction of social relations and in the organization of the social division of labor*.[47] It plays an indispensable role in the development of the processes of production, distribution, and management in developing them in the interest of monopolies. This intervention is manifested in regulations that affect the functioning of education, health, mass media, housing and transportation. This intervention increases unproductive expenditures because it acts on the means for reproducing labor power toward ends that are essentially tied to reproducing the dominant social relations.

The intervention of the state in the economy is a countertendency essential to keeping monopoly capitalism out of crisis. This intervention requires a continuous flow of public expenditures in order to act *at the same time and in a permanent manner on the five functions we have analyzed*. Now, where do these resources come from? There are only two possible sources.

First, they come from fiscal measures in different forms—that is, a levy on the surplus value. Although it has continued to grow, this levy does have a double limit. It can only operate on profits or revenues distributed in the form of wages and transfers.

However, the profit rate cannot be seriously reduced by the state in a capitalist society below certain levels unless there is strong political pressure from the working class that forces such a move.

Wages (direct or indirect) also cannot be reduced below a certain point because to do so would cause a great decrease in consumer demand and lead to social and political unrest. In spite of the rapid increase in the taxation of revenues in advanced capitalism, fiscal policies face a mounting opposition. The limits on the state's ability to draw on fiscal resources to match its growing expenses provokes the development of what James O'Connor calls "the fiscal crisis of the State" as one of the fundamental trends of advanced capitalism.[48] Fiscal policy does not have the capacity to cope with the huge increases in public expenditures. Out of this limitation has come the necessity of finding new sources.

These sources can only be currency and credit in various forms, such as the traditional public debt loans given for certain activities. As the demand for means of payment increases without a corresponding expansion of material production, the state is forced to make its currency nonconvertible and to abandon all economic controls on the issuing of money, which becomes more and more dependent on political relations of power.

The growing mass of liquidities in relation to the goods placed on the market is one of the primary and fundamental sources of inflation. However, this situation is not a purely monetary phenomenon. It is an expression of the structural gap existing between value and prices. And one of the fundamental causes of this gap is the growing demand for the state to develop its expenditures above and beyond the productive capacities of the society as the only means for artificially maintaining the rate of profit of monopoly capital.

In this way, monopoly capital, state intervention, and creeping inflation are structurally tied to each other. And these contradictions become more and more acute because they are developing at a time when the internationalization of capital has entwined the majority of societies in the world framework of the capitalist mode of production.[49]

3.3.6. Capital Accumulation and the Internationalization of Capital: The New Imperialism, Transnational Corporations, and World Inflation

Among the countertendencies to the fall of the profit rate cited in Volume III of *Capital*, Marx includes the "development of foreign trade." This can be interpreted as opening outlets and internationalizing the market. This is, indeed, one of the fundamental characteristics of present-day capitalism. One can also extend the reasoning, as Lenin did, to the internationalization of capital. Surplus accumulation leads to monopoly capital investment throughout the world, not only in order to pillage natural resources but as an opportunity to invest great amounts of capital that risk overaccumulating in the financial markets of the capitalist metropolises.

Advanced capitalism is made up of economic units related to each other on a world scale in capital, markets, and the labor process (internationalization of labor power, international interdependent chains of production and distribution, etc.), all benefiting from the development of transportation and communication technology.[50] Today's capitalism is marked by the domination of transnational corporations. It is not that capital does not have a nation. In reality most of these corporations are American, and it is mainly the American government that defends their interests, which extend over the entire globe. Their operations intermix in articulated links from one country to another, depending on how favorable they find the conditions. But they are not placed above the state institutions of the different countries. On the contrary, they are joined to them in a specific manner, playing one against the other and organizing in a different way their ties to the "internal bourgeoisies" of each society.[51]

This process underlies the phenomenon of peripheral industrialization that has taken place in the last decade. Dominant and dependent capitalist societies are seeing their relationships deeply transformed on these grounds. For instance, when the German branch of Volkswagen, Inc. stopped producing the legendary Beetle, its production in Brazil and Mexico was greatly increased in order to supply the market in the United States. Of course, this tendency does *not* imply that now the "Arabs" and other "nouveaux riches" have reversed the trend, using their oil resources to take control over American and European economies. Peripheral industrialization is mostly directed by the transnational corporations. What is true, however, is that the new international division of labor embraces the whole world economy in a much closer way by developing new interdependent relationships of which the transnational corporations are the nerve centers.

Capitalist internationalization has played an extraordinary role in increasing the profit rate for big business for the following reasons:

1. The transnational corporation has profited from the com-

parative advantages of each economic or political location in each operation in the process of production and distribution.

2. There has been a considerable acceleration in the speed of the rotation of capital invested under these conditions.

3. The transnational corporation receives aid from each state in which it operates, instead of being limited to receiving aid only from its home state. American corporations in Europe, for example, were developed essentially with loans and subsidies from the European states.

4. There has been a huge expansion of markets for goods as well as capital.

5. The transnational corporation has been able to circumvent all state economic frontiers: financial and fiscal controls are bypassed by simple bookkeeping transfers within the transnational corporations.

At the same time, *this fundamental countertendency to avoid capitalist crisis is one of the greatest sources of inflation given the close linkage of all capital flows on a world scale*. Individual countries are unable to defend themselves against inflation because their economies are so dependent on each other.

Charles Levinson has analyzed in a striking manner the relationship between transnational corporations and inflation in a book that provides some decisive insights into the problem.[52] Transnational corporations have a great impact on structural inflation because they are able to put considerable pressure on financial markets all over the world. They are responsible also for accelerating inflation in three fundamental ways: by contributing to the instantaneous spread of economic movements to each economy because they increase sensitivity to business cycles; by making it impossible for individual states to develop national policies of economic planning; and by bringing into existence a transnational cash-flow, which is necessary to these corporations because it determines the amount of "floating capital" available for short-term investments. Gradually, the large corporations begin to use their cash-flow for systematic speculation, which is one of the causes of the monetary crisis.

Such massive displacements, practiced with a high degree of skill and knowledge on the evolution of business cycles, provoke virtual financial and monetary catastrophes and make all economies vulnerable because they are unable to resist these back-and-forth movements. An example of what happens when extreme and unstable solutions are used can be seen in the practice of making West Germany a sponge capable of absorbing floating capital through successive revaluations of the mark owing to a surplus trade balance. Since this solution is not feasible except in a world environment untouched by recession, these "remedy" risks are being transformed into a potential tragedy. The tragedy will happen one day when the Federal Bank of Germany decides to apply the same restrictive measures as the American Treasury if its position in the export markets comes to be threatened.

One of the most visible effects of the new contradictions generated by the process of internationalization of capital was the crisis of the international monetary system, which was the first important sign of the structural economic crisis. Since this is fundamentally the crisis of the dollar, on which the system was relying as the exchange currency, we will analyze later its causes and effects in the framework of the development of the economic crisis in the United States.[53]

4. A THEORETICAL FRAMEWORK FOR ANALYZING THE WORLD ECONOMIC CRISIS

We can now summarize the different elements we have developed during the preceding discussion and organize them in a way that will provide a tentative explanation of the structural causes of the current economic crisis.

The process of capitalist accumulation is a process of class struggle. Because of the historical social domination of capital, it is able to expand through development of the productive forces under its control and through competition between different capital units. This process has to face increasing obstacles: class struggle limits the appropriation of surplus value by reducing absolute exploitation; the development of productive forces increases the technical composition of capital and, under certain conditions, the organic composition, which tends to lead to a falling rate of profit; intercapitalist competition leads toward monopoly concentration posing very serious problems at the level of the realization of commodities and devaluation of fixed capital. To overcome the tendencies toward overaccumulation and crisis, the state becomes the nerve center of the whole process, and capital expands its accumulation worldwide. The major counter-tendencies used to prevent the profit rate from falling (particularly state intervention) provoke structural inflation. Therefore, advanced capitalist economies oscillate between stagnation and inflation. And because it has been a process of internationalization of capital and markets, the crisis becomes a world crisis. Figure 4 tries to organize in a systematic way the set of relationships underlying the economic crisis of the seventies, as postulated in the analysis we have presented.

The basic principle of this approach is that an economic crisis, like all historical processes, has to be understood from a dialectical point of view. That is, a given reality must be seen as the result of the contradictory forces, not only because reality is shaped by struggles between classes but also because it is the practical synthesis of structural tendencies toward opposed systemic effects. The outcome of this set of contradictory forces is not undetermined. It depends upon human action. As is well know, humankind makes its own history, but does so under specifically defined social conditions. We have tried to show, on the one hand, the interplay in the production of the structural trends of capital accumulation by the historical practices of classes and, on the other hand, the constraints that this structure *continuously* creates for such historical practices.

The fruitfulness of the theoretical framework presented here can only be tested by concrete analyses of economic crises in particular historical situations. Because the United States is the center of the capitalist system, any attempt to understand the present worldwide crisis must start from the study of the development of the crisis in American capitalism. But if the analysis is going to explain certain historical processes, we may proceed, according to our theoretical approach, by studying societies, and not capital flows. So we must consider the economic crisis as an expression of the contradictions of a class society—that is, class struggle—and as a process closely linked to political conflicts and decisions in the American state. Therefore, this book should be considered as both an attempt to understand the contradictory evolution of American society and an effort to recast and reformulate a social theory of economic crises.

Figure 4

Tendencies and Countertendencies toward the Crisis of Accumulation

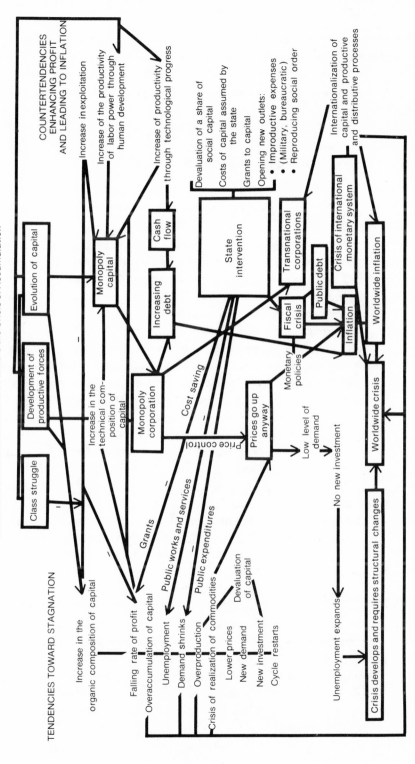

2

■■■

What Happened: The Roots and the Development of the Economic Crisis in the United States

T HE WORST economic crisis of American capitalism since World War II openly appeared in 1974. It was characterized by the simultaneous spread of stagnation, unemployment, and inflationary pressure. After a short recovery in 1973, the balance of payment continued its deteriorating trend. Corporation profits fell dramatically, and capital consequently reduced its investment plans. Figures 5, 6, 7, and 8 provide some indications of the acuteness of the cycle's downturn. From the beginning the crisis was considered serious because for the first time since the 1930s the business cycle was synchronized throughout the world, reinforcing the tendencies toward recession in all capitalist nations.[1]

Furthermore, the crisis struck the United States at a time when its political foundations were being shaken both internally and externally. Watergate was a major breach in the legitimacy of the highly integrated American political system, and it showed the limits of the concentration of power in the top levels of the executive branch. The historical defeat in Indochina proved that there were also limits to an imperial policy that was being resisted all over the world as well as in the United States.

These political trends, together with some major corresponding ideological crises (the ecological and feminist movements, among others), are a very significant part of the picture. Understanding their precise meaning depends on a general sociological analysis that must proceed step by step and must link the economic cycle to the economic structure, then to the social structure, and then to the political conflicts. In fact, the connection

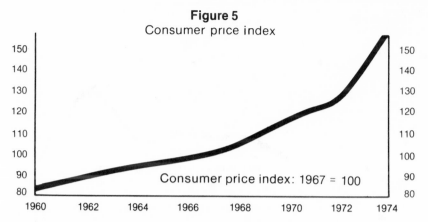

Figure 5
Consumer price index

1960-1973 are yearly figures; 1973-1974 are monthly averages
Source: *Monthly Labor Review*, Jan. 1975.

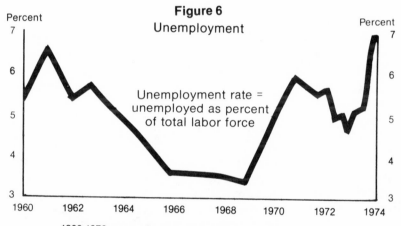

Figure 6
Unemployment

1960-1972 are yearly rates; 1972-1974 are monthly rates
Source: *Monthly Labor Review*, Jan. 1975.

between political conflicts and economic contradictions appears
to be the most immediate and striking trend of the phenomenon
under analysis. How could such a crisis happen in an economy
that had sustained a long-term expansionary cycle? How was
this destabilization possible in a society that had developed such
a powerful system of social integration? Let us turn to the history
of the 1960s.

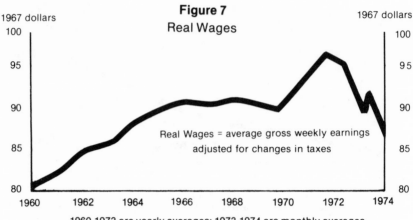

Figure 7
Real Wages

1967 dollars

Real Wages = average gross weekly earnings
adjusted for changes in taxes

1960-1973 are yearly averages; 1973-1974 are monthly averages
Source: *Monthly Labor Review*, Jan. 1975.

Figure 8

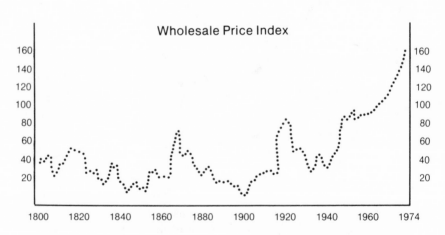

Wholesale Price Index

Source: Bureau of Labor Statistics , as compiled by Union of Radical Political
Economics, *Radical Perspectives on the Crisis of Monopoly Capitalism*, New York:
URPE-PEA, 1975.

1. THE EVOLUTION OF THE BUSINESS CYCLE
IN THE LATE SIXTIES

A combination of several stimulating factors had allowed the
United States economy to have a sustained long-term economic
growth regulated by periodic business cycles. These factors included qualitative improvements in technology, the expansion of
markets at the world level, a huge increase in the debt and credit
system, development of public spending and state support of the
economy, and a high level of military expenditures.

In the early sixties the New Frontier policies were designed to
treat the major bottlenecks of the American economy by rationalizing the system, increasing consumer demand, and stimulating the economy through public spending in research, education, health, fixed capital, and the development of military
supplies. Having disciplined the labor movement through the
1958 recession, the American economy, powerfully stimulated by
the state and the demand from European markets, made one of
its most spectacular upturns in the period from 1960 to 1965. In
1965-1966 the economy required a new recession from the point
of view of corporate capital to curb wages and improve productivity of the workers, thus raising the rate of exploitation, and to reduce inflation that was endangering the credit system and creating social and economic instability.[2]

However, even though the United States needed a recession
economically, the government could not afford it politically. The
warfare-welfare state was more important than ever at the peak
of the Vietnam War because of the massive involvement of U.S.
troops and because of the first waves of social unrest that were
breaking in the ghettos. This situation required more welfare to
promote integration and more police to facilitate repression.
Without a reduction in public expenditures, which could have
started the recession, the boom continued. Unemployment rates
remained *relatively* low. Wages increased in relation to profits
because workers in the monopoly sector were able to take advantage of the labor shortage during this sustained expansionary
phase.[3] As a result, the ratio of profits to wages declined sharply.
The share of profits of nonfinancial corporations in the GNP went
down from 10 percent in 1965 to 5.3 percent in 1970. Real profits
(calculated in 1958 dollars) were reduced from $78.4 billion in

1966 to $63.5 billion in 1970. This trend seriously affected the dynamics of capitalist growth, since the reduction of profits threatened to accelerate the shift from investments in the United States to investments in Western Europe, which were much more profitable.

At the same time, such a long boom accentuated the structural trend toward inflation. Furthermore, the same political factors that had enabled the government to engineer a recession were also decisive in stimulating inflation. Because the Vietnam War was highly unpopular, military expenditures were financed by increases in the public debt and the money supply rather than by new taxes. People thus had more money to spend without an equivalent creation of new value. Not only did the state add new demand to the economy, but it also failed to cut down on purchasing power by raising taxes. Full employment and expanding demand and purchasing power were political measures used to prevent the potential alignment of students, blacks, and labor in the antiwar movement.

Faced with a continuously expanding demand, public and private corporate capital maintained their investments in spite of the decreasing profitability of capital. The only way out was to borrow from financial lenders. Corporate debt increased dangerously. Such an increase in private debt was one of the major accelerating factors in the creeping inflation because it increased dramatically the means of payment without inducing a corresponding increase in commodities produced.

Because the U.S. economy had become so closely linked to the world economy, these threatening trends were reinforced by the deterioration of the U.S. position in the international exchanges. The crisis of the dollar and the deterioration of the balance of trade undermined the economic and political hegemony that were major factors in the formation of profits for the leading U.S. corporations.[4] This development also accentuated the outflow of American capital and increased the competition from foreign-made commodities in the American market.[5]

This deterioration in the international position of the United States played a very important part in the economic policies of the Nixon administration. In 1969-1970 Nixon engineered a recession in order to fight inflation and restore the rate of exploitation in the overheated industries. But the recession was too short. In August 1971 he launched his "New Economic Policy" in order to restart the economy, provoking a major upswing from 1971 to 1973. Many observers have interpreted this change of direction in Nixon's economic policy as an electoral maneuver to keep the economy working for his 1972 election. This is a plausible inference if we consider the Republican party tradition in that sense. However, if we examine in detail the measures undertaken in the period from August to December 1971, such as the devaluation of the dollar, wage controls, deficit spending, and export aids, we will find that they were measures undertaken to restore the U.S. position in the world economy. At the same time, they were intended to aid the major corporations by compensating them for their relative loss in not being able to use dollars so widely as a major tool of economic power. Although Nixon paid a great deal of attention to his personal political interests, he also had to remember what the major requirements were for the reproduction of a system that structurally favored the large U.S. corporations in the international economy. As we will explain in the following paragraphs, such a system was endangered by the simultaneous deterioration of the U.S. balance of payments and its political hegemony. To act in the interest of big corporations on the economic level it was necessary to end the recession and to stimulate exports. However, the measures implemented by Nixon had several immediate consequences that precipitated inflation and started the crisis.

The two major elements that triggered this inflationary process were food prices and oil prices. Both have to be considered in a broader context. Their effect was mostly to accelerate (and not to cause) an inflation that had been growing steadily since 1961. Furthermore, these price increases were the result of policies being pursued in order to restore the economic hegemony of the United States at the international level. Let us examine the two precipitating factors of inflation.

In the first half of 1973 retail food prices rose by more than 10 percent. Why this increase? Except for the United States, 1972 was a year of crop failure, especially in the Soviet Union. But the decisive factor in the increase of food prices was the support by the Nixon administration of food production for export, particularly grain, in order to restore the balance of trade. Agricultural exports from the United States averaged about $5 billion a year from 1966 to 1969. This increased to $9.4 billion in 1972, and then rose to $17.5 billion in 1973. The government favored and systematically followed this policy in order to allow the agricultural sector higher profit margins on exports.[6] Obviously, food prices began to rise dramatically on the internal market because in 1973 and subsequent years the United States exported half of its grain crop.

A similar trend determined the oil-price increase in the fall of 1973. Increases in food and oil prices accounted for 60 percent of the cost of the increased prices in 1973 and triggered the inflationary process that caused the economy to collapse in 1974, as a consequence of the sudden acceleration of the structural trends toward inflation linked to the boom that lasted almost without interruption for fourteen years.

Is the "oil crisis" an exogenous factor, which suddenly attacked the unstable U.S. economy provoking a major disruption? Not at all, for several reasons.[7]

As we have seen in the Introduction, we cannot speak of an oil crisis in terms of shortage of supply. The proper way to analyze the crisis is to focus on the dramatic rise in oil *prices* and the consequent rise in the cost of energy in general.

The increase in the price of oil and the importance of its impact on the Western economies is a contradictory consequence of the rise and fall of American hegemony in the world. The United States, Britain, and the transnational corporations were able to dominate the oil-producing countries without any possible opposition (remember Mossadegh), and their entire economic expansion has been based on the assumption of unlimited cheap energy. However, because of the unstable political balance of forces in the Middle East, the oil-producing countries were able to challenge the United States and other dominant countries by increasing the price of oil after years and years of artificial price leveling during a period of world inflation.

Once the historical patterns of power in the Middle East were eroded, it became clear to the big oil companies that they could not refuse, in the long term, a move that gave them in the short term (because of the sudden and dramatic character of the event) two major advantages: immediate high profits from revaluation of stocks and short-term speculation; and public support and incentives to explore new fields in safer regions (Alaska, North Atlantic Ocean) and to develop, *under their own control*, new sources of energy (especially nuclear power).

The United States used the "oil crisis" to improve its balance-of-payments position with respect to its major creditors in Western Europe and Japan. The European countries and Japan had to assemble a huge amount of dollars in order to pay for their oil imports since they were much more dependent on them than the United States was.[8] This outflow of dollars from the banks in Europe and Japan greatly improved the U.S. balance of payments. This, perhaps, explains the relatively mild reaction of the United States toward such Arab countries as Saudi Arabia, which had traditionally been dominated by the United States. Nevertheless, we reject the explanation of some observers in Europe[9] who have argued that the United States manipulated the crisis. In fact, the movement did spread to other countries more important to the United States (such as Venezuela and Mexico); the rise in the price of foreign oil had an impact on the price of domestic oil; and the inflationary crackdown in Europe also had dramatic consequences for the United States and for the U.S. corporations in Europe. In summary, then, if it is true that the United States did think about taking advantage of the situation in the beginning to restore its balance of payments with respect to its competitors, it became clear later that such a policy could seriously damage its political and economic interests in the long run. For proof we can point to the threats the United States made to intervene unilaterally against the oil producers and to the diplomatic pressures applied on Israel and Egypt to stabilize the political situation in the area. What is implied here is the existence of some level of contradiction between the interests of the oil companies in the crisis and the interest of the capitalist system as a whole.

Thus, the sudden acceleration of inflation at the world level, stimulated by the increases in food and oil prices and public and private debt, inevitably led to a major recession under the combined impact of shrinking demand (because of the increase in prices) and falling investment determined mostly by the deterioration of the profits-to-wages ratio and by the cost of money and credit in a financial market shaken by uncontrolled expanding debt and falling profitability of capital. In addition to this, some anti-inflationary public policies, mostly for controlling credit and reducing public spending, were initiated. Their result was to deepen the recession. The economy was in a crisis. Recession and inflation were to develop simultaneously.

This situation was a clear indication that a new and disturbing economic trend was under way in the advanced capitalist societies. Can it be explained *only* by the cyclical factors we have presented? Certainly not. It is true that these elements played a decisive role in triggering the crisis at a particular time as well as in shaping it. But, as we shall see, both the recession and the inflation and their effects had been determined by the major structural contradictions of capitalist accumulation and the particular form these contradictions took in American society.

2. TOWARD A STRUCTURAL EXPLANATION OF THE CRISIS IN THE U.S. ECONOMY

Capitalist accumulation is characterized by its economic instability and its potential for social disruption. Between the Civil War and World War II the U.S. economy experienced eleven major recessions, the most serious one being, of course, the Depression of 1929 to 1935. After this giant collapse of the economy, which spread throughout the world, only the war combined with so-called Keynesian policies, which introduced the state as a major economic force, were able to restart the process of accumulation within the framework of monopoly capitalism. However, after this structural transformation in 1945, and in spite of six additional downturns in the business cycle, a long-term period of economic growth was experienced. But this upward movement has been abruptly stopped and subsequently modified by the current crisis. *It is our hypothesis that the same major socioeconomic trends that allowed this long-term expansion are the structural roots of the crisis of the seventies.*

We have to understand this as a complex *contradictory process* where the structural problems inherent to the capitalist mode of production are temporarily overcome by the historical practice of the bourgeoisie and the state. But the elements introduced to handle the obstacles that had appeared in the accumulation process led to a new set of contradictions, which eventually produced a new form of economic crisis.

Our method will be first to examine the major structural contradictions that U.S. capitalism had to solve in order to develop itself and then to turn to the historical pattern used in dealing with these contradictions. Finally, we will try to relate the profile of the crisis we have described to the contradictions arising from the interaction between the structural problems and the process of problem solving.[10]

2.1. THE MAJOR CONTRADICTIONS OF CAPITALIST ACCUMULATION IN THE POSTWAR U.S. ECONOMY

The major requirements for a capitalist process of accumulation to expand at a general level are: first, to be able to exploit labor power, appropriating the largest possible share of surplus value produced in the process of productive work; second, to realize this appropriated surplus value by transforming it into commodities to be sold in a continuously expanding market; and, third, to maintain and, if possible, raise the rate of profit, always searching for higher profits and reproducing the social and economic conditions for such a move in changing technological and political environments. This trend, which involves the evolution of the rate of profit, requires more and more state support of the entire capitalist social organization. In fact, it is the decisive point in a capitalist economy. If the rate of profit decreases regularly over a long period, investments will fall and the economy will stagnate in spite of many unsatisfied social needs. Obviously, the level and evolution of the rate of profit are linked directly to the rate of exploitation and to the possibility of its realization through the selling of commodities. However, the profit rate is also determined by additional factors, generally social and political, particularly in the stage of state monopoly capitalism. Let us consider how these problems have been treated in American capitalism since 1945.

2.1.1. *Increasing Difficulties in the Process of Exploitation*

Capitalist accumulation depends on the rate of profit. And the main structural basis for the rate of profit is the rate of exploitation; that is, the relationship between the surplus value produced by labor and appropriated by capital and the cost of living labor for capital: $e = s/v$.

For a given surplus value, the rate of exploitation depends upon the size of v. And since labor power is a commodity, the actual pattern of capital investment in the business cycle is largely determined (at the first level of analysis) by the cost of labor power. This cost includes not only direct wages but also indirect wages (welfare, unemployment insurance, collective consumption expenditures, etc.) socially necessary for the reproduction of labor power.

The commodity character of labor power makes its price dependent upon the conditions of the labor market: the tighter the labor market, the more expensive is labor power. On the other hand, labor power is a very special commodity, able to defend itself and to enhance its own value by withdrawing its contribution in crucial moments of the productive process in order to get higher wages or better working conditions from capital. In other words, the cost of labor power will vary according to the evolution of the economic class struggle between capital and labor. But this class struggle at the economic level will depend on the general relationships of power between capital and labor at the level of society. In particular, it will be determined by the ability of each class to favor its own interests structurally through laws and institutions. Therefore, the cost of labor power for capital will ultimately depend on the conditions and evolution of the political class struggle.

On the other hand, the size of the surplus value obtained by capital will depend, in the process of production, on the amount of labor appropriated and on the productivity of labor. The amount of labor appropriated will also be determined by the capacity of capital to impose its conditions in the work process, as determined by the economic and political class struggle. Increases in productivity will depend on state support of technological research and capital's ability to reorganize the process of production according to productivity requirements without considering labor interests.

Thus, the basic determinants of the rate of exploitation, which is the basis of the rate of profit, will be the labor market, the economic class struggle, and the political class struggle as well as the network of effects of their interaction. How did these factors develop in the postwar U.S. economy?

The labor market became increasingly tighter because the long-term expansionary cycle created, in the monopoly sector, a relatively low rate of unemployment, giving the workers in that sector a stronger bargaining position. This bargaining power was exercised to obtain higher wages, better working conditions, and more social benefits, while resisting to some extent the attempts to increase absolute surplus value through speeding up the work process.

This is the basic argument proposed by Boddy and Crotty in "Class Conflict and Macro-policy" to explain the increasing fall in the rate of profit on American capital. Relying on a statistical study by Albert E. Burger[11] as well as on other studies on the evolution of the ratio between profits and wages, they show a direct relationship between this ratio and the business cycle for the period 1952 to 1972. While in the first phase of the expansion in each cycle the ratio clearly favors profits, halfway through this upward trend the ratio declines and profits fall rapidly until investments drop, starting a recession. The recession spreads unemployment, curbs wages, and disciplines labor, allowing the ratio of profit to wages to be restored. Investments pick up again, causing an upswing in the cycle. Figure 9 and Table 5 show the close relationship between the evolution of the cycle and the profit squeeze.

The relatively high level of employment and the high level of wages for workers in the monopoly sector,* as well as the lack of communication between the labor market in the monopoly sector and that in the other sectors, are in large measure the consequences of the level and form of economic class struggle in the United States. As Table 6 shows, there was a high level of strike activity in American industry until the mid-fifties, imposing on capital many concessions to labor demands, particularly in the crucial period after World War II. Even more important, workers' resistance on the shop floor made it increasingly difficult to extract additional surplus value by speeding up the work process.

* As we shall see in Chapter 3, a low rate of unemployment in the U.S. economy would be considered a high rate in most Western European economies.

Figure 9

Ratio of Profits to Wages

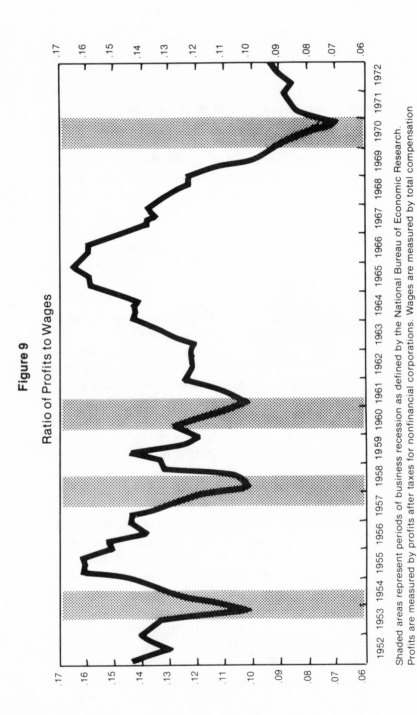

Shaded areas represent periods of business recession as defined by the National Bureau of Economic Research. Profits are measured by profits after taxes for nonfinancial corporations. Wages are measured by total compensation in nonfinancial corporations.

Source: Albert E. Burger, "Relative Movements in Wages and Profits," *Federal Reserve Bank of St. Louis*, Feb. 1973, p. 13.

TABLE. 5. FACTORS INFLUENCING PROFITS/WAGES RATIO
(ANNUAL RATES OF CHANGE IN %) TROUGH TO MID-POINT OF
EXPANSION AND MID-POINT OF EXPANSION TO PEAK

	Wage rate[a]	Unit labor cost[b]	Wholesale prices of industrial commodities	Output price[c]
III/54—I/56				
(6 quarters)	4.6	2.3	3.5	0.2
I/56—III/57				
(6 quarters)	6.8	4.1	3.1	2.8
II/58—II/59				
(4 quarters)	4.9	4.1	2.3	1.3
II/59—II/60				
(4 quarters)	4.5	4.7	0.0	0.6
I/61—III/65				
(18 quarters)	3.9	1.4	0.4	0.7
III/65—IV/69				
(17 quarters)	6.5	4.2	2.7	3.3

	Output per person	Capacity utilization	Output	Profits[d]	Compensation of employees[e]
III/54—I/56					
(6 quarters)	3.5	5.6	8.7	21.6	11.9
I/56—III/57					
(6 quarters)	1.4	4.0	0.9	4.2	5.7
II/58—II/59					
(4 quarters)	12.9	16.4	20.8	63.0	13.2
II/59—II/60					
(4 quarters)	1.7	3.8	0.9	13.9	4.9
I/61—III/65					
(18 quarters)	6.5	4.5	10.1	25.6	7.8
III/65—IV/69					
(17 quarters)	1.6	1.3	4.2	4.0	10.2

Note: Profits and compensation pertain to nonfinancial corporations. All other
data pertain to total manufacturing.
[a] Employee compensation divided by manhours.
[b] Compensation divided by output.
[c] Consumer price index of commodities less food.
[d] Corporate profits after tax liability for nonfinancial corporations.
[e] Compensation of employees in nonfinancial corporations.
Source: Albert E. Burger, "Relative Movements in Wages and Profits," *Federal
Reserve Bank of St. Louis.*, Feb. 1973, p. 13.

Labor's economic gains were obtained mostly through collective bargaining and increased union activity as a consequence of
the more favorable conditions for organizing workers after the
upsurge of more militant unions during the thirties. But this
process is twofold. On the one hand, unionized workers (mostly
in the monopoly sector) obtained higher wages, social benefits,

TABLE 6. WORK STOPPAGES IN THE U.S., 1950-1974

Year	Workers involved (percent of total employed)
1946	10.5
1947	4.7
1948	4.2
1949	6.7
1950	5.1
1951	4.5
1952	7.3
1953	4.7
1954	3.1
1955	5.2
1956	3.6
1957	2.6
1958	3.9
1959	3.3
1960	2.4
1961	2.6
1962	2.2
1963	1.1
1964	2.7
1965	2.5
1966	3.0
1967	4.3
1968	3.8
1969	3.5
1970	4.7
1971	4.6
1972	2.3
1973	2.9
1974	3.4

Source: *Statistical Abstract of the U.S., 1976*, p. 386.

and more professional stability, while the unions improved their position within the workplace. On the other hand, after the bitter struggles of the late forties, capital obtained a decisive victory: collective bargaining could settle wages and benefits but would not interfere with the organization of the work process, which remained entirely under the control of management. Furthermore, in exchange for higher unemployment benefits, the unions accepted the necessity of suppressing jobs to improve productivity. The result was that monopoly capital could stabilize capital-labor relations, undertake long-term planning of production, and introduce labor-saving investments, which would enhance its profits through large-scale production for a mass market. A tendency toward expanding capitalist accumulation followed. But the basic condition for such stability was the maintenance of a relatively high level of wages and benefits within an increasingly isolated and self-reproducing labor market in the monopoly sector. This was done by a series of arrangements strongly enforced by the unions, which had become a powerful pressure group after the merger of the AFL and CIO in 1955. Because of the strength of labor's bargaining power at the economic level, each time that the expansionary cycle allowed new demands without endangering the stability of the system, the unions pushed toward higher direct and indirect wages. And when in the late sixties capital tried to resist this course, a series of strikes started again, some of them out of union control, putting the level of strike activity back up to that of the early fifties. The ratio of profits to wages went down again, helping cause investment to fall.

This argument needs further specification; otherwise, it might appear to suggest that there was in the relationship between supply and demand an automatic effect of labor power on the business cycle, the rate of profit, and the process of accumulation. In fact, the tightening of American labor markets in the postwar period emerged because of two specific conditions: the particular segmentation of the labor market and the intensity of the class struggle at the economic level.

The segmentation of the labor market between monopoly and competitive sectors is a decisive element in the functioning of American capitalism because of its effect on the division among workers. It also makes possible the transfer to monopoly capital of a significant portion of the value produced in the competitive sector. Furthermore, within the monopoly sector, ethnic and sex characteristics introduce additional cleavages, which are essential for weakening the potential unity of the workers and for over-exploiting some categories. The labor market in the monopoly sector is thus restricted to certain categories of workers already participating in it. The tightening of the market does not come from a shortage of supply but from the constraints preventing capital from extending the market during the expansionary cycle to include the surplus population without endangering the crucial mechanism of labor-market segmentation.

The tensions in the labor market during the expansionary stage of the cycle are the specific effect of characteristics of the economic class struggle in the United States. The importance of this economic level of class struggle for labor in the monopoly sector comes from the particular evolution of the whole class struggle in America since the 1930s.[12] During the Great Depression, an important labor movement developed at a mass level for the first time in the United States. This led to the formation, in 1935, of the Congress of Industrial Organizations, which not only challenged the economic position of capital but also started to question the social organization underlying the economy. The Wagner Act decisively improved working conditions and made it possible for the unions to defend themselves legally against the traditional brutality of American capitalist management. This was, on the one hand, a victory for the workers, obtained by means of hard and painful struggles; on the other hand, it was also the first move toward the integration of the labor movement into the "Keynesian coalition." This coalition, organized around the Democratic party, grew out of the New Deal and had as its goal the reform of U.S. capitalism on more solid grounds.[13] The aftermath of World War II was dominated by the expansion of this political trend, through two complementary processes. One was the repression and control of the labor movement. During the Cold War period, Communist and left-wing labor leaders were isolated and expelled from the unions, and the leadership of the AFL-CIO was held more and more by politically conservative bureaucrats who built their careers on the basis of an outrageous witch-hunt campaign. At the same time, Congress, reacting against a series of powerful and violent strikes, passed the Taft-Hartley Act of 1947. This law reversed most of the gains obtained during the thirties and conceded substantial institutional weapons to business interests, enclosed labor-capital relations within a collective bargaining procedure that restricted the autonomy of workers, and charged the state with the continuous supervision of the established system. This led to a slow but continuous decline of union membership and strength, while increasing the unions' social influence as a full political partner on the grounds of their complete loyalty to capitalism. The complementary process was to reward the unions' loyalty: politically, organized labor became one of the most influential elements of the Democratic party; economically, labor obtained substantial advantages in terms of wages, cost-of-living escalation clauses, participation in capital's profits, and social benefits, both private and public.[14]

Thus, in order to stabilize the whole society, socially and politically, capital had to integrate the labor movement. Combining repression and cooptation, and taking advantage of the Cold War and the ideological weakness of the American Left,[15] the operation was successful. This is how American capitalism in the postwar period was able to gain enough maneuvering room to reorganize itself, creating the conditions favorable to a long-term economic boom. But the price paid for this crucial historical step was a high cost of labor in the monopoly sector and a rigid internal segmentation of the labor market essential for weakening the working class. Under these conditions, the bargaining power of workers in the monopoly sector led to increasing economic demands, fully legitimated within the historical agreements reached to coopt the unions. These demands were subsequently extended to the area of welfare and indirect wages and became particularly acute in the periods of expansion, contributing to the cyclical deterioration of the ratio of profits to wages: this is one of the main tendencies leading toward a falling rate of profit and toward subsequent stagnation in American capitalism.

Nevertheless, although the wages of the workers were raised, the rate of exploitation actually increased, and real take-home pay went down, as shown by Victor Perlo's interesting calculations. How can this phenomenon be explained?

First of all, there was the huge increase in productivity and its differential appropriation. Second, the increased labor costs were added on to the cost of the products by the monopoly corporations that had control over the market. This does not mean that workers are spreading inflation because they ask for higher wages. In fact, the famous Phillips curve, which statistically relates the level of employment and inflation, is based upon one implicit postulate—the maintenance of the rate of profit. What is to say that an upturn in wages is inflationary when the capitalists do not pay for it but force the consumers (that is, the workers) to do so instead?[16] It is too easy to accuse labor unions of being irre-

Figure 10

Prices, Labor Costs, and Workers' Share in Production, U.S.
1946-1970 (1946 = 100)

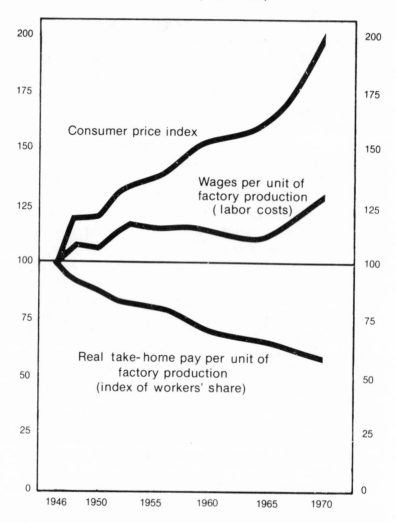

Source: Victor Perlo, *The Unstable Economy: Booms and Recessions in the U.S. Since 1945*, New York: International Publishers, 1973, p. 31.

TABLE 7. TRENDS IN RATE OF EXPLOITATION OF LABOR, U.S. MANUFACTURING INDUSTRY, 1946-1969*

(1957-1959 = 100)

Year	Volume of production	Man-hours of production workers	Productivity per man-hour (Col. 1/Col. 2)	Real take-home pay per week	Average weekly hours	Real take-home pay per man-hour (Col. 4/Col. 5)	Exploitation of labor (Col. 3/Col. 6)	Labor's share in production (Col. 6/Col. 3)
1946	60.0	98.7	60.8	81.2	101.3	80.2	75.8	131.9
1947	66.4	104.7	63.4	79.5	101.6	78.2	81.1	123.3
1948	68.9	103.2	66.8	81.3	100.6	80.8	82.7	121.0
1949	65.1	92.1	70.7	83.2	98.3	84.6	83.6	119.7
1950	75.8	101.2	74.9	87.7	101.8	86.1	87.0	115.0
1951	81.9	108.5	75.5	86.2	102.1	84.4	89.5	111.8
1952	85.2	108.5	78.5	88.0	102.3	86.0	91.3	109.6
1953	92.7	113.7	81.5	91.1	101.8	89.5	91.1	109.8
1954	86.3	101.4	85.1	91.4	99.6	91.8	92.7	107.9
1955	97.3	108.0	90.1	97.7	102.3	95.5	94.3	106.0
1956	100.2	108.4	92.4	99.8	101.6	98.2	94.1	106.3
1957	100.8	104.8	96.2	99.3	100.1	99.2	97.0	103.1
1958	93.2	93.8	99.4	97.9	98.6	99.3	100.1	99.9
1959	106.0	101.3	104.6	102.7	101.3	101.4	103.2	96.9
1960	108.9	99.7	109.2	102.1	99.8	102.3	106.7	93.7
1961	109.6	96.1	114.0	103.7	100.1	103.6	110.0	90.9
1962	118.7	100.6	118.0	106.9	101.6	105.2	112.2	89.2
1963	124.9	101.4	123.2	108.1	101.8	106.2	116.0	86.2
1964	133.1	103.9	128.1	112.6	102.3	110.1	116.3	85.9
1965	145.0	110.4	131.3	116.6	103.6	112.5	116.7	85.7
1966	158.6	118.0	134.4	116.4	103.9	112.0	120.0	83.3
1967	159.7	115.9	137.8	115.3	102.1	112.9	122.1	81.9
1968	166.8	117.9	141.5	116.3	102.3	113.7	124.5	80.4
1969	173.9	119.5	145.5	115.2	102.1	112.8	129.0	77.5

Sources:

Col. 1. *Business Statistics*, 1969, p. 16; *Survey of Current Business*, May 1970, p. S-3.

Col. 2. *Business Statistics*, 1969, pp. 72 and 74; *Survey of Current Business*, May 1970, p. S-14.

Col. 4. *Handbook of Labor Statistics*, 1969, Table 88; *Monthly Labor Review*, May 1970, Table 22 (average of no dependent and 3 dependents).

Col. 5. *Business Statistics*, 1969, p. 74; *Survey of Current Business*, May 1970, p. S-14.

Business Statistics and *Survey of Current Business* are published by the Commerce Department. *Handbook of Labor Statistics* and *Monthly Labor Review* are publications of the Labor Department.

* Computed by Victor Perlo, *The Unstable Economy*, New York: International Publishers, 1973.

sponsible and widening the gap between organized and unorganized workers on the basis of their differential capacity to keep up with prices during an inflationary period.

In sum, U.S. capitalism had to keep the labor market fragmented to stabilize capital-labor relations in the monopoly sector, thereby preserving relative social peace with the mainstream of labor unions. It did this by paying more to one fraction of the working class. The development of this pattern in an expansionary phase implied a higher cost of labor and threatened the rate of exploitation, which underlies the rate of profit. However, capital was able to keep ahead because of its ability to appropriate productivity gains and pass on labor costs in prices charged for goods. Capital would obviously have preferred to increase exploitation rather than increase productivity because it required less investment. But it was forced to labor-saving investments by labor's resistance to absolute exploitation.

By following the path of greater productivity, it accentuated the contradictions inherent in a higher technical composition of capital and developed a surplus population that threatened the expansion of the internal market and the stability of the social order. By using its control over the market to increase prices, it encouraged inflation and threatened both the consumers' purchasing ability and the financial stability required for the circulation of capital.

Thus, the evolution of the rate of exploitation appears to be linked to the problem of realization and to the structural determinants of the rate of profit.

2.1.2. *The Outlets Problem: The Crisis of Realization in the U.S. Economy*

One of the major problems in capitalist accumulation is the imbalance between the expansion of the sectors that Marx calls Department I (production of the means of production) and Department II (production of the means of consumption). In order to realize profit by selling commodities, a capitalist economy needs enough consumers to pay for the commodities produced by Department II so that this department can be kept working at a level high enough to buy the means of production from Department I. But with the increase in the technical composition of capital required to improve productivity, which in turn raises the rate of profit through increasing relative surplus value, a tendency toward overpopulation and unemployment develops. More and more value is produced by (relatively) fewer and fewer workers. If other sources of employment and income are not expanded, demand shrinks and the commodities are unsold, leading to overproduction, a fall in investment, and then to stagnation. The continuous expansion of the outlets for commodities (and for the kind of commodities that are more profitable) is thus a major requirement for the smooth functioning of a capitalist economy.

The evolution of the composition of demand in the United States shows a clear contradictory pattern. Private consumption amounted to 76.9 percent of the GNP in 1929, providing the essential portion of the outlets. After World War II the share of private consumption declined steadily, falling to 62.9 percent of the GNP in the period from 1961 to 1969. This trend is important because it has continued in spite of a systematic selling effort directed against the progressive shrinking of consumer demand.

The contradiction between the requirements of accumulation and the proportionate expansion of outlets is, as is generally known, the basis of Baran and Sweezy's analysis of the dynamics of U.S. capitalism.[17] We can summarize their argument in the following way. The more national income grows, the larger a share must be devoted to investment in order to maintain the rate of growth. At the same time, if the proportion of income allowed to investment purposes grows steadily, an increasing proportion of the goods produced will be in the sector producing means of production (Department I). Consequently, the share of consumption in the GNP will decrease, and there will be a growing disequilibrium between fixed capital formation and consumption expansion. Under these conditions, major crises of realization can only be avoided by a continuous unlimited expansion of the market for the means of production or by rigorous centralized planning able to foresee and to regulate the lack of adjustment between industrial sectors. Neither of these conditions is realized in American capitalism. Therefore, a rate of growth of investment in the formation of fixed capital higher than the rate of growth of the GNP tends to create excess capacity in relation to the development of new outlets. The shrinking of demand and the existence of idle capital goods leads toward a crisis of overproduction. This is not because all the needs of society are satisfied but because the solvent demand does not match the acceleration of capital investment in the sectors producing means of production. Thus, this pattern of investment is self-limiting and continuously tends toward depression.[18]

Stimulating demand is therefore one of the key factors in keeping a difficult balance in the disequilibrating process of capitalist expansion. If one accepts this argument and considers this to be one of the main contradictions in advanced capitalism, then it seems quite clear that it is one of the most important causes of stagnation. In the absence of counteracting forces it can lead to a catastrophic crisis, as in 1929. The problem of realization is so vital to capitalism that any sign of underconsumption is counteracted by stimuli introduced by the state or by the corporations themselves. Nevertheless, sales efforts in the sixties were not strong enough to counteract the tendencies toward stagnation. The utilization of manufacturing capacity never reached full capacity. On the contrary, in the late sixties it began to decline sharply, falling to 78 percent of capacity utilization in 1970.

The inability to absorb the economic surplus through profitable capitalist consumption, in spite of all the stimulation of demand, will clearly lead to permanent economic stagnation in the absence of some structural change.[19] In advanced capitalism the problem of realization is, in fact, the problem of the limits of the system to stimulate increased demand, to find an adequate form for this demand, and to regulate the new contradictions triggered by such an uneasy manipulation of consumption mechanisms.

2.1.3. *The Falling Rate of Profit*

The key element of a dynamic capitalist economy is in the long run the evolution of the rate of profit. This evolution depends on the rate of exploitation, the organic composition of capital, the expansion of the market, the rate of turnover of capital, the increase in productivity, the amount of levy that has to be imposed on profits in order to cover expenditures essential for the system, the articulation with other economies, and a number of conjunctural factors, especially those concerning the business cycle.

At the structural level, particularly in the United States, the increase in the organic composition of capital tends to lower the ratio of labor to capital and then to decrease the source of production of surplus value, a *tendency* we discussed in Chapter 1. In the United States this tendency is accentuated because of the importance of research and technology in the development of productive forces. Obviously, the impact of such a tendency on profits cannot be directly observed because of a number of historical factors and countertendencies that intervene. But this analysis is useful because it helps us to understand why the more the productive forces (especially technology and science) develop in advanced capitalist countries, the more the rate of profit tends to fall without the introduction of some major countertendencies. In fact, we must learn to distinguish between: 1) the amount of surplus value and the amount of profit; 2) the amount of profit and the rate of profit; 3) the amount and rate of profit for the whole economy and the amount and rate of profit for private corporations; 4) the distribution of profits among different corporate groups, the rate of profit in each sector of the economy, and the rate of profit to capital as a whole.

Clearly, such a study is too complex to be carried out here, but we can point out what seem to be some major trends. It appears from the estimate by Phillips, which underlies Baran and Sweezy's analysis,[20] that surplus value grew steadily between 1929 and 1963. Also, according to the same source, the amount of profit, which is largely determined by the amount of surplus value, increased sharply during the same period. But the rate of profit is a very different thing. This is the ratio of the profit obtained to the capital invested. For the society as a whole, it would correspond to the rate of total surplus value, which is the ratio of the value produced to the value consumed in its production. To our knowledge, such a total and inclusive analysis has not been done for the United States. This could only be done by estimating with some accuracy the productivity or lack of productivity of the different "services," which represent a growing share of public and private investments.

However, in a capitalist society the essential concern is not the rate of social surplus value but the actual profitability for corporate capital. Some reliable estimates seem to indicate that there has been a rapid decline in the profits of nonfinancial corporations in the United States since 1950, measured either in terms of their share of the GNP (Figure 11) or in terms of the rate of return.[21] Nevertheless, two aspects of this trend must be qualified.

First, in monopoly capitalism the law of equalization of the rate of profit between sectors and firms does not work, since the leading trusts have imposed an unequal share on the "competitive sector." The decline in the profitability of capital could mean that there has been a greater accentuation of the law of uneven development between monopoly corporations and the competitive sector, which seems to be what is happening in the United States.[22]

Figure 11

Evolution of the Share of Profits in the Gross Corporate Product of Nonfinancial Corporations, U.S., 1950-1974

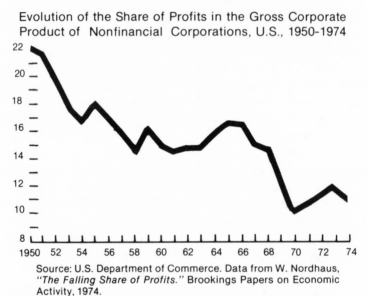

Source: U.S. Department of Commerce. Data from W. Nordhaus, *"The Falling Share of Profits."* Brookings Papers on Economic Activity, 1974.

Second, the rate of profit varies in each conjuncture for each monopoly group according to the competition between them, that is, in terms of the position of power they occupy in the economic *and* in the social system. Particularly important have been the increasing assessments of financial corporations on nonfinancial profits. There is no contradiction between banks and industries implied here, because they are interrelated in financial groups.* The point is rather that an increasing amount of profits have to be used to circulate capital instead of being invested in the production of value and commodities. Although this mechanism does not affect the financial group as a whole, it does affect the level of productive investment and hence the source of surplus value and, in the long run, the source of profit.

In sum, the evolution of the profits of the leading corporations is the result of major structural contradictions and the ultimate expression of the problems generated in the process of production and circulation. There has been a trend in the U.S. economy toward a decrease in the share of corporate profits in the GNP. Such a tendency has led to the bankruptcy of some major corporations, such as Penn Central in 1970. It has also contributed to the recession since expected profits determine the rate of investment and economic growth. Since falling profits were a potential threat to the U.S. economy, once the expansionary effects of World War II were over, several major countertendencies were introduced to restore the rate of profit for corporate capital. The analysis of these countertendencies and of the contradictions they triggered leads to an understanding of the dynamics of the U.S. economy and of the actual roots of the golden period of capitalist miracles.

2.2. SOLVING PROBLEMS AND TRIGGERING CONTRADICTIONS: THE COUNTERTENDENCIES INTRODUCED BY CAPITAL AND THEIR CONSEQUENCES

A capitalist society is *not* a cybernetic system functioning along the lines of an ideal model of accumulation, as outlined by Marx, which comes to a catastrophic end by the deepening of its own contradictions. Capital is incarnated in a social class, the bourgeoisie, and capitalism is a particular form of social organization preserved and expanded by institutions and the state. When major breakdowns occur, when economic, social, and political contradictions develop to the point where they threaten the existence of the system itself, then major structural arrangements

* A financial group is a system of interrelated corporations where the rate of profit comes both from direct appropriation of surplus value and from capital interests, in a network of interdependent units of production and circulation.

are provided through a combination of policies implemented by the state and adjustments made consciously or unconsciously (depending on the circumstances) by corporations.

In the postwar economy of the United States three major countertendencies were introduced to fight the tendencies toward stagnation represented by the difficulty of developing the rate of absolute exploitation, by the continuous shrinking of markets, and by the falling rate of profit.

In order to enhance the rate of exploitation on a new basis and avoid the overaccumulation of capital, corporations expanded throughout the entire world, triggering an accelerated internationalization of capital, productive processes, labor power, and markets.

In order to provide a continuous expansion of demand, consumer credit has been developed in all of its forms. Corporations have borrowed more and more money in order to keep up with the increasing demand for goods, and the economy has been progressively transformed into a debt economy.

In order to coordinate the attack against the falling rate of profit and to link closely social conditions to the economic process required by the new functioning of corporate capital, the state has developed a system of massive intervention into the whole process of production, reproduction, circulation, and regulation of capital, commodities, resources, and labor.

Each of these three major countertendencies, which explain the astonishing capitalist growth from 1945 to 1970, has developed a specific set of deep contradictions that have led to the economic crisis of the seventies along the lines described in our analysis of the conjuncture. Let us now consider in some detail each of these countertendencies and its corresponding contradictory consequences.

2.2.1. The Internationalization of Capital and the Role of a Changing World Hegemony in American Capitalist Expansion

The internationalization of capital and of its units of production, distribution, and management has been one of the major sources of expansion for large American corporations in the last thirty years. This is not to say that capital has become internationalized only recently. Immanuel Wallerstein has clearly shown (following Marx, Lenin, and Rosa Luxemburg) that capitalism from its origin has been a world system.[23] What is new is the form of capitalist exploitation at the international level and the strategic role played by foreign investments in the expansion of monopoly capital. While maintaining the traditional neocolonial pillage of raw materials and natural resources, international capital has shifted progressively from emphasizing investment in mining and agriculture to emphasizing investment in manufacturing and services. This shift has been translated geographically in the switch of U.S. capital from Latin America to Western Europe.[24] Whereas from 1920 to 1930 42 percent of American foreign investments were in Latin America, against 20 percent in Europe, in 1970 the percentages were reversed: 50 percent of American foreign investments went to Europe and only 12 percent to Latin America. This move was implemented especially through the Marshall Plan, which provided, under certain conditions, American economic assistance to the European countries in order to reconstruct the economies destroyed by the war. American corporations used this occasion to penetrate deeply the European economies, the depth of the penetration being a function of the potential market and the degree of political subordination to the United States. West Germany became the most obvious target for American businesses, followed by the United Kingdom.[25] This pattern of investment grew out of the need to find profitable new outlets to invest overaccumulated capital, and it resulted from several interrelated factors:

1. *Lower wages than in the United States.*

2. *Enough industrial and technological capacity and skilled labor power.* This factor is very important because it clearly explains the preference for manufacturing in Europe rather than in Third World countries where wages were even lower.

3. *Support from European governments and businesses.* The greatest part of American investments in Europe was financed through both private and public European loans. The costs of large industrial infrastructures, social services, research, education, reproduction of labor power, and transportation, have been assumed by European states at the national, regional, and local level.[26]

4. *The very large market represented by the massive investment in fixed capital needed for the reconstruction of Europe.* To
some extent World War II represented an incredible double benefit for American capital. First, it provided a huge outlet for investment in military equipment during the war; second, because
American productive capacity was totally preserved, it was the
only economy able to provide (in exchange for high profits) capital and resources to rebuild the continent destroyed by the
weapons whose production provided an opportunity for capital
accumulation.

One of the most decisive developments was the creation of the
European Common Market in 1957, providing the American
corporations with a market comparable in size and, potentially,
in purchasing power to the United States market. By taking advantage of national differences in monetary and wage policies
without being limited by national borders in the circulation of
commodities, the European Common Market allowed the U.S.
corporations abroad to become the second largest economic
power in the capitalist world.

This trend was made possible largely by the economic, political, and military hegemony of the United States throughout the
world. The concrete expression of this hegemony was the use of
U.S. currency as a reserve currency. By being able to use the dollar without any restrictions and without any counterpart (since
the central banks of Europe, with the exception of the national
bank in Gaullist France in the early sixties, could hardly ask for
gold in exchange for their dollars), American corporations were
able to buy a significant share of assets throughout the world by
using "paper dollars," which were increasingly inflated, and fic-
titious credit, calculated on the basis of these dollars that were
circulated at an accelerated speed in the Eurodollar market.

The immense concentration of wealth and power generated by
this process led to the formation of the so-called transnational
corporations (mostly American), which have become the hard
core of advanced capitalism. The most important characteristic of
these corporations have been the integration of their operations
at the world level, enabling them to take advantage of the best
conditions in each country for the performance of each part of
the process of production, circulation, distribution, and man-

agement.[27] Moreover, the maximization of these advantages, which have included the accelerated turnover of capital and the control over the source of production and labor, has allowed the worldwide network to dramatically improve the rate of profit and the rate of exploitation of the world's people. This trend is being increasingly expanded. Faced with problems in exploiting highly organized European labor, the corporations developed new manufacturing networks in such Third World countries as Brazil, Mexico, Iran, Taiwan, Singapore, South Korea, and Malaysia to provide cheap labor to operate the assembly lines. The advanced technology, however, remained concentrated in the United States and Western Europe, with management staying mostly in American metropolises.

U.S. transnational corporations have obtained huge profits by using this strategy.[28] In 1945 U.S. corporations received $1 billion in profits from investments abroad. In 1970 this had increased to $8 to $10 billion. Officially, more than 20 percent of their profits came from investments abroad. However, the real share is much larger, perhaps as much as 35 to 40 percent. And it is expanding at an accelerated rate. A survey by the U.S. Department of Commerce of 298 large American firms that accounted for two-thirds of all international exchanges shows that the percentage of profits obtained abroad was 25 percent in 1966 and 44 percent in 1970. This explains, perhaps, why new corporate investments are being switched abroad in increasing proportions: 21 percent of all new investments in 1960, 25 percent in 1966, and 40 percent in 1970 were made abroad.

The same pattern is being followed by banks. The nine largest banks in New York City controlled more than 50 percent of the dollars deposited abroad. In 1965 they had only 30 percent of their deposits abroad. In 1972 this percentage was 70. Table 8 will give us a more precise idea of the development of U.S. investment abroad.

This evolution has created a considerable number of new problems for the U.S. economy and has triggered a number of contradictions that threaten the stability of the whole system. For one thing, *there is an increasing contradiction between the internationalization of capital and the persistence of national states*, including the United States. In a period when the state

TABLE 8. U.S. DIRECT INVESTMENT ABROAD: BOOK VALUE AT YEAR
END, BY GEOGRAPHIC AREA AND SECTOR OF ACTIVITY
(IN MILLIONS OF U.S. DOLLARS)

	Year	Total	Mining & smelting	Petroleum	Manufacturing
World total	1950	11,788	1,129	3,390	3,831
	1957	25,394	2,634	8,991	7,898
	1960	31,865	2,997	10,810	11.051
	1965	49,474	3,931	15,298	19,339
	1970ᵃ	78,090	6,137	21,790	32,231
Canada	1950	3,579	334	418	1,897
	1957	8,769	996	2,154	3,512
	1960	11,179	1,325	2,664	4,827
	1965	15,318	1,851	3,356	6,872
	1970	22,801	3,014	4,809	10,050
Other Western Hemisphere	1950ᵇ	4,576	628	1,416	781
	1957	8,052	1,238	3,060	1,675
	1960	8,365	1,319	3,122	1,521
	1965	10,886	1,474	3,546	2,945
	1970	14,683	2,037	3,929	4,604
Europe	1950	1,733	21	424	933
	1957	4,151	50	1,184	2,077
	1960	6,691	49	1,763	3,804
	1965	13,985	54	3,427	7,606
	1970	24,471	71	5,487	13,704
United Kingdom	1950	847	3	123	542
	1965	5,123	2	1,093	3,306
	1970	8,015	1	1,852	4,988
ECC	1950	637	+	210	313
	1965	6,304	16	1,624	3,725
	1970	11,695	15	2,525	7,126
Japan	1950	19	. . .	+	+
	1960	254	. . .	125	91
	1965	675	. . .	321	275
	1970	1,491	. . .	540	753
Australia, New Zealand, South Africa	1950	366	+	+	+
	1960	1,195	79	373	692
	1970	4,348	572	909	2,241

ᵃ Preliminary data.
ᵇ Excluding European dependencies.
+ Included in totals, but not itemized.
Source: *Survey of Current Business*, Oct. 1971, Aug. 1964, Sept. 1960, Aug.
1957, Jan. 1951.

must develop its regulatory functions over economic activities, the world expansion of capital in the absence of a world capitalist government has created a structural obstacle for the self-sustaining mechanisms of the system. One of the major problems created for the U.S. government by the transnationals is their failure to pay federal taxes. In 1958 corporate taxes represented 25 percent of the total federal revenue. By 1973, however, their contribution had dropped to 15 percent. The government has been unable to control the discount rate, the amount of liquidities actually introduced in the economy, or the fluctuation of prices. Nor has it been able to get accurate information on crucial economic trends.

Nevertheless, the real contradictions provided by the internationalization of capital concern the roots of the system itself. One of the most important is the accelerated deterioration of U.S. balance of payments as a result of three combined factors (see Figure 12):

1. *The continuous outflow of U.S. capital searching for higher profits abroad.*

2. *The deterioration of the balance of trade as a result of the increasing competition in the American market from Japanese and European products* (some of them being produced by American corporations abroad). The export of American capital and expansion at the world level have produced a pattern of uneven development threatening U.S. hegemony, as shown in Table 9. In spite of the efforts made by the United States during the sixties, all of the advanced capitalist countries, with the exception of the United Kingdom, have performed much better in the process of accumulation than the United States. This is undermining American economic supremacy, which was the cornerstone of the system's stability.

3. *The huge amount of military expenditures abroad required to back up the political domination of the United States*—the most important factor of the three. These expenditures support the transnational corporations and maintain the mechanisms that provide the structural requirements for the corporations' undisputed expansion. Table 10 gives an estimate of the importance of military expenditures abroad. They are a basic contradiction of the U.S. economy. What must be emphasized is that the

military expression of U.S. domination is linked to a model of accumulation based more and more on the internationalization of U.S. corporate capital and the process of exploitation on a world scale.

At another level, then, the more monopoly capital expands its frontiers, the more it sharpens and expands its contradictions. The accelerated capitalist growth in Western Europe and Japan

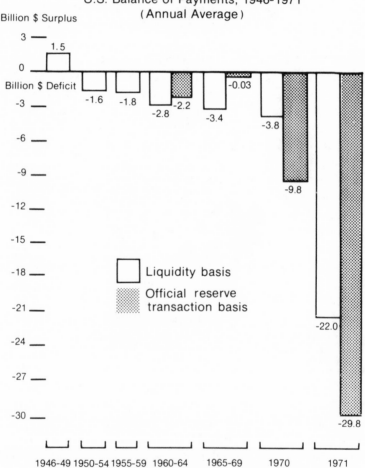

Figure 12

U.S. Balance of Payments, 1946-1971
(Annual Average)

Source: U.S. Department of Commerce: as printed in Victor Perlo, *The Unstable Economy: Booms and Recessions in the U.S. Since 1945*, New York: International Publishers, 1973, p. 182.

TABLE 9. ANNUAL AVERAGE GROWTH RATES OF PER CAPITA REAL GROSS NATIONAL PRODUCT (LEADING CAPITALIST COUNTRIES, 1870-1969)

	1870-1913	1913-1929	1929-1950	1950-1964	1960-1969
United States	2.2	1.3	1.6	1.8	3.2
Japan[a]	—	—	—	8.7	9.9
West Germany[b]	1.7	0.0	0.7	5.9	3.6
United Kingdom	1.2	0.3	1.2	2.4	2.1
France	1.4	1.8	0.0	3.8	4.7
Italy	0.7	1.2	0.3	5.2	4.9

[a] Per capita figures for Japan are not given for periods prior to 1950, but rate of absolute growth in real gross national product is slightly lower than that of the United States, suggesting a moderately lower per capita growth rate.
[b] All Germany prior to 1945.
Sources: 1870-1964: U.S. Department of Commerce, Census Bureau, *Long-Term Economic Growth, 1960-1965*, 1966, p. 101.
       1960-1969: computed from *United Nations Monthly Statistical Bulletin*, Nov. 1970, Table 63 (real gross domestic product) and Table 1 (population).

TABLE 10. U.S. CONVERTIBLE CURRENCY MILITARY AND GIFT TRANSACTIONS, 1946-1970 (ANNUAL AVERAGES IN MILLIONS OF DOLLARS)

Year	Military expenditures	Net unilateral transfers, excluding military	Total
1946-49	992	3,928	4,920
1950-54	1,831	2,965	4,796
1955-59	3,122	2,415	5,537
1960-64	3,007	2,554	5,561
1965-69	4,096	2,839	6,935
1970	4,851	3,148	7,999

Source: *Survey of Current Business*, June 1970, Table 1, pp. 34-35, and Feb. 1972, pp. S-2, S-3.

has been accompanied by an increase in the class struggle, with labor unions forcing capital to pay higher wages and improve working conditions. In the period from 1963 to 1969 the real wages of workers in manufacturing increased at an annual rate of 1 percent in the United States, but in Japan they increased 7 percent, in West Germany 5 percent, in France 3 percent, and in the United Kingdom 1 percent.[29] One of the major incentives for profitable investments disappeared with the increase in wages in these countries, and there was a shift to "quieter" regions such as Taiwan and Korea where the transnational corporations were able to take advantage of terrorist dictatorships. But experience shows that such processes will eventually create the same problems from which capital is trying to escape. For instance, the massive inflow of U.S. capital into Spain to take advantage of lower wages and of Franco's repression of the working class resulted paradoxically in a process of industrialization that strengthened the working class and helped develop mass movements against government repression, leading to the end of the dictatorship itself.

Also, the accumulation of capital on a world scale has made the system much more sensitive to localized crises, which were isolated until recent years. The uprisings of people in nations of the Third World have led to increasingly acute conflicts over the exploitation of raw materials (from coffee to oil), since the world chain of production requires a steady supply of raw materials to operate efficiently. The interpenetration into all economies has led to a synchronization of the business cycle during the crisis. This has made recovery more difficult and has deepened the depression while inflation continues to spread because of the increasing instability of international movements of capital.

This whole set of contradictions generated by the international expansion of U.S. corporations and its attached complement of military expenditures have been responsible for bringing about two major critical developments: the international monetary crisis and the decline of the dollar as a reserve currency; and difficulty in perpetuating the economic and political hegemony of the United States and its corporate world interests.

The *international monetary crisis* is the crisis of the dollar because of the increasing conflict between the two terms of its double use as a means of payment and a means of exchange. *This crisis has been motivated by the necessary contradiction between the use of dollars as international means of payment (which requires the stability of its value) and the use of dollars as an instrument of accumulation (which requires its flexibility).*[30] The deterioration of the balance of payments for the United States has led to the inconvertibility of the dollar, to its devaluation, and to its declining role as a reserve currency on the international exchanges. What must be emphasized here is the fact that although the deficit in the U.S. balance of payments has existed since 1950, confidence in the dollar was not shaken until the sixties. It was this lack of confidence that led to the demand for gold, then to speculation, then to an actual devaluation of the dollar. The loss of confidence was caused by the questioning of U.S. hegemony, which triggered speculation about the ability of the United States to reestablish its dominance in the future. The two phenomena (the monetary crisis and the end of U.S. hegemony) are, in fact, linked.[31] This decline in hegemony has two interrelated dimensions. One is the differential economic growth that has led to the accumulation in West German and Japanese banks of a disproportionate amount of dollars whose sudden devaluation could provoke catastrophic losses. The other is the political disability that has come from the relative loss of American political and military power following the defeat in Indochina, the uncertainties in the Middle East, the uprisings of nationalism in the Third World, the progress of the Left in Western Europe, and the growing desire for autonomous governments in the advanced capitalist countries.

Until 1971 the dollar had been structurally overvalued, but in the mid-seventies it became structurally undervalued. For political reasons the dollar was sometimes rejected as a means of exchange and a deposit currency despite the fact that since 1974 the economic position of the United States in relation to its partners had improved.[32] This has created an extremely dangerous situation for the U.S. economy. The existence of almost $200 billion in floating capital around the world may provoke a major breakdown at any time. This is the reason for the accelerated search by the United States through the International Monetary Fund for a new international means of exchange, such as the Special Drawing Rights, based on the dollar for only 33 percent of its value. The most unmistakable expression of the end of economic hegemony was the loss of the cherished benefits of holding the reserve currency. Perhaps it would be more accurate to say that this involved losing only two-thirds of the dollar's capacity to decide the movements of money in a world dominated by money.

The internationalization of U.S. capital, which has been used as a major countertendency to the falling rate of exploitation, has expanded and increased exploitation on a world scale. However, in doing so, it has encountered new contradictions: transnational corporations have undermined the structural conditions that made possible their movement, and they have found new difficulties in an unstable world where there are now millions of people who have become conscious and organized through the process of contradictions that constitute for them, day by day, their personal and political experiences.

2.2.2. *The Roots of Inflation: The Debt Economy*

The problem of realization has been at the center of economic policies since 1945. The idea has been to stimulate the steady expansion of the demand for those commodities the large corporations consider profitable. The problem was to generate demand without so raising the cost of wages as to threaten the rate of profit. Two major tools were used. One was public expenditures, and the other the incredible expansion of consumer credit. We will examine later the role of the state in the creation of markets within the general framework of state intervention in the economy. First, however, we will analyze the mechanisms that have developed consumer demand and their relationship to the new contradictions brought on by creeping inflation.

One of the major sources of the development of consumer demand has been the deliberate efforts undertaken by the large corporations to manipulate demand in order to direct it toward the most profitable commodities the corporations are able to produce. What Baran and Sweezy call "the sales effort"[33] gives a powerful stimulus to demand. In his book *Economics and the Public Purpose* John Kenneth Galbraith has accurately depicted the relationship between the functioning of large corporations and the formation of demand.[34]

The corporations have stimulated the desire for consumption through *marketing* and *advertising*. Marketing has allowed them to understand consumer preferences and to convert these preferences into a demand for what is most profitable to produce. Advertising has become one of the most powerful ideological apparatuses in history and entirely dominates the content and functioning of mass media. Advertising is not just commercials on television or advertisements in newspapers. It is a whole culture shaped symbolically by the topics, attitudes, and reactions adequate to consumption patterns. This development has reached the point that one of the innovations in advertising in the United States in the mid-seventies has been the distribution of relatively high quality free magazines to well-to-do neighborhoods in order to target particularly desirable sectors of the market. This example shows the final consequence of the trend—the informational media have become purely the support of commercial advertising. News and entertainment have become mainly the means to penetrate a market. They would not exist without their utility to enhance the distribution of profitable commodities.

Nevertheless, it is not enough to stimulate the consumer's demand. The customer must also be able to pay for the commodities he wants. The contradiction between the required increase in demand and the decrease in the proportion of value appropriated by wage earners has been overcome by drawing on expected future producing ability through a massive and steady development of *consumer credit*. This is mostly in the form of installment credit, which amounted to $8.4 billion in 1946 and jumped to $122.5 billion in 1969. The total household debt in 1955 represented 65 percent of disposable income. In 1974 the percentage reached 93. This explains why American families used 6 percent of their income to pay the interest on the loans they had in 1947, and why in 1969 interest payments had risen to 15 percent of their income.[35]

This increase in private debt accelerated considerably during the sixties. One of the more insidious mechanisms of the hysterical expansion of demand to solve the problem of realization in the short run was the proliferation of credit cards during the sixties. Americans owned 70 million credit cards in 1973, and the interest rates on these cards ran as high as 18 percent. In 1973 there were 63 million bank-credit transactions amounting to $14 billion.

Another powerful tool for the expansion of demand through debt has been the development of the federal government-backed housing mortgages. By creating a mass market for single-family suburban dwellings, this has been a major factor in the improvement of housing conditions in the United States. The number of home mortgages multiplied by fifteen from 1965 to 1974 and grew at an increasing rate during the sixties. When more and more individuals and small mutual fund companies defaulted on their loans, federal agencies were forced to absorb the foreclosures in increasing numbers, which demonstrated the impact of the growing disequilibrium between private indebtedness and family income.

But perhaps the most dangerous trend has been the mechanisms of creating demand through debt that has been used not only by the consumer but by the corporations themselves. The corporations have borrowed from the banks and have issued bonds at an increasing rate in order to be able to mobilize quickly the resources needed for profitable investments caused by the expansion of private and public demand. This practice also increases demand by activating the circulation of commodities and capital among the corporations themselves.[36]

This trend accelerated considerably during the sixties in response to the uninterrupted expansionary phase generated by the internationalization of capital, the rising military and government expenditures, and stimulated consumer demands. Figure 13 gives an idea of the growing dimensions of debt during the 1960s.

To complete our overview of this journey toward financial catastrophe, we need only observe that the federal government has used the same procedure to finance the huge expenditures required by state capitalism. As a consequence of these different and articulated financial trends, the U.S. economy has been converted into a *debt economy* (see Figure 14). *The total U.S. debt has jumped from $400 billion in 1946 to $2.5 trillion in 1974.* This includes $1 trillion in corporate debt, $600 million in mortgage debt, $200 billion in state and local government debt, and $200 billion in consumer debt. In other words, U.S. expansion has been fueled by borrowing, since 1946, at the rate of *$200 million a day*! This has been a self-accelerating process, which has been expanding rapidly each year. It took fifteen years (1945-1960) for the U.S. debt to double, but only ten years (1960-1970) to double again. In 1974 there was $8 in debt for each $1 of money supply.

This pattern of growth through expanding debt is due not just to a shortage of capital but also to the desire to take advantage of opportunities for profitable investment. It is a deliberate proce-

Figure 13

Evolution of U.S. Debt, 1955-1974

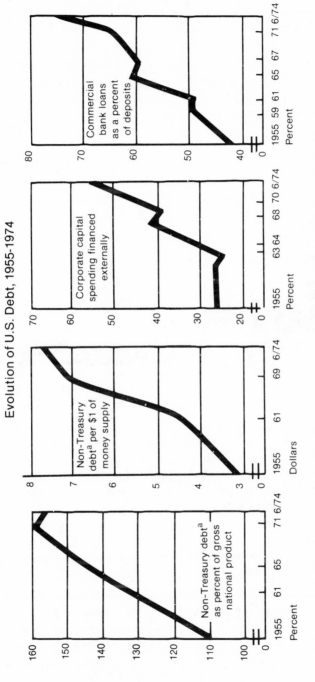

Source: *Business Week*, Oct. 12, 1974, p. 46.

aTotal dept of all borrowers except the U.S. Treasury.

Figure 14

The Debt Economy

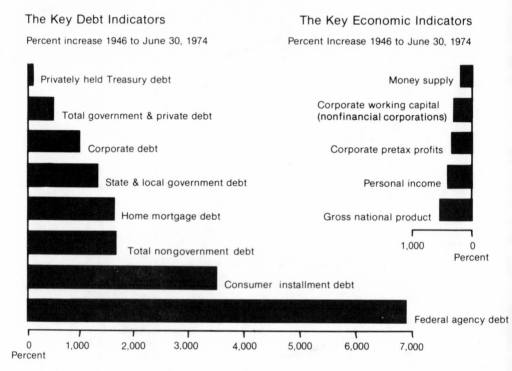

The Key Debt Indicators

Percent increase 1946 to June 30, 1974

Privately held Treasury debt

Total government & private debt

Corporate debt

State & local government debt

Home mortgage debt

Total nongovernment debt

Consumer installment debt

Federal agency debt

0   1,000   2,000   3,000   4,000   5,000   6,000   7,000
Percent

The Key Economic Indicators

Percent Increase 1946 to June 30, 1974

Money supply

Corporate working capital
(nonfinancial corporations)

Corporate pretax profits

Personal income

Gross national product

1,000   0
Percent

Source: *Business Week*, Oct. 12, 1974, p. 47

dure to fuel the economy, to accelerate the circulation of capital, and to transform into commodities everything possible everywhere in the world.

This economic pattern also has important consequences at the level of social relationships. There seem to be very few alternatives for individuals, families, or organizations that wish to reverse this process and change their way of living.

In order to qualify for consumer credit, a person must have a stable job or career as well as normal behavior, which is defined by the financial institutions as a prerequisite for reliable purchasing power. However, any unexpected changes in this predicted pattern of purchasing power can result in a breakdown in the re-

lationship between the consumer and the social and economic
system.

This means that the debt economy is a very powerful instrument of social control, since access to the channels of consumption is defined in terms of certain social characteristics and the
ability of the consumer to maintain them. But, at the same time,
any major disruption of the system threatens the stability of the
whole network of social relationships.

The same thing has happened to the corporations. They have
had to use more and more of their profits to pay the interest on
their borrowed capital and to cover their obligations, thus producing a vicious circle. Furthermore, this process draws the financial institutions into the same spiral, creating a major source of
instability for the whole system. As the editors of the *Monthly
Review* have shown in a keystone article written in February
1975:

There are two sides to the debt explosion: 1) capitalists borrow
as much as possible not only from necessity, but more impor-
tantly, as a way to increase their individual profit rates and 2)
banks and other institutions aggressively increase their lend-
ings as a means of maximizing their own profits. . . . This
means as Marx said "driving capitalist production beyond its
own limits" and means relying on debt because of the insuffi-
ciency of funds capitalists are able to generate internally or
through flotation of new stock issues to finance capital expansion.

. . . As much as this long-term debt of corporations has
grown, it has nevertheless proven to be insufficient to appease
the capitalist appetite for accumulation. And hence corporations, with the collaboration of the banks and other financial
institutions, began to depend more and more on short-term
borrowing. . . . Bank loans increased in the decade of the
1950s, but pretty much in line with the general expansion of
nonfinancial corporate business: bank loans as a percent of
nonfinancial corporate GNP were 12.1 in 1950 and 13.8 in
1960. . . . Now look at the decisive change that begins with
1960. Between 1960 and 1974 bank loans grew at much faster
rates than non-financial business activity: from 13.8% in 1960

to 25.2% in the first half of 1974. Still more interesting is the acceleration in the dependence on bank credit. . . . Business borrowers can still absorb this expanding debt only as long as they can make enough profit to meet the rising interest payments. Eventually, if the debt load keeps accelerating, the interest on the debt begins to choke off profits and hence also the incentive, as well as the financial ability, to keep the underlying accumulation process going on. The capitalist answer to this dilemma up to now has been to feed the fires of inflation. As interest burdens increase capitalists raise prices to meet these obligations. And as price hikes spread throughout the economy, the need for even more borrowing follows. Thus, debt obligation, interest charges, and prices chase each other in the upward spiral of inflation. . . . [S]hort of such a runaway inflation, we are beginning to see the obstacles emerging in the ability of the banks to keep on supplying credit at the accelerated rate of the past. It is true that the banks, in pursuit of ever more profit for themselves, have tried to keep up with the demand for loans. But in doing so, they have stretched themselves so thin that their own liquidity is in question, and legitimate fears have been raised about the possible collapse of the financial system.[37]

Now, growth through an expanding debt economy can only reestablish an equilibrium if in the long run the mass of goods and services produced can reduce the level of the liquidity existing in money and debt. But this is not the case in the United States. On the contrary, if the gap between production and its liquidity expression is increasing, the result is *inflation*. It seems clear that there is a relationship between the quantity of money and the worsening of inflation.

There is evidence consistent with the proposition that inflation is primarily a monetary phenomenon. This proposition holds that an increase in the trend growth of money is followed by an increase in the rate of inflation. This proposition attributes the basic cause of our inflation to the accelerating trend growth of money since the mid 1960s. Money rose at about a 2% annual rate from 1952 to 1962, accelerated to a 4% rate to 1966, accelerated further to 6% to 1971, and has been about a 7% rate

TABLE 11. LIQUIDITY OF LARGE COMMERCIAL BANKS (BILLIONS OF DOLLARS)

End of year	Cash reserves[a]	U.S. Treasury Bonds[b]	Short-term U.S. Treasury Notes[c]	Cash & All Treasuries as a percent of total deposits	Cash & Short-term Treasuries as a percent of total deposits
1950	13.7	33.7	n.a.	54.0	n.a.
1955	14.9	30.1	n.a.	42.7	n.a.
1960	14.0	30.2	8.2	34.7	17.5
1965	16.3	24.3	8.6	22.3	13.7
1970	20.2	28.1	10.3	18.3	11.4
1974	29.5	28.4	7.9	13.6	9.6

n.a.: not available.
[a] Cash in vault plus reserves with Federal Reserve banks, as required by the Federal Reserve Board.
[b] Bonds here include bills, certificates, notes, as well as bonds.
[c] All Treasury securities that mature in less than one year.
Source: Data prior to 1974 are from various issues of the *Federal Reserve Bulletin*. Data for 1974 are from *Federal Reserve Statistical Release* H.4.4. for the last week in 1974.

TABLE 12. SHORT-TERM BORROWING BY LARGE COMMERCIAL BANKS (BILLIONS OF DOLLARS)

End of year	From Federal Reserve Banks	Federal funds purchased[a] and others	Large negotiable certificates of deposit[b]	Eurodollars[c]	Total	Short-term borrowing as a percent of total loans outstanding
1950	0.7				0.7	2.2
1960	1.8	1.4			3.2	4.5
1965	6.2	2.8	16.1		24.9	20.7
1970	1.5	18.8	26.1	7.7	54.1	28.7
1974	4.8	54.0	92.2	4.0	155.0	48.5

[a] The data for 1960 and 1965 are from a special series designed by the Federal Reserve Board based on the 46 most active commercial banks in the federal funds market. The data for these years are not comparable with those for later years, but are given here to indicate the trend. The data for 1970 and 1974 include, in addition to federal funds purchased, securities sold under agreements to repurchase identical or similar securities and sales of participations in pools of securities.
[b] These are short-term certificates of deposit in minimum amounts of $100,000.
[c] These data are the reported "Gross Liabilities of Banks to Their Foreign Branches." According to the Federal Reserve Bank of New York, *Glossary Weekly Federal Reserve Statements*, this item is often used as a proxy for Eurodollar borrowings, though these data include some other types of transactions between domestic banks and their foreign branches.
Source: Data prior to 1974 are from various issues of the *Federal Reserve Bulletin*. Data for 1974 are from *Federal Reserve Statistical Release* H.4.4. for the last week in 1974.

since then. Studies present evidence consistent with the proposition that short-run accelerations and deceleration in the rate of money growth are followed by similar movements in growth of real output. It is thus concluded that monetary actions are an important cause of the business cycle.

Another lesson is that government deficits are an important

cause of accelerating money growth. The amount of government debt held by the Federal Reserve System has risen at a much faster rate since the early 1960s than debt outstanding. As a result, the System's holdings of government debt rose from 11% of the total outstanding in 1961 to 23% in 1973. These rapidly growing purchases of government securities provided much of the basis for the accelerating growth of money.[38]

But it is also clear that the money supply is a function of the general debt of the economy and the impact that debt has on Federal Reserve Board policies. *Thus, the statistical relationship between the amount of money and inflation is the expression of the gap between the production of value and the required artificial expansion of demand.*

The relationship between the debt economy and the acceleration of inflation is a dialectical one. If inflation accelerates very fast, it can wipe out a significant portion of the debt through devaluation. This is a nice automatic mechanism for an eventual self-regulation of the system. But it so happens that we are not dealing with a cybernetic system, but with a historical society dominated by financial capital with its center of economic power within the financial institutions. What this means is that the major economic interests are going to do everything possible to recover the real interest rates they expected when they invested their capital. The financial corporations react to inflation by raising the interest rates in order to prevent devaluation. However, when it becomes clear that inflation is a structural trend that threatens the whole system, the financial corporations ask for a global economic policy that has two major targets: to wipe out part of the debt in some sectors where monopoly capital has little interest, such as mutual savings and public debt (witness, in particular, the case of New York City municipal bonds); and, more important, to provide the structural requirements for financial capital to fight inflation, that is, to reduce it, to control it, to channel it before its geometrical progression is able to devastate the very foundations of the financial markets. This is the reason why the fight against inflation has top priority for financial capital. Thus, we are on the threshold of a new economic policy necessitated by the new contradictions that have been generated by the attempt to create demand for capital and capital for demand without a corresponding creation of value. *The debt economy is the structural background of our age of inflation.*

2.2.3. *The American State in a State Capitalist Economy*

The most important transformation characterizing advanced capitalism is the decisive role taken by the state in the functioning of the economy. To the traditional functions of social control, repression, legitimation, and political leadership, the state has now added new economic functions that have steadily grown in size and importance since the Great Depression. One crucial problem, which we can hardly consider here, has been the interaction between the classical political-ideological functions and the new economic ones.

The economic intervention of the state developed after it became clear that the spontaneous rules of the market could provoke major catastrophes that would undermine the self-reproduction of capitalist social relationships. Functions of regulation and programming, from data collection to coordination of individual economic units, became the usual practice of the state in capitalism after World War II, with different institutional expression according to the particular historical situation. However, it was clear from the beginning that systematic state intervention in the economy would be necessary to overcome the trends toward stagnation, sustain investments, provide employment, and create demand. The New Deal was the first attempt to translate such a program into government initiatives, and Keynesianism became, particularly in 1960 with the Kennedy administration, the orthodoxy underlying economic policies.[39]

Because of these new trends, total government spending in the United States jumped from less than 8 percent of the GNP in 1890 to almost 30 percent of the GNP in 1960. This increase was particularly important in nonmilitary expenditures. Military expenditures, even though they increased greatly in absolute terms, remained fairly stable or declined in relation to the GNP.

Since World War II total expenditures by all levels of government have risen from an average of 12.8 percent of the GNP in 1945-1950 to an average of 22.4 percent of the GNP in 1966-1970. State and local government spending rose from 5.9 percent of the GNP in 1946-1950 to 11.5 percent in 1966-1970. This steady accelerated expansion of public expenditures between 1950 and 1972 is shown in absolute terms in Table 13 for the federal government and in Table 14 for state and local governments.

Why this accelerated growth of public expenditures? James O'Connor has developed an insightful analysis that provides some of the most important elements for our answer to this question in terms of social dynamics.[40]

Capitalism, in order to expand, has to perform the two major functions of accumulating capital and legitimizing social order that makes this accumulation possible. The expansion of public spending and state intervention develop in two closely interacting ways. Spending for social capital provides a stimulus to accumulation, and spending for social expenses serves the purpose of legitimization. Social expenses include the maintenance of channels of integration (social welfare, income maintenance, social security, etc.) and the development of institutions for repression (police, army, justice, etc.). Expenditures on social capital take two different and complementary forms. Expenditures to sustain the formation of constant capital (what O'Connor calls social investment) are concentrated on physical capital (industrial infrastructure, fixed capital, technological improvements, transportation, etc.) and human capital (research, education, etc.). Expenditures for the improvement of variable capital—that is, expenses in social consumption—are directed to the reproduction of labor power, lowering its cost for private capital in housing, schools, health services, etc.

As O'Connor shows, the requirements of all these expenditures by the state come from several articulated trends in the evolution of advanced capitalism:

1. Production increases in complexity and interdependence, especially because of the progress in technology and the rapid adolescence of capital equipment.

2. Human capital assumes a greater role in the growth of productivity.

3. The multifaceted long-term impact of indivisible physical social investments means that private capital seeks control of all collective equipment shaping economic factors and social life. The state has then to intervene in order to coordinate and to socialize for the whole capitalist class requirements that are necessarily collective. This is a contradictory process since it will express at the same time the state's tendency to appropriate some fractions of capital and its required intervention on behalf of the ruling class.

4. The cost of such huge infrastructural projects is too large to be assumed by one single corporation or even by a group of them.

5. Some investments in social consumption and social capital are absolutely necessary for capital but hardly profitable in the short term. Therefore, the state assumes the initial expense and transfers the function to the private sector once it has become profitable. An example of this kind of function would be basic research and development. Many other services required for the reproduction of labor power that would be unprofitable to capital are also assumed by the state.

6. Pressure from the grassroots increasingly forces the state to provide services that are not supplied by private investment. As social needs grow and consumption becomes ever more socialized, the state has to increase social consumption expenditures and social expenses in order to reproduce power and social relationships.[41]

The intervention of the state is required by capital (in its process of accumulation and legitimization) and forced by labor (which demands a larger share of the product through forced socialized consumption). This raises the profits for capital by transferring public resources to it, lowers the cost of labor power, and creates a social environment suitable for exploitation.

Public expenditures play a major role in the right to expand employment and create new markets for the realization of capitalist commodities. Military expenditures have been important in both these respects.[42] Public expenditures have also accounted for an increase in civilian employment in the United States, especially at state and local levels. *Approximately one-sixth of the U.S. labor force is employed by the state.* If we were to consider all employment that is dependent on public expenditures, includ-

TABLE 13. STATE AND LOCAL REVENUES AND EXPENDITURES, SELECTED YEARS 1955-1972 AND PROJECTED FOR 1980 AND 1985

Category	1955	1958	1959	1963	1965	1968	1970	1971	1972	Projected 1980	Projected 1985
					Billions of current dollars						
Revenues	31.4	41.6	46.0	63.4	75.5	107.1	135.0	152.3	177.2	349.8	505.8
Personal tax and nontax receipts	4.1	5.6	6.3	9.4	11.8	18.3	24.4	27.7	34.3	73.5	108.0
Corporate profits taxes	1.0	1.0	1.2	1.7	2.1	3.2	3.8	4.1	4.9	9.1	14.6
Indirect business tax and nontax receipts	21.4	27.0	28.9	39.4	45.9	60.6	74.1	82.0	89.6	156.4	213.9
Contributions for social insurance	1.8	2.5	2.7	3.8	4.5	6.4	8.3	9.4	10.7	20.7	31.8
Federal grants-in-aid	3.1	5.6	6.8	9.1	11.1	18.7	24.4	29.1	37.7	90.2	137.5
Expenditures	32.7	44.0	46.8	62.2	74.5	107.5	133.2	[a]148.3	[a]164.0	353.0	514.7
Purchases of goods and services	30.1	40.6	43.3	58.2	70.2	100.8	123.3	136.2	150.5	326 0	480.8
Transfer payments to persons	3.7	4.6	4.8	6.0	6.9	10.0	14.1	16.6	18.2	31.0	38.2
Net interest paid	.5	.6	.7	.8	.5	[b]	–.4	–.2	–.4	.5	.7
Less current surplus of government enterprises	1.6	1.8	2.0	2.8	3.0	3.4	3.8	4.1	4.4	4.5	4.9
Surplus or deficit (–)	–1.3	–2.3	–.8	1.2	1.0	–.3	1.8	4.0	13.1	–3.2	–8.9
					Percent distribution						
Revenues	100.0	100.0	100.0	100.0	100.0	100.0	100.0	100.0	100.0	100.0	100.0
Personal tax and nontax receipts	13.1	13.4	13.7	14.8	15.7	17.1	18.1	18.2	19.4	21.0	21.4
Corporate profits taxes	3.1	2.4	2.7	2.7	2.7	2.9	2.8	2.7	2.7	2.6	2.9
Indirect business tax and nontax receipts	68.1	64.7	62.9	62.1	60.9	56.6	54.9	53.8	50.6	44.7	42.3
Contributions for social insurance	5.8	6.0	5.9	6.0	5.9	6.0	6.1	6.2	6.0	5.9	6.3
Federal grants-in-aid	9.9	13.5	14.8	14.4	14.7	17.4	18.1	19.1	21.3	25.8	27.2

Expenditures	100.0	100.0	100.0	100.0	100.0	100.0	100.0	100.0	100.0	100.0
Purchases of goods and services	92.2	92.6	93.6	94.2	93.8	92.6	91.9	91.8	92.4	93.4
Transfer payments to persons	10.4	10.3	9.7	9.2	9.3	10.6	11.2	11.1	8.8	7.4
Net interest paid	1.4	1.5	1.2	.7	—	-.3	-.1	-.3	.1	.1
Less current surplus of government enterprises	4.0	4.3	4.6	4.0	3.2	2.9	2.8	2.7	1.3	1.0

	Average annual rates of change[c]			Projected		
	1955-68	1965-72	1972-80	1968-85	1968-80	1980-85
Revenues	9.90	12.97	8.88	9.56	10.36	7.65
Personal tax and nontax receipts	12.17	16.40	10.00	11.02	12.30	8.00
Corporate profits taxes	9.50	13.09	8.16	9.44	9.24	9.92
Indirect business tax and nontax receipts	8.34	10.02	7.21	7.70	8.22	6.46
Contributions for social insurance	10.23	13.23	8.59	9.87	10.25	8.97
Federal grants-in-aid	14.76	19.04	11.53	12.46	14.02	8.80
Expenditures	9.59	11.92	10.05	9.65	10.42	7.83
Purchases of goods and services	9.74	11.52	10.14	9.63	10.28	8.08
Transfer payments to persons	8.07	14.89[d]	6.88[d]	8.19	9.87	4.27
Net interest paid	17.41			18.51	23.69	6.96
Less current surplus of government enterprises	6.12	5.62	.22	2.20	2.40	1.72

[a] Detail does not include wage accruals less disbursements.
[b] Less than $50 million.
[c] Compound interest rates between terminal years.
[d] Not calculated.
Source: Historical data from U.S. Department of Commerce, Bureau of Economic Analysis; projections by Bureau of Labor Statistics.

TABLE 14. FEDERAL GOVERNMENT REVENUES AND EXPENDITURES, SELECTED YEARS 1955-1972 AND PROJECTED FOR 1980 AND 1985 (NATIONAL INCOME ACCOUNTS BASIS)

Category	1955	1958	1959	1963	1965	1968	1970	1971	1972	Projected	
										1980	1985
	Billions of current dollars										
Revenues	72.1	78.7	89.7	114.5	124.7	175.0	192.0	198.9	228.7	421.0	570.0
Personal tax and nontax receipts	31.4	36.8	39.9	51.6	53.8	79.7	92.2	89.9	107.9	195.8	289.0
Corporate profits taxes	20.6	18.0	22.5	24.6	29.3	36.7	31.0	33.3	37.8	86.5	112.1
Indirect business tax and nontax receipts	10.7	11.5	12.5	15.3	16.5	18.0	19.3	20.4	19.9	30.2	36.5
Contributions for social insurance	9.3	12.4	14.8	23.1	25.1	40.7	49.5	55.2	63.0	108.6	132.3
Expenditures	68.1	88.9	91.0	113.9	123.5	181.5	203.9	221.0	244.6	431.7	574.5
Purchases of goods and services	44.1	53.6	53.7	64.2	66.9	98.8	96.2	98.1	104.4	166.6	218.5
Transfer payments to persons	14.5	21.3	21.9	29.1	32.5	48.2	63.2	74.9	82.9	149.7	191.9
Grants-in-aid to state and local governments	3.1	5.6	6.8	9.1	11.1	18.7	24.4	29.1	37.7	90.2	137.5
Net interest paid	4.9	5.6	6.4	7.7	8.7	11.7	14.6	13.6	13.5	18.1	18.7
Other[a]	1.5	2.7	2.1	3.6	4.3	4.1	5.5	5.4	6.1	7.0	8.0
Federal surplus or deficit (−)	4.0	−10.2	−1.2	.7	1.2	−6.5	−11.9	−22.2	−15.9	−10.6	−4.5
	Percent distribution										
Revenues	100.0	100.0	100.0	100.0	100.0	100.0	100.0	100.0	100.0	100.0	100.0
Personal tax and nontax receipts	43.6	46.8	44.5	45.0	43.1	45.5	48.0	45.2	47.2	46.5	50.7
Corporate profits taxes	28.6	22.9	25.1	21.5	23.5	21.0	16.1	16.7	16.5	20.5	19.7
Indirect business tax and nontax receipts	14.8	14.6	13.9	13.4	13.2	10.3	10.1	10.3	8.7	7.2	6.4
Contributions for social insurance	12.9	15.8	16.5	20.2	20.1	23.3	25.8	27.8	27.5	25.8	23.2

Distribution (percent):

Expenditures	100.0	100.0	100.0	100.0	100.0	100.0	100.0	100.0	100.0	100.0	100.0
Purchases of goods and services	64.8	60.3	59.0	56.4	54.2	54.4	47.2	44.4	42.7	38.6	33.0
Transfer payments to persons	21.3	24.0	24.1	25.5	26.3	26.6	31.0	33.9	33.9	34.7	33.4
Grants-in-aid to state and local governments	4.6	6.3	7.5	8.0	9.0	10.3	12.0	13.2	15.4	20.9	23.9
Net interest paid	7.2	6.3	7.0	6.8	7.0	6.4	7.2	6.2	5.5	4.2	3.3
Other[a]	2.2	3.0	2.3	3.2	3.5	2.3	2.7	2.4	2.5	1.6	6.4

Average annual rates of change[b]

				Projected		
	1955-68	1965-72	1972-80	1968-85	1968-80	1980-85
Revenues	7.1	9.1	7.9	7.2	7.6	6.3
Personal tax and nontax receipts	7.4	10.5	7.7	7.9	7.8	8.1
Corporate profits taxes	4.5	3.7	10.9	6.8	7.4	5.3
Indirect business tax and nontax receipts	4.1	2.7	5.4	4.3	4.4	3.9
Contributions for social insurance	12.0	14.1	7.0	7.2	8.5	4.0
Expenditures	7.8	10.3	7.4	7.0	7.5	5.9
Purchases of goods and services	6.4	6.6	6.1	4.8	4.5	5.6
Transfer payments	9.7	14.3	7.7	8.5	9.9	5.1
Grants-in-aid to state and local governments	14.8	19.1	11.5	12.5	14.0	8.3
Net interest paid	6.9	6.5	3.7	2.8	3.7	.6
Other[a]	8.0	5.1	1.7	4.0	4.6	2.7

[a] Includes subsidies less current surplus of government enterprises plus a small amount of wage accruals less disbursements in 1971 and 1972.

[b] Compound interest rates between terminal years.

Source: Historical data from U.S. Department of Commerce, Bureau of Economic Analysis; projections by Bureau of Labor Statistics.

ing the production of military supplies, we would find that *almost one-third of the labor force is dependent on the economic activity of the state.*

The state thus plays a decisive role in the U.S. economy, sustaining capital accumulation, providing services, creating markets, and absorbing surplus population into public employment. In fact, the different economic functions of the social and political mechanisms are interrelated in a complementary way. They form a structural set of relationships that O'Connor aptly describes as the "warfare-welfare state."

The complexity of these relationships can be summarized in one simple sentence. *The state has become the center of the process of accumulation and realization in advanced capitalism.* Without the state the process could be neither expanded nor reproduced. Are we then in a different mode of production? Not at all. The intervention of the state takes place within the structural rules of capitalism for the purpose of overcoming the historical contradictions that arise during the latter stages of its development. The crucial mechanism that reveals the capitalist logic of public policies is the fact that we can observe *a systematic trend toward the socialization of costs and the privatization of profits.* This is the most profitable pattern of state intervention for corporate capital. But it is also the basis for increasing contradictions that support the trends toward a new type of economic crisis.

One of the major contradictions is that as the state increases its intervention in the economy with a corresponding expansion in its outlays, it reduces its base of revenue. This happens not only because most of the profitable operations are transferred to corporate capital but also because the state's absorption of surplus population forces the state into less productive activities. The monopoly sector produces more and more value but distributes less and less income. What happens in the public sector is just the opposite. The state employs more and more people and distributes more and more revenue, but does not take over productive activities that would increase the productivity of the public services.

To pay for its massive expenditures in the absence of a large sector of public enterprises, the state must raise revenue from sources other than itself. It does this in two ways: through taxation on capital and people (appropriating a share of the value); and through debt and increases in the money supply (without respecting the necessary relationship to the value created).

Taxation has obvious limits. To collect taxes on profits defeats the purpose of increasing the rate of profit in order to make the capitalist economy more dynamic. Collecting taxes on personal income reduces demand and can provoke social unrest.

Despite the increase in taxes, the gap between state resources and state expenditures expanded at an accelerated rate for the period 1960-1972, as shown by Figure 15. (There was an exception in 1969-1970, when budgetary restrictions were used by Nixon to engineer a short recession.) Total spending rose at an annual rate of 5 percent from 1952 to 1960, 7 percent from 1960 to 1968, and 8 percent from 1968 to 1975.[43]

To fill the gap, *the U.S. government has created public debt and increased the money supply without a corresponding in-*

Figure 15

Federal Budget Receipts and Outlays: 1960-1976

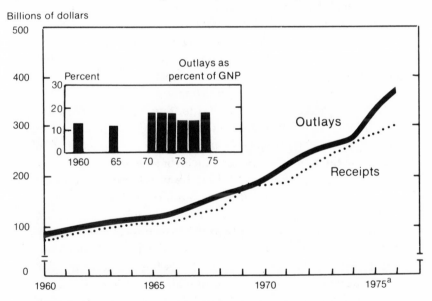

^aEstimate

Source: Chart prepared by U.S. Bureau of the Census. Data from U.S. Office of Management and Budget. *Statistical Abstract Yearbook, 1976.*

crease in the actual levels of production. Figure 16 shows the size of the federal debt, and Tables 15 and 16 show the increasing rate of growth in money supply and in debt per capita. The situation is even more unfavorable for local governments, which have been required to bear increasing costs for social consumption expenditures, especially in education. *The structural gap between the socialization of costs and the privatization of profits has led to the fiscal crisis of the state.*

In order to pay for the expenditures required by the warfare-welfare state, the U.S. government has used the only tool possible within the limits of the system—the expansion of the debt and the money supply—which has spurred inflation. Why does the expansion of public debt and the money supply lead to inflation? There are several reasons. First, their rate of growth exceeds the rate of growth of the GNP. Thus, for a given amount of commodities (goods and services), there is an increasing proportion of means-of-payment units: the same value will be represented by a higher nominal price. Second, the increased borrowing of the state in the financial markets (particularly in the form of municipal debt) will raise the rate of interest for capital, further increasing the cost of money, which we have seen to be one of the primary sources of inflation. Third, most state expenditures (nurtured through debt) do not correspond to the production of goods and services but to the expansion of unproductive services and to increased employment in the public sector. Therefore, by paying its employees the state introduces more and more money into the market without increasing the existing quantity of commodities. Thus, in addition to the direct effect of increasing the money supply and the debt (the first factor), there is also an indirect effect caused by the way these increases are used—demand is stimulated through unproductive activities.

Nevertheless, it would be theoretically possible to balance production and the money supply in the long run. The state would stimulate the economy just to pump it and withdraw when equilibrium was established. Actually, this is impossible in the current pattern of U.S. capitalist accumulation for two reasons:

1. There is an imbalance of growth between Department I and Department II of the economy, requiring a *preexisting solvent demand* for capital to invest in Department I at a level high

Figure 16

The Big Increase in Government Borrowing

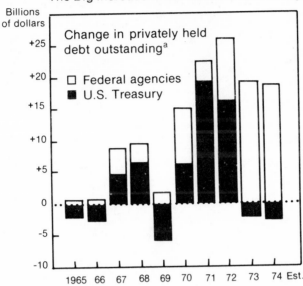

ªExcludes holdings of Federal Reserve. U.S. trust funds, and federal agencies.

Data: Solomon Bros.

TABLE 15. GROWTH OF THE U.S. MONEY SUPPLY

Year	Billions of dollars	Percentage increase
1965	463	—
1966	485	4.8
1967	533	9.9
1968	577	8.3
1969	594	3.0
1970	641	7.9
1971	727	13.4
1972	822	13.1
1973	893	8.6

Source: *The Economic Report of the President*, Feb. 1974, p. 310.

enough to ensure a profitable return on the increasing quantity of fixed capital. Therefore, state-stimulated demand always has to be ahead of the general rate of growth in the economy, and the gap between the quantity of commodities and the means of payment will never be closed.

2. As it develops, corporate capital increasingly relies on the

TABLE 16. PUBLIC DEBT OF THE FEDERAL GOVERNMENT, 1900-1975

Year	Total billions of dollars[a]	Gross Debt Percent annual change[b]	Per capita dollars[c]
1900	1.3	2.9	17
1905	1.1	−2.2	14
1910	1.1	0.3	12
1915	1.2	0.8	12
1920	24.3	80.0	228
1925	20.5	−3.3	177
1930	16.2	−4.6	132
1935	28.7	12.1	226
1940	43.0	8.4	325
1945	258.7	43.0	1,849
1950	256.1	−0.1	1,688
1955	272.8	1.3	1,651
1960	284.1	0.9	1,572
1961	286.4	0.9	1,559
1962	295.4	3.1	1,582
1963	302.7	2.5	1,598
1964	308.1	1.8	1,604
1965	313.8	1.9	1,613
1966	316.1	0.7	1,605
1967	322.9	2.2	1,622
1968	345.4	7.0	1,717
1969	352.9	2.2	1,737
1970	370.1	4.9	1,807
1971	397.3	7.4	1,919
1972	426.4	7.3	2,042
1973	457.3	7.2	2,174
1974	474.2	3.7	2,238
1975	533.2	12.4	2,496

Note: As of June 30. See also *Historical Statistics, Colonial Times to 1970*, series Y, pp. 461, 493, and 494.

[a] Adjusted to include nonmarketable issues to the International Monetary Fund and other international institutions for each year as follows (in billions of dollars): 1950, 0.9; 1955, 1.6; 1960, 2.2; 1962, 2.8; 1963, 3.2; 1964, 3.6; 1965, 3.5; 1966, 3.8; 1967, 3.3; 1968, 2.2; and from 1969 through 1976, 0.8.

[b] Change from previous year: e.g., 1900 from 1899; 1905 from 1904, etc. Minus sign (−) denotes decrease.

[c] Based on estimated July 1 population; prior to 1960, excludes Alaska and Hawaii.

Source: U.S. Department of the Treasury, *Statistical Appendix to the Annual Report of the Secretary of the Treasury of the State of the Finances and Final Monthly Treasury Statement of Receipts and Outlays of the U.S. Government*, taken from *Statistical Abstract of the U.S., 1977*, p. 266.

state to support technological innovations and to assume the cost of capital devaluation. Since this is a self-accelerating process that also has to be ahead of the rate of accumulation, the state needs to mobilize over and over again a quantity of resources larger than the value it can appropriate.

Therefore, the "monetary school" is not wrong when it claims its statistical findings establishing the correlation between inflation and the expansion of the debt and the money supply are valid. But such a "discovery" is a blind observation as long as it is not put into the broader context of the dynamics of accumulation in advanced capitalism. In fact, the state has tried from time to time to stop this movement by applying a more restrictive budgetary policy. By doing so, however, it threatened the whole equilibrium of the system whose expansion was based on the ability of the state to provide jobs and demand to counteract the tendencies toward stagnation. For instance, the restrictions in 1969 drastically reduced the government's addition to consuming power ($11 billion less in consumer demand), provoking a reduction in investment and a rise in unemployment. Inflation and recession have become the two benchmarks between which the capitalist state must follow an increasingly adventurous path.

THE CAPITALIST mode of production is an expanding contradictory system. Capitalist societies are shaped by the particular way these contradictions develop through the conflicts and interactions defined *on* the social classes and *by* their political expression. The major structural problems created by the process of capitalist accumulation in the United States were determined by the upheavals caused by new economic policies and the transformation of the system on the basis of a new relationship between the state and the large corporations. The internationalization of capital, the creation of the debt economy, and the decisive role of the state in the process of accumulation and realization of profit were major structural trends that allowed for sustained capitalist growth during almost three decades. But the introduction of these countertendencies to fight stagnation triggered new contradictions that were increasingly expressed through the monetary crisis and the sprawl of structural inflation. In this particular situation, dominated by the defeat of imperialism in

Indochina, increasing intercapitalist competition, and the development of social unrest within advanced capitalist societies, the new structural contradictions came together in certain conjunctural factors that, in return, made them more acute and precipitated the latest crisis. The worldwide interdependency of the American economy permitted the crisis to expand through the whole system. Figure 17 gives a schematic summary of the process.

In this analysis we have oversimplified some trends by reducing them to their effect on the process of production and circulation of capital and commodities. Nevertheless, in order to understand the dynamics of U.S. *society* we must now consider the specific American class structure and the reciprocal relationship between its transformation and the major trends of the economic crisis.

Figure 17

Mechanisms of the Production of the Crisis in the U.S. Economy, 1965-1975

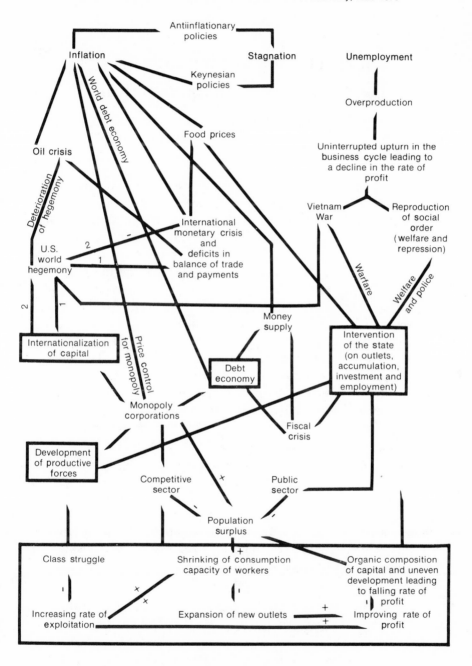

3

■■■

Capitalist Contradictions and
Class Relationships in the American
Social Structure

THE ECONOMIC CRISIS, which has developed as a consequence
of structural conditions triggered by the process of capital accumulation, results from contradictions that are an expression of
social relationships of production, distribution, and management.
The policies that will be used to deal with the crisis will be determined less by structural requirements than by the political
process of American society (even if the possible alternatives and
the specific problems are structurally conditioned). This political
process will be largely determined by the interplay of political and
ideological factors with the structural positions of different social
groups in the process of production and consumption. Therefore,
we need to introduce the characteristics of American class structure and their relation to the development of the economic crisis
as the next step in understanding the crisis as a social process.

Our analysis will not simply describe the distribution of the
labor force and the pattern of income stratification. It will relate
these characteristics, their changing pattern, and the interests
they represent to the dynamics of *capitalist accumulation*, to the
development of *productive forces*, and to the transformation of
social relationships. Obviously, we cannot develop the whole
analysis of this point here (namely, a general interpretation of
American class structure and class struggle), but we must consider some of the major trends in order to be able to relate them to
the economic crisis.

1. THE PATTERN OF CAPITALIST
ACCUMULATION IN THE UNITED STATES

We must begin by reviewing the main trends of the pattern of capitalist accumulation in the United States.[1] This pattern, working on a world scale, is defined by increasing productivity in an expanding monopoly sector, which centralizes and concentrates more and more capital and productive labor, produces more and more value, develops and controls more and more technology and knowledge, and employs, proportionally, less and less labor power. This creates an interdependent trend toward extraordinary excess productive capacity in this sector with an increasing surplus population that is not required for production purposes. The major contradiction is that this population is, nevertheless, required for consumption purposes and has to be integrated or repressed or both in order to preserve the social relationships that support the private appropriation of surplus value in the form of profit.

The process of capitalist expansion proceeds by destroying the existing precapitalist forms of production and consumption as well as the more primitive forms of capitalist production that include small shops, handicraft businesses, and labor-intensive agriculture. Advances in science and technology (innovation concentrated mainly in the monopoly sector) are used to take advantage of competitive capital sectors. The process of development is fulfilled through endless competition and through an increasing alignment of social relationships following the rules of the most advanced fractions of capital in the monopoly sector. This process of intersectoral domination takes two forms: mass destruction of backward firms and subordination to the interests and patterns of the monopoly sector.

The "competitive sector" plays a major role in the accumulation of the monopoly sector in at least two ways. It is the first line of defense in a depression. It also functions as a mechanism of overexploitation: because it is forced to accept low prices in interfirm transactions, a share of surplus value must be transferred to the monopoly sector.

The process of uneven development and capitalist accumulation through penetration, destruction, and absorption of previous forms of economic and social relationships "free" a considerable amount of resources and labor, which constitute an additional source of surplus population. Some of this surplus is recycled into the monopoly sector; some is absorbed by the remaining competitive sector; some is absorbed by the state; and the rest joins the ranks of the unemployed and the underemployed. The expansion of the monopoly sector tends to generate its own demand and its own basis of social integration by increasing the standard of living. But only part of the population benefits. This particular pattern of development can only survive economically and politically because massive state intervention in the economy provides jobs, services, and income. The state thus becomes a center of regulation of the entire system under the conditions of structural domination of corporate capital.

This pattern of development relies on the ability of the "system" (that is, the ruling class and the state apparatus) to cope with the different contradictions in order to preserve the most important sources of its dynamic stability. This means maintaining the ability of the monopoly sector to:

1. Increase the rate of profit, through the combination of:

a. The appropriation of surplus value permitted by the stability of the relationship between capital and labor, based on the repression and integration of the working-class movement.[2]

b. The development and appropriation of science, technology, and general knowledge, the increase in the productivity of work, enhancing the rate of relative surplus value.[3]

c. The maintenance and expansion of economic and political domination over the world.

2. Concentrate and centralize capital, the means of production, and labor and to combine them in an increasingly efficient way, as exemplified by the large corporations developing the functions of management and control and structuring the market and the social processes required for the achievement of corporation goals. This results in a deepening of the social division of labor, in expansion of the activities called "services," and in a transition from a market-oriented economy to a market-manipulated society.

3. Absorb and recycle the increasing surplus population.

4. Preserve the fragmentation of labor power in order to achieve greater exploitation.

5. Rely more and more on state intervention to support the needs of the process of accumulation, to provide the required social services, and to assume the legitimization crucial for the reproduction of the social order.

Now, the American social structure is shaped by the requirements of this specific pattern of capitalist accumulation and by the contradictions they cause. Such contradictions are ultimately expressed by social movements and political conflicts that will determine the final consequences of the economic crisis. Therefore, we will try to analyze the major trends of this social structure as the expression of the particular dynamics of capitalist accumulation in the United States and as the basis of social contradictions that led to the current crisis. Since a class society is shaped largely on the basis of its structurally dominant interests, we will begin with an analysis of these interests, namely, those of large corporations and their relationship to the ruling class. Then we will trace the major characteristics of the relations of production and distribution, giving some attention to certain important issues, such as "services," the "dualist" structure, the sexual division of labor, the "minorities," and the urban crisis. The whole discussion will be oriented toward the causes and implications of the economic crisis.

2. CORPORATE CAPITAL AND THE RULING CLASS

A class society is organized around processes that reproduce and contradict the exploitation and domination of structurally dominated classes by the structurally dominant class. A social class is a relationship or, better said, a position in a relationship. Individuals and groups are defined by the social relationships they generate in the work process and by the appropriation of their work product.[4] They do not decide their class position, and they do not often define themselves in terms of class. But classes are not merely an intellectual tool. They exist in practice even though individuals cannot control their own class affiliation. At the same time, classes as collective agents are able to transform and modify their own positions and the class relationships that define them in the overall structure of social organization.

The ruling class is formed by people who in each historically defined society have structural advantages because of the rules of social organization relating to the disposal of surplus value and the goals and orientations of processes of production and distribution. In a capitalist society such structural privilege is acquired through the control of the organization, use, and ownership of the means of production and the sources of productivity required to produce value through human labor. In an advanced capitalist society the control over the means of production is exercised by corporate monopoly capital. Corporate monopoly capital controls extremely large units of production, distribution, and management. It does so as a result of the historical processes of concentration and centralization of capital, made possible by the domination of capitalist social relationships and the corresponding capital's control over the means of production and human labor. By concentration we mean the tremendous growth of individual capital units through the intensive use of labor power, capital, and machinery. By centralization we mean there are fewer and fewer firms, which control more and more labor power, either directly or indirectly, and which organize and direct an increasing share of the production of surplus value.

In an advanced capitalist society contradictions, which are triggered by the expansion of capitalism, are solved temporarily by the systematic intervention of the state in the production of surplus value, the reproduction of labor power, and the realization of profits. This particular type of capitalism[5] has specific historical characteristics. In spite of the great importance of state intervention, *the control of the means of production and the structural rules of the production process still depend on the units of management of monopoly-capital corporations and on private ownership of that capital.* This point is fundamental. If it were not true, we would no longer be dealing with a capitalist society, and consequently the mechanisms of the crisis would have to be analyzed on the basis of another hypothesis. *Capitalism without capitalists is an unthinkable entity.*[6]

If the functioning of the economy and the society were not based on the interests of monopoly corporations controlled through private ownership of capital, we would not have a "state capitalist society" but a "technocratic society" or something else. Capitalism is a society where corporate capitalist interests are the basis of the social structure. We cannot conceive of a capitalist social structure without the historical existence of a capitalist class, which is defined as such because of its control over the means of production (including science) through capital.

It is important that we consider this point carefully in order to understand who the ruling class is in the United States today, what the structurally dominant interests are, and where the important decisions will be made in dealing with the crisis.

The United States is a capitalist society at the stage of monopoly capital for the following reasons:

1. The economy organizes society.

2. The economy relies on a highly concentrated and centralized corporate structure.

3. The corporations are controlled by small groups of major shareholders and their representatives.

4. The intervention of the state is linked to: explicit support to large corporations; support to the implementation of rules that structurally favor the corporations; responses to grassroots movements that can be maintained only by continued pressure from the grassroots, when the reforms are contradictory to state policies.

5. Access to the sources of productivity (labor and science) are controlled either by the corporations or by the state in the interests of the corporations.

Let us consider these different points. We will not demonstrate here the economy's domination of social relationships. This is very obvious in the United States: everyone can observe the crucial role money plays in the organization of social positions. It is true that economic factors do not explain everything, but it would appear that the way people produce and consume affects decisively the entire social organization.*

Let us consider carefully the other points, taking as a postulate that the interests prevailing in production, distribution, and consumption will be the dominant interests in the overall society.

The United States economy relies on a very small number of large corporations that concentrate and centralize capital, labor, and resources. To make the discussion simpler, we will support this point with evidence gathered by Charles Anderson from the

---

* This statement could appear as an economistic understanding of a class society. It is not. Actually, if "money organizes society," it is because the production of commodities for profit is the socially dominant value. That is, the economy determines society because capital imposes its structural interests in the historical process of class struggle.

main sources existing before 1974.[7] In 1968 there were 1.5 million firms in the United States. Firms with less than $1 million in assets represented 94 percent of the total number of firms but only 9 percent of the total capital. On the other hand, firms with assets over $250 million accounted for 0.1 percent of the firms but held 55 percent of the assets. The largest 200 corporations had 60 percent of the manufacturing assets in 1969, while the same number had only 68 percent in 1950. The top 100 corporations in 1969 accounted for 48 percent of the assets, while they accounted for only 40 percent in 1950. The larger the firm, the greater the centralization of capital: according to data from Gardiner Means, in 1962 there were 50 industrial firms holding 36 percent of the capital, 20 corporations 25 percent of the capital, 10 corporations 18 percent, and the top 5 firms 12 percent of the capital. This concentration and centralization of capital are particularly strong in aluminum, chemicals, glass, coffee, rubber, synthetic fibers, foods, electrical equipment, and steel. Concentration of capital leads to concentration of profits. The largest 500 corporations take four-fifths of all after-tax corporate profits in manufacturing, the 200 largest two-thirds of profits, the 100 largest almost three-fifths, the 50 largest almost one-half, the 20 largest almost two-fifths, the 10 largest three-tenths, and the largest one-fifth of total manufacturing profit. The amount of profits becomes overwhelming: in 1960 after-tax corporate profits amounted to $17 billion; in 1970 they amounted to $44 billion. Undistributed profits and depreciation allowances led to a $73 billion cash-flow. In 1971 ATT had profits of $2.24 billion, General Motors $1.94 billion, Standard Oil (N.J.) $1.46 billion, and IBM $1.08.

Monopolization of capital has been furthered by a continuous merger process, with peaks during the 1920s and the 1960s. The predominant form is not direct acquisition but the formation of conglomerates that link firms in very different sectors of activity. Among the most important conglomerate groups are ITT, General Motors, Ling-Tenco-Vought, Litton Industries, Gulf and Western, National General Corporation, and Leasco Data Processing. The banks are a crucial element in the development of this process. And banks are even more concentrated than industrial corporations. In 1970 the 50 largest commercial banks held 48 percent of banking assets (39 percent in 1960); 6 New York banks accounted for almost one-sixth of all bank assets in 1971. Furthermore, concentration in banking is increasing. Insurance companies are also concentrated: in 1970 the 50 largest companies held 83 percent of the assets, amounting to a total of $207 billion. And while 800 companies are in the business, the top 10 hold 60 percent of the assets. Additional data, which are incontrovertible on the point we are trying to prove, can be found in the sources gathered by Maurice Zeitlin.[8]

Once we have established the fact that the large corporations control the economy, we can turn to the decisive questions underlying the relationship between this fact and the class structure and dynamics of United States society:

1. What is the role played by corporations in the general organization of the ruling class? Is there some structural self-reproducing role, or is there a specific social group that holds that privilege through its control of the leverage of wealth and power? How do corporate goals and mechanisms affect the dynamics of society?

2. What is the relationship between corporate directors and the group that forms the social elite of the United States, not only in terms of prestige but in terms of social and political power (for instance, as opinion makers working through the mass media, or policy makers working through powerful lobbies)?

3. What is the relationship between the corporations, the social elite, and the state?

4. What are the historical and immediate interests of the American ruling class, as defined by the interaction between the above-cited elements, and how do they relate to the current crisis?

We will go into some detail on the first point, that is, how they each relate to the capitalists, the corporations, and the dynamics of the economy. We must therefore answer three different, but interrelated questions:[9] Who controls the corporations? What are the goals of the corporations? What are the new mechanisms introduced by the existence of the corporations in the economy, and how do they affect the dynamics of society? Let us proceed step by step to answer this series of specific questions.

Who controls the corporations is a classic subject and a fundamental issue in the characterization of modern industrial societies. One of the most uncritically accepted theses about the transformations of modern capitalism is that referring to the so-called managerial revolution. It argues, first, that there is a separation of ownership and control in large corporations because ownership is scattered among thousands of stockholders. Actually, the direction of a corporation is concentrated in the hands of the top managers, who are appointed according to professional criteria. Second, the managers in running the corporations search more for rational and economic effectiveness than for profit. This thesis, developed on the basis of the empirical evidence in the classic study by Adolph Berle and Gardiner Means[10] and popularized by James Burnham in *The Managerial Revolution*, has been redeveloped by other authors, particularly Galbraith.[11]

Whether expressed in terms of managers or technostructure, the basic idea is that the roots of corporate functioning have shifted from ownership and profit to control and rationality. The ruling class dissolves itself into a process of managerial organization in search of rationality and technological development. In fact, however, several empirical studies of American capitalism have seriously challenged the so-called observations provided by the ideologists of the post-industrial society.[12]

The most important one is an article by Maurice Zeitlin,[13] published in 1974, which systematically reviews all the existing evidence and theories. Zeitlin's discoveries are so striking that the whole question should be reexamined. The study's lack of impact shows clearly that the roots of the managerial ideologies are social and political and that these ideologies do not dominate simply on the basis of a scientific debate relying on empirical evidence: this is merely the first line of defense in the argument. Because this is a strategic point in our analysis, we will summarize Zeitlin's findings and propositions in some detail.

First, Zeitlin examines carefully the evidence presented by Berle and Means and finds that, according to their own data, they could classify as being definitely under management control only 22 percent of the largest corporations and only 3.8 percent of the 106 industrials. Then he reviews the conflicting statements of different empirical studies. In 1936 and 1937 the studies by Anna Rochester and Ferdinand Lundberg concluded, unlike Berle and Means, that a small group of families, through their ownership interests and control of the major banks, were still in control of the industrial system. Also, a National Resources Committee study carried out by Paul Sweezy discovered major centers of control along family lines when the 20 largest banks were added to the 200 largest nonfinancial corporations. While it is true that in a more recent study Robert Larner found 84 percent of the 200 largest nonfinancial corporations in 1963 under management control (providing the empirical support for Galbraith's theory), yet Don Villarejo concluded that at least 54 percent (and perhaps 61 percent) of the 232 large industrial corporations in the *Fortune* list for 1960 were controlled by ownership interests. The most important study in recent years carried out by Philip Burch, who searched through *Fortune, Time, Business Week, Forbes,* and *The New York Times* for the period 1950-1971 to collect information on the 300 largest manufacturing and mining corporations as well as on the top 50 merchandising and transportation companies, supplementing his data with material from other sources. He found that 40 percent were probably under management control, 45 percent probably under family control, and 15 percent possibly under family control. The main explanation for these contradictory findings is that Larner underestimated the control exercised through minority stockholders.

Next, Zeitlin turns to the question of who are the minority stockholders that control the crucial positions in the management of the corporations. The banks and financial institutions appear decisive not only because the banks control the corporations but because, in monopoly capital, industries and banks are highly interconnected. The banks play in the United States the role of coordinating financial groups including industrial corporations; because there are laws that explicitly forbid interlocking directorates between nonfinancial corporations, the connections are established through the banking system. Moreover, the connections are strengthened by the increasing dependence of large corporations on external financing, an empirical trend contrary to Galbraith's assumption. Financial capital, following Lenin's analysis, is the particular form of merger between banking and industrial capital in a decisive network of economic power in monopoly capitalism. As Zeitlin says:

If, contrary to managerialist assumptions, the large corporations must continue to rely on the capital market no less than in the past that is of critical importance; since the distribution of banking assets and deposits is highly skewed, this means that "reliance on external financing" is, in fact, dependence on a small number of very large financial corporations. As of 1964, the 100 largest commercial banks in the United States held 46% of all the deposits of the 13,775 commercial banks in the country. The 14 largest alone, representing one-tenth of 1% of all commercial banks, held 24% of all commercial bank deposits (Patman Report 1966, p. 804). Thus, the relationships between the large banks and corporations are essential to our understanding of the locus of corporate control.

This may mean that the conceptualization of the largest corporations, banks, and insurance companies as independent institutions may obscure the actual coalescence of financial and industrial capital which has occurred. On the one hand, as noted above, large banks and insurance companies frequently are themselves principal shareholders in the large corporations. On the other, the very same individuals and families may be principal shareholders in large banks and large corporations, even when these do not have institutional holdings in one another. Aside from the Mellons, with controlling interests in at least four of the 500 largest nonfinancial corporations and in an investment bank, insurance company, and the fifteenth largest commercial bank, whom we noted above, other well-known industrialist families in the United States may be cited who also have dominant and/or controlling interests in the largest banks. For example there are both branches of the Rockefeller families, as well as other principal families in the Standard Oil corporations. The Rockefellers and associates reportedly (*Time*, September 7, 1962; Abels 1965, p. 358) held over 5% of the stock in the Chase Manhattan Bank (ranking second by deposits of all banks in 1963), whose chairman of the board is David Rockefeller; the Stillman-Rockefeller families and associates are said to be dominant in the First National City Bank (ranking third in 1963) (*Fortune*, September 1965, p. 138). The Fisher and Mott families, among the principal shareowning families in General Motors, reportedly held over 5% of the stock of the National Bank of Detroit (U.S. Congress, 1963, pp. 227, 416), the country's sixteenth largest bank

in 1963. The Henry Ford family owns 4% of the thirtieth ranking Manufacturer's National which, in turn own 7% of Ford
Motor Company common stock (Patman Report 1968, p. 664).
The M. A. Hanna family that controls at least two of the 500
largest corporations, National Steel and Consolidated Coal
(Larner 1970, p. 120; Burch 1972, p. 58), has a dominant
minority interest of at least 3% in the thirty-fourth ranking National City Bank of Cleveland (U.S. Congress 1963, p. 165),
which, in turn holds 11% of the stock of Hanna Mining Company. These are, of course, merely instances, as I said of prom-
inent families whose interests overlap banking and industry.

. . . Do such "finance capitalists" or representatives of banks
who sit on the board of the large American corporations today,
have a special role in coordinating the interest of these corporations?

. . . One relevant issue, however, on which we do have some
information, is the extent to which they are likely to sit on a
number of large nonfinancial corporation boards, compared
with "outside directors" (i.e. those who do not actually hold
posts as officers in the corporate management) who are not
bankers. I have analyzed raw data presented elsewhere (Smith
and Desfosses 1972) on interlocking directorates among the
500 largest industrial corporations, ranked by sales, in 1968.
What we find is that commercial and investment bankers are
disproportionately over represented among the occupants of
multiple corporate directorships. Bankers constituted 21% of
all outside directors in the 500 largest industrials but well over
twice that proportion among the outside directors with seats on
three or more corporate boards. Indeed, the proportion of
bankers who are outside directors rises directly with the numbers of corporate posts held. And among the select few (N =
16) outside directors who have five or more posts, 56% were
bankers: of the five outside directors with six or seven posts,
four were bankers. Viewing the same relationship differently
commercial and investment bankers stand out in marked contrast to other outside directors in the top 500 corporations: a far
higher proportion of them have multiple corporation posts than
do outside directors from other top 500 corporations, law firms,
consulting firms, or other types of companies and institutions.

Outside directors from other top 500 corporations are second only to the bankers in the proportion with multiple directorships. But well over twice the proportion of bankers occupy multiple posts: 11% of the commercial bankers and 15% of the investment bankers have seats on three or more top 500 corporate boards compared with 6% of the directors from other top 500 firms.[14]

Because of the data presented by Zeitlin and other recent studies, particularly those by Robert Fitch and Mary Oppenheimer,[15] we should not only question the empirical evidence for the managerial theories but accept as a *probable* trend the idea that corporations are controlled by small groups of stockholders often organized along individual and group lines. We have seen, particularly in our analysis of the economic evolution of the United States, that the idea that corporations are self-financing is a myth since one of the roots of the crisis is the accelerated expansion of corporate debt. The top managers are certainly selected on the basis of their efficiency, but they either come from the "inner circle" or, more frequently, are coopted through the distribution to them of important stocks and sometimes through adoption by means of selected marriages. The capitalists exist in monopoly capitalism, and they still rule the corporations (certainly as rationally as possible) on the basis of their stock ownership even if it is minority ownership (sometimes 5 percent of the stock is enough) and even if the mechanisms linking minority ownership and effective control are extremely complex and are exercised through networks of interlocking directorates and remote policy control.[16]

The crucial goal of the corporations still is the search for high profits. The recent empirical study used as a basis to establish the separation between ownership and control, by Robert Larner,[17] provides systematic data to show that profit maximization is the definite target of the large corporations. Using multiple-regression analysis and taking into account assets, industrial concentration, Federal Reserve Board indices of economic growth and fluctuation of profit rates, and equity-asset ratios, Larner found, first, that the rate of profit earned by "management" and by "owner-controlled" firms was about the same; both were equally profit oriented. Second, the evidence on fluctuations in profit rates suggested no support for the view that allegedly nonowning managements avoid risk taking more than owners do. Third, Larner found that the corporation's dollar profit and the rate of return on equity were the major determinants of the level of "executive compensation." Compensation of executives, he concluded, has been "effectively harnessed" to the stockholders' interests in profits.

O'Connor also gathered convincing material indicating that the search for profits is the major mechanism underlying corporate policies,[18] but it would be simplistic not to qualify this finding. We are speaking of a search for profit, but not in the short term or for each operation of the corporation. Rather, we are dealing with a rate of profit normalized over the long term, through the operations of the entire financial group in a world market. What this implies is that the major sources of such profit lie in a growing control over the conditions of production and realization of profit, over the supply of capital, raw materials, labor, and technology. Thus, the search for profits is translated into sequences of operations that only make sense as an expression of corporate strategies designed to attain an advantageous position in terms of economic and social power. Nevertheless, though it is true that this overall long-term strategy characterizes the general pattern of the corporations, it is also clear that the complexity of the system makes it impossible to have a totally rational optimization of the financial group. Thus, there is often a return to the simple rule of requiring profit maximization at the level of each firm in one particular situation, not coordinating the whole group, except for some major initiative. The search for profits is the goal of the corporation, but in each case the significance of profits for the particular corporation acting in a given situation has to be considered.

What changes in the capitalist mechanisms are introduced by the new corporate policies? Intercapitalist competition exists within monopoly capitalism. In fact, competition is intrinsic to the capitalist system, since accumulation relies both on the exploitation of workers and on control over the markets won from other competing capitalist units. The size of these units is not an obstacle to competition; it only changes the way of competing.

But we must carefully consider these changes in order to understand advanced capitalism.

Monopoly competition consists primarily of attempts to control different zones of the world, to expand markets for new products, to appropriate science, to keep accessibility to financial sources, and to exercise influence over key centers of decision in the state apparatus.

Thus, appropriation of knowledge is a major factor in corporate policies. This is done not just to make use of knowledge, but sometimes to neutralize it or keep it in reserve. The close ties between corporations and universities have to be considered in this perspective as more important than the so-called growing social responsibility of the giant firms.

For if the control of the "scientific revolution" becomes crucial for the production of value, the control of prices will become a major element in the realization of profit. Through control of prices, which is made possible by their manipulation of the market, corporations are able to absorb the high profits coming from the decrease in the costs of production and recover whatever concessions are made to workers through wage increases.

One of the major new mechanisms is the function of planning and coordination, which obviously requires large management. However, this function does not redefine the class content of the corporation. It simply transforms the organizational means to achieve the structural target of profit maximization. While the rise of new forms of large rationally oriented organization is a very important trend, it does not substantially modify the capitalist policies these new organizations implement.

The most important transformation concerns the close links the corporations maintain with the state. As we have observed, the state in the United States has been an indispensable help in overcoming the contradictions faced by the capitalist corporations. The strategic economic role of the state makes it even more important to corporate capitalists to become more openly a ruling class in strictly political terms. In advanced capitalist societies the corporations are becoming more politically involved, and the state is becoming more openly procapitalist and not just pro-bourgeois, in social terms. Thus, what we have is a state capitalist society.

In summary, the most important factor in maintaining corporate profits is corporate control over the process of accumulation and realization throughout the whole system. However, this introduces a major contradiction since the functioning of the capitalist economy becomes objectively socialized while competition and profit maximizing by particular corporations still remain a major determinant of the economy.

We will not comment here in detail on the other factors regarding the existence of the ruling class and its relationship with the state. We will simply recall some basic trends in order to be able to use them as "constant values" in our analysis.

As G. William Domhoff has repeatedly established in several syntheses of the existing empirical research (including some of his own),[19] there is a ruling class in the United States. This class is an inner group that links corporate directors, the social elite, institutions of higher learning, opinion makers, the mass media, and the circles having access to the top positions in the political system. But the relationship between the ruling class and the state is extremely complex. On the one hand, the state cannot be seen as a pure instrument of the ruling class. It has resulted historically from a process of contradictory class struggle, where both the dominating and the dominated classes have produced effects. Also, at any moment in a given society the class struggle cuts across the existing institutions, including the state. Thus, the state is shaped by contradictions of the society and continuously affected by changing power relationships. On the other hand, the state is not an even mirror of the class struggle. It is the product of a historical process characterized, in a capitalist society, by the continuous domination of capital. Therefore, the state is the crystallization of this class domination, and its institutions will reflect fundamentally the interests of the bourgeoisie, although the purity of this expression will vary according to the historical capacities of contradictory classes.[20] *In the United States the overwhelming hegemony of capital in society has produced a state that responds almost entirely to capitalist interests.*

To support this statement, we need analyses of the relationship between corporate interests and state policies. One excellent study carried out in the Department of Sociology at the University of Wisconsin demonstrates that the policies of redistribution of the American states do not depend on the political system but on the strength of the relationship between capital and labor, in such a way that they only become actively redistributive when the labor movement is sufficiently strong.[21] There are also studies on the logic of social services that show the hegemony of corporate policies in shaping programs in the fields of health,[22] housing,[23] social security,[24] and transportation.[25] On the other hand, Frances Piven and Richard Cloward have shown that reforms (for instance, the improvement of social welfare) are directly linked to pressure from the grassroots generated by social unrest.[26]

Rather than summarize the entire literature on the existing relationship between class interests and state policies in the United States, we are going to investigate how they interrelate in regard to the policies now being used to deal with the current economic crisis. To proceed in this direction, it is crucial that we have a clear, even if somewhat schematic, idea of the structural interests of the ruling class in relationship to the economic crisis.

We have to differentiate between immediate interests and historical interests at the economic, political, and ideological levels.[27] The historical interests of the large corporations are to normalize the rate of profit in the long term and to reproduce capitalism. Their immediate interests are to solve the problem of the falling rate of profit, to realize profit, and to preserve the social order. However, this characterization is too general, and it is necessary to identify these interests in each historical situation.

In the economic crisis of the seventies the historical interests are to maintain the general dynamics of the system as described, introducing some corrections to smooth its functioning. The immediate interests of corporate capital during the current crisis can be summarized briefly as follows: to curb inflation and absorb part of the debt; to increase productivity both through absolute and relative surplus value; to obtain help from the state for investment, shifting some expenditures from social consumption and social expenses to social investment; to increase productivity in the service sector; to keep social unrest under control as much as possible.[28]

The immediate interests at the political level are to combine mechanisms of integration with tough new policies enabling the ruling class to maneuver in dangerous situations and reestablish control over the empire. The immediate interests at the ideological level are to issue a call to national solidarity in the name of free enterprise.

A national opinion survey in 1975 showed that 72 percent of the Americans interviewed were confident about the future of the United States. However, only 42 percent were confident about the future of "the American economic system, namely free enterprise." Also, in most national elections in recent years, almost half of Americans did not vote. This political "dropping out" of the American people is potentially threatening the legitimacy of the system. The situation must be restored by an appeal to the old virtues of hard work, family life, patriotism, and community solidarity, with more austerity and less consumption, more "natural life" and less "sophisticated urbanism." Carter's campaign was centered on this attempt to restore confidence in the fundamental values of the system. The question is whether or not this appeal, mostly packaged for middle-class Americans, will be heard in the inner city ghettos, on the campuses, in the factories, in the kitchens.

3. THE IMPACT OF THE PATTERN OF
   DEVELOPMENT ON THE RELATIONS OF
   PRODUCTION AND MANAGEMENT:
   OLD AND NEW WORKING CLASS[29]

The pattern of capitalist accumulation determines the social structure by placing people in positions defined by the social division of labor in the process of production, by destroying or reorganizing former positions, and by continuously transforming this structure through the contradictory dynamics of its process of expansion.

In order to be able to understand the specific effects of the particular pattern of U.S. capitalism on the social structure, we must look at the most important transformations of the occupational structure. Before establishing any kind of relationship, let us see what these trends are.

The American occupational structure is overwhelmingly com-

TABLE 17. CLASS OF THE EMPLOYED AS A PERCENTAGE OF THE LABOR FORCE

	Wage and salary workers A	Self-employed B	Unpaid family workers	Ratio of A/B
1940	75.1	21.6	3.2	3.5
1947	77.5	19.0	3.2	4.1
1950	79.6	17.3	3.1	4.6
1955	81.9	15.2	2.9	5.3
1960	83.7	13.7	2.5	6.1
1965	86.3	11.8	2.0	7.3
1969	89.5	9.1	1.4	9.8

Sources: U.S. Census, 1940, *Special Reports: The Labor Force*, Table A11, p. 228; *Manpower Report of the President*, 1970, Table 19, pp. 36-37.

posed of wage and salary workers. As shown in Table 17, they comprised 89.5 percent of the work force in 1969. This fact is extremely important because most of these salaried workers are selling their labor power in exchange for payment in order to get access to the means of production and management. The entire society is dependent on capitalist rules, rooted ultimately in the power of the large corporations. This has been the argument used to explain both the disappearance of the working class and its generalization. The debate concerns the fact that, as Table 18 shows, the percentage of so-called nonmanual workers (all but farm workers and manual workers) has increased steadily, reaching 63.3 percent in 1970. By including all these "nonmanual workers" in the middle class, theorists of the mass society have achieved a very rough ideological manipulation. At the same time, other authors have tried desperately to show that the working class defined in the traditional terms of manual labor still constitutes a majority of the population. To do this Andrew Levison in the first part of his excellent book[30] and Richard Hamilton[31] use the same argument: if we only take into consideration the occupations of the men, almost half the labor force is made up of manual laborers. If we include some service workers who should be manual laborers, then we have a working-class majority. Levison actually calculated that 57.5 percent of the male labor force was working class by adding craftsmen, foremen, operatives, laborers, and service workers in 1969, which would have been a normal year before the recession began in 1970. The argument is that most women are married and live in the class

TABLE 18. OCCUPATIONAL GROUPS, BOTH SEXES

	1900	1920	1940	1950	1960	1970
Managers, officials, proprietors, farm owners and managers	7,460 25.6%	9,245 21.9%	9,132 17.7%	9,530 16.1%	10,400 15.5%	9,998 12.7%
Professional and technical	1,234 4.3%	2,283 5.4%	3,879 7.5%	5,031 8.6%	7,475 11.1%	11,322 14.4%
Independent professional and technical	320 1.1%	420 1.0%	570 1.1%	654 1.1%	873 1.3%	1,200 1.5%
Professional and technical workers	910 3.1%	1,860 4.4%	3,310 6.4%	4,427 7.5%	6,602 9.9%	10,100 12.9%
Clerical and sales workers	2,184 7.5%	5,443 12.9%	8,432 16.3%	11,365 19.3%	14,184 21.2%	18,548 23.6%
Service workers	2,626 9.1%	3,313 7.9%	6,069 11.8%	6,180 10.5%	3,349 12.5%	9,724 12.4%
Manual workers	10,401 35.8%	16,974 40.2%	20,597 39.8%	24,266 41.1%	24,211 36.1%	27,542 34.9%
Craftsmen and foremen	3,062 10.5%	5,482 13.0%	6,203 12.0%	8,350 14.2%	8,560 12.8%	10,027 12.8%
Operatives	3,720 12.8%	6,587 15.6%	9,518 18.4%	12,030 20.4%	11,986 17.9%	13,311 17.6%
Nonfarm laborers	3,620 12.5%	4,905 11.6%	4,875 9.4%	3,885 6.6%	3,665 5.5%	3,614 4.6%
Farm workers	5,125 17.7%	4,948 11.7%	3,632 7.0%	2,578 4.3%	2,057 3.1%	1,400 1.8%
Total	29,030	42,206	51,742	58,999	66,681	78,408

Source: *Historical Statistics of the United States*, 1970, p. 74, *Statistical Abstract of the U.S., 1970*, p. 225. U.S. Department of Labor, *The U.S. Economy in 1980*. Table A-24, p. 57.

and culture of their husbands. They follow their husbands' lead in politics, and their social life is with their husbands' class. Therefore, men's occupations give a much clearer indication of the relative size of the working class in America.

We reject such arguments because they oversimplify the issues and confuse the level of analysis. It is one thing to analyze the relationships, associations, and contradictions between different positions in the social division of labor held by the members of the family and another very different one to decide in advance that the class structure is determined only by the position of males. We have to consider both sexes and to think about their differential evolution. Why do we have to show that there is a majority of manual workers? Does the working class disappear because the conditions of work and exploitation are transformed? The class structure is reflected in the social division of labor in each society. This division of labor defines the working class under capitalism as a result of the following: the selling of workers' labor power as their only resource; the working conditions; the sharing of power in the organization, that is, the role played in the mechanisms of social control and in the process of management; the relationship between productive and unproductive labor.

If selling one's labor power were the only criterion to consider a position as working class, the overwhelming majority of Americans would be considered working class. Obviously, we have to correct by other criteria, but in what terms? The essential distinction in the division of labor is not merely between manual and nonmanual. At best, such a distinction is extremely ambiguous. What is manual labor? Is it operating an automatic machine in the factory or punching IBM cards in a computer-center assembly line? The working conditions of clerical employees have been transformed into unskilled, subordinated, and piecemeal labor.[32] In terms of earnings, clerical workers and service workers are below the level of traditional manual workers (Table 19). Also, the most important cleavages in earnings are related not to occupational position but to the sector of the economy, as shown in Table 20.

As for sharing power in the organization, an almost continuous line of hierarchy only gives real power (the ability to decide) to the top level.[33] This means that most salaried workers are not in a position to make decisions.

Therefore, according to Marxist theory, what remains as the major cleavage between the working class and "the others" is not the distinction between manual and nonmanual labor but participation in the process of the actual production of value. Indeed, the former criterion is more and more blurred by technological progress and the increasing socialization of the process of production.[34]

The distinction between productive and unproductive does not relate to any judgment on the social usefulness of an activity or to the material form of the result of the activity. An activity is productive if it contributes to the formation of what the mode of

TABLE 19. WEEKLY EARNINGS BY U.S. PROFESSIONAL GROUPS

Occupational group	Median usual weekly earnings of full-time workers
Craftsmen and foremen	$167
Operatives and kindred workers	120
Nonfarm laborers	117
Clerical workers	115
Service workers (except private household)	96

Source: Harry Braverman, *Labor and Monopoly Capital*, New York: Monthly Review Press, 1974, p. 297. Copyright © 1974 by Harry Braverman. Reprinted by permission of Monthly Review Press.

TABLE 20. GROSS AVERAGE WEEKLY EARNINGS OF PRODUCTION OR NONSUPERVISORY WORKERS ON PRIVATE NONAGRICULTURAL PAYROLLS, 1971–

Relatively stagnant industries		Rapidly growing industries	
Mining	$171.74	Wholesale and retail trade	$100.74
Contract construction	212.24	Finance, insurance, and real estate.	121.36
Manufacturing	142.04	Service industries	102.94
Transportation and public utilities	168.84		

Source: Harry Braverman, *Labor and Monopoly Capital*, New York: Monthly Review Press, 1974, p. 393. Copyright © 1974 by Harry Braverman. Reprinted by permission of Monthly Review Press.

production relies on. What is productive in capitalism, is what produces surplus value for capital—namely profit—not what produces use value or what increases the amount of money (as in a profitable commercial exchange). It is the process of production of goods or services where a part of human labor embodied in the process is appropriated by capital and transformed into a commodity to realize profit in the market.

This is still a basic distinction for understanding the structure of a capitalist society. However, this distinction does not overlap much with the distinctions resulting from the three preceding criteria. The reason is that with the development of socially necessary unproductive expenditures for the realization and management of capitalist profits, labor employed in these management functions is less and less distinct, in the process of actual work, from labor engaged in the production of surplus value. As Braverman says: "Although productive and unproductive labor are technically distinct, although productive labor has tended to decrease in proportion as its productivity has grown, while nonproductive labor has increased *only as a result of the increase in surpluses thrown off by productive labor*—despite these distinctions, the two masses of labor are not otherwise in striking contrast and need not be counterposed to each other. They form a continuous mass of employment which, at present and unlike the situation in Marx's day, has everything in common."[35]

What this development means, in fact, is that although the distinction between productive and unproductive labor is fundamental to the dynamics of capitalism and the future organization of society, it no longer forms a major line of differentiation between social classes. Their conditions of existence have become structurally homogenized in terms of class interests, but highly differentiated on other new lines: sector of the economy, place in the hierarchy, place in the structural causes of discrimination (sex and race).

If the profile of the working class in the United States appears less sharply defined than in the past, it is not because there is a lower proportion of manual workers but because the labor movement historically grounded in the industrial working class does not define itself as such. What distinguishes the American working class from other working classes is not its historical class interests but its weak class organizational *capacities*.[36]

The second major characteristic of the evolution of the division of labor in the United States is the spectacular decrease—almost disappearance—of the labor force in agriculture, as shown in Table 21. This has had extremely important consequences as agricultural workers (especially Southern blacks) had to move to other sectors of the economy where they have not been absorbed. The transformation of agriculture is one of the clearest expressions of the process of uneven development. An increasingly productive monopoly sector is at the same time destructive because it does not generate enough new opportunities to absorb the labor power no longer needed in the more productive areas.

A correlated major trend is the expansion of the labor force in the service sector, as shown in Table 22. It is important to remember that the ratio of the industrial labor force to the total

TABLE 21. LABOR FORCE IN AGRICULTURE

Year	Total labor force	Labor force in agriculture	Percentage	Farm laborers as a percentage of agriculturally employed
1900	29,070,000	10,710,000	36.8	48.0
1920	41,610,000	11,120,000	26.0	44.0
1940	55,640,000	9,540,000	17.1	40.9
1950	63,099,000	7,507,000	11.9	36.2
1960	66,681,000	5,723,000	8.6	36.0
1970	68,408,000	3,531,000	4.5	40.0
1980	95,100,000	2,600,000	2.7	48.1

Source: U.S. Department of Labor, *The U.S. Economy in 1980*, Table A-16, p. 49; *Statistical Abstract of the U.S., 1970*, p. 225; *Historical Statistics of the U.S.*, p. 72.

TABLE 22. PERCENTAGE DISTRIBUTION OF EMPLOYED WORKERS

		Agriculture	Industry	Services
U.S.:	1900	38	38	24
	1970	4	35	61
France:	1950	35	45	20
	1970	17	39	44
West Germany:	1950	24	48	28
	1968	10	48	42

Source: Alan Gartner and Frank Riessman, *The Service Society and the Consumer Vanguard*, New York: Harper & Row, 1974, p. 125. Copyright © 1974 by Alan Gartner and Frank Riessman. Reprinted by permission of Harper & Row, Publishers, Inc.

labor force has been quite stable for the last seventy years; the main changes are the disappearance of agricultural workers and the steady growth of workers employed in the so-called services. It is clear that to understand the relationship between the pattern of capitalist accumulation and the new social structure, we need a more rigorous analysis of the social and economic content of the service sector.

The increase of the labor force in the service sector is due mostly to a massive increase of clerical workers, 66.5 percent of whom are women (see Table 23). The dramatic increase in the employment of women as wage earners, shifting from 23 percent of the labor force in 1920 to 42 percent in 1970, has been a major factor in altering the entire structure of the society given the growing contradiction between the ideological meaning of sex roles and the new connection of this meaning to the social division of labor.

The greatest increase has been in professional and technical workers, who have grown from 4.3 percent of the labor force in 1900 to 14.4 percent in 1970. These people are sometimes called the "new working class." However, if we look at their specific jobs (Table 24), we will find that these middle-level workers face problems increasingly similar to those of other workers. They are salaried workers, productive and unproductive, suffering from increased workloads, lack of responsibility for the organization of their jobs, job insecurity, and absence of social services. They are unique in the sense that they do not have a tradition of organization and struggle. That is why they are "new." The evolution, perspective, and interests of this "group" will be decisive in determining the class struggle in the United States since they have traditionally been the most effective supporters of the ruling class.

Finally, about 40 percent of the American people over sixteen are outside the labor force in positions with a loosely defined rela-

TABLE 23. PERCENTAGE OF FEMALES IN EACH OCCUPATION

	1900	1920	1940	1950	1960	1970
Managers, officials, proprietors, farm owners, and managers	5.2	5.1	6.3	8.6	15.1	16.1
Professional and technical	35.2	44.0	41.3	39.5	36.3	38.2
Independent professional	—	—	19.4	16.8	16.7	26.6
Professional workers	—	—	45.3	42.9	38.6	40.4
Clerical and sales	20.0	39.5	43.0	52.2	58.8	66.5
Service workers	71.8	62.1	61.0	57.3	65.1	67.0
Manual workers	14.2	12.1	13.2	15.2	15.1	17.0
Craftsmen and foremen	2.5	1.9	2.2	3.0	2.6	2.9
Operatives	34.0	26.5	25.7	27.4	27.8	30.9
Nonfarm laborers	3.8	4.0	2.7	3.7	2.2	3.2
Farm workers	13.6	18.0	9.6	18.7	26.0	14.3
Total	18.5	20.5	24.4	28.0	33.2	37.9

Sources: *Historical Statistics of the United States*, 1970, p. 74; *Statistical Abstract of the U.S., 1970*, p. 225.

TABLE 24. NEW WORKING CLASS OCCUPATIONS, 1960

	Males		Females	
	1,000s	% of total	1,000s	% of total
Professional, technical and kindred workers (including self-employed)	4,543	100.0	2,793	100.0
Accountants and auditors	396	8.7	80	2.9
Actors, dancers, etc.	—	—	25	.9
Architects	30	.7	—	—
Artists and art teachers	68	1.5	37	1.3
Authors, editors and reporters	86	1.9	46	1.6
Chemists	77	1.7	—	—
Clergymen	197	4.3	—	—
College teachers	140	3.1	39	1.4
Dentists	81	1.8	—	—
Designers and draftsmen	262	5.8	25	.9
Dieticians and nutritionists	25	—	25	.9
Engineers	864	19.0	—	—
Lawyers and judges	206	4.5	8	.3
Librarians	—	—	72	2.6
Musicians and music teachers	86	1.9	111	4.0
Natural scientists	59	1.3	15	.5
Pharmacists	85	1.9	—	—
Physicians and surgeons	214	4.7	16	.6
Professional nurses	—	—	634	22.6
Social scientists	43	.9	14	.5
Social, welfare, and recreation workers	58	1.3	78	2.8
Elementary and secondary school teachers	478	10.5	1,206	43.2
Medical and dental technicians	53	1.2	88	3.1
Electrical and electronic technicians	89	2.0	—	—
Therapists and assimilated	—	—	20	.7
Others	971	21.4	254	9.1

Source: *Statistical Abstract of the U.S., 1970*, Table 337, pp. 227-228.

tionship to the occupational structure. More than thirty-five million of these people are "keeping house." In fact, without being paid, they are essential to the reproduction of labor power and the maintenance of the family, one of the basic apparatuses for preserving social order. An additional nine million are in school, and a large portion are undergoing an unpaid apprenticeship and thus constitute a subsidy to the system. Both housekeepers and students are making free and substantial social contributions to the economic viability of the system, yet are largely dependent for such necessities as medical care on the breadwinning fortunes of the family head. Among the remaining twelve million adults not in the labor force are an unknown but significant number who have simply dropped out of it.[37]

In fact, the number of adults in the labor force has increased from one-half the adult population at the beginning of the century to three-fifths in 1970, in spite of longer schooling and early retirement. The main factor accounting for this increase is the accelerated participation of women in the process of paid labor.

This trend in the evolution of the occupational structure raises a number of specific questions, which we will discuss in regard to their relationship to the contradictions of capitalist development in the United States. The main issues seem to be: the trend toward a "service society"; the internal cleavages between workers on the bases of race and sex; the persistence of widespread unemployment and underemployment; and the increasing fragmentation of the labor market.

4. THE SERVICE ECONOMY AND THE "POSTINDUSTRIAL SOCIETY"

Underlying the interpretation of the transformation of capitalism is the thesis of the appearance of a new society ("postscarcity," "postindustrial," "technological," etc.). The empirical basis for this argument is usually that workers who produce goods are continuously being replaced by workers who produce services (see Table 25). If this is a major trend of the U.S. economy, it is a very ambiguous one, because it does not differentiate among the very different kinds of economic activities labeled "services." Table 26 clearly shows that the services we are talking about in 1971 are not the same kind of services there were in 1870. The expansion of the service sector has caused the relative decay of transportation and personal services, but an increase in trade, finance, and real estate, with a very rapid absolute and relative increase in government activities.

An important study by Joachim Singelmann has differentiated among distributive services, producer services, social services, and personal services, recalculating the evolution of the labor force using these different labels (see Table 27).[38] The study shows clearly that although distributive services represent a very important proportion even at a stabilized rate of growth, the most rapidly growing services, which have been responsible for the transformation of the whole sector, have been the social services.

TABLE 25. GOODS-PRODUCING AND SERVICES-PRODUCING WORKERS IN
CIVILIAN LABOR FORCE (IN MILLIONS)[a]

Year	Total	Goods-producing workers	Services-producing workers
1940	49.3	25.6	24.5
1947	51.7	26.3	25.4
1968	80.7	28.9	51.8

[a] This trend is continuing with a projected ratio in 1980 of 32 goods-producing to 68 services-producing workers.
Source: Daniel Bell, *The Coming of the Post-Industrial Society: A Venture in Social Forecasting*, New York: Basic Books, 1973, p. 20.

TABLE 26. DISTRIBUTION OF EMPLOYMENT WITHIN THE
SERVICES-PRODUCING SECTOR, 1870-1971 (IN %)

	1870	1900	1920	1940	1947	1971
Transportation and utilities	20	23	27	17	16	9
Trade, finance, real estate, insurance	28	30	31	36	42	39
Personal services	48	42	36	40	20	25
Government	4	5	6	7	22	26

Source: Daniel Bell, *The Coming of the Post-industrial Society: A Venture in Social Forecasting*, New York: Basic Books, 1973, p. 21.

The data for 1970 reveal the acceleration of this trend, particularly in education and health. While employment in the transformative sector went down to 33.1 percent, producer services jumped to 8.2 percent and social services reached a peak of 21.9 percent. Therefore, we have to consider social services specifically in order to understand the relationship between the "service economy" and the pattern of capital accumulation.

Another trend that has been used as empirical support for arguing that advanced capitalism has been transformed into a service economy is the increase in professional-technical jobs as compared to operatives-craftsmen and managers-proprietors (see Table 28). Again, however, the statistical trends are ambiguous. Are we saying that we have had an increasing reevaluation of job qualifications? Yet many of the observations presented by Braverman show that for the majority of clerical workers, professionals, and technicians, working conditions and status in the division of labor are not essentially different from those of the industrial workers. Are we saying, then, that "services" are new

TABLE 27. PERCENTAGE DISTRIBUTION OF U.S. LABOR FORCE BY INDUSTRY SECTORS AND INTERMEDIATE INDUSTRY GROUPS, 1920-1970*

Sectors and Industries	1920	1930	1940	1950	1960	1970
I. Extractive	28.9	25.4	21.3	14.4	8.1	4.5
1) Agriculture	26.3	22.9	19.2	12.7	7.0	3.7
2) Mining	2.6	2.5	2.1	1.7	1.1	0.8
II. Transformative	32.9	31.5	29.8	33.9	35.9	33.1
3) Construction		6.5	4.7	6.2	6.2	5.8
4) Food		2.3	2.7	2.7	3.1	2.0
5) Textile		4.2	2.6	2.2	3.3	3.0
6) Metal		7.7	2.9	3.6	3.9	3.3
7) Machinery	32.9		2.4	3.7	7.5	8.3
8) Chemical		1.3	1.5	1.7	1.8	1.6
9) Misc. manufacturing		9.0	11.8	12.3	8.7	7.7
10) Utilities		0.6	1.2	1.4	1.4	1.4
III. Distributive Services	18.7	19.6	20.4	22.4	21.9	22.3
11) Transportation	7.6	6.0	4.9	5.3	4.4	3.9
12) Communication		1.0	0.9	1.2	1.3	1.5
13) Wholesale	11.1	12.6	2.7	3.5	3.5	4.1
14) Retail			11.8	12.3	12.5	12.8
IV. Producer Services	2.8	3.2	4.6	4.8	6.6	8.2
15) Banking		1.3	1.1	1.1	1.6	2.6
16) Insurance		1.1	1.2	1.4	1.7	1.8
17) Real Estate		0.6	1.1	1.0	1.0	1.0
18) Engineering	2.8	—		0.2	0.3	0.4
19) Accounting		—	1.3	0.2	0.3	0.4
20) Misc. business serv.		0.1		0.6	1.2	1.8
21) Legal services		—		0.4	0.5	0.5
V. Social Services	8.7	9.2	10.0	12.4	16.3	21.9
22) Medical services		—	2.3	1.1	1.4	2.2
23) Hospitals		—		1.8	2.7	3.7
24) Education		—	3.5	3.8	5.4	8.6
25) Welfare	8.7	—	0.9	0.7	1.0	1.2
26) Nonprofit		—		0.3	0.4	0.4
27) Postal services		0.6	0.7	0.8	0.9	1.0
28) Government		2.2	2.6	3.7	4.3	4.6
29) Misc. social serv.		6.3	—	0.1	0.2	0.3
VI. Personal Services	8.2	11.2	14.0	12.1	11.3	10.0
30) Domestic services		6.5	5.3	3.2	3.1	1.7
31) Hotels		2.9	1.3	1.0	1.0	1.0
32) Eating & drinking			2.5	3.0	2.9	3.3
33) Repair	8.2	—	1.5	1.7	1.4	1.3
34) Laundry		—	1.0	1.2	1.0	0.8
35) Barber & beauty shop		0.9	—	—	0.8	0.9
36) Entertainment		0.9	0.9	1.0	0.8	0.8
37) Misc. personal serv.		—	1.6	1.2	0.4	0.3
Total Labor Force	100.2	100.1	100.1	100.0	100.1	100.0

* Compiled by Joachim Singelmann, *The Transformation of Industry from Agriculture to Service Employment*, Beverly Hills, Calif.: Sage Publications, 1977, p. 145.

forms of production and organization that distinguish the service workers in terms of their relationship to the productive forces?[39] The growing "service" sector is a major indicator of social transformation, and to emphasize this trend is always to link it to a particular theory of value. Table 29 shows the typical pattern as presented by Daniel Bell in what is probably the most famous book on this subject, one that develops the technocratic version of the "postindustrial society."[40] The basis of Bell's theory is that productivity depends primarily on the organizational capacity to generate, diffuse, and exchange information and knowledge. Therefore, the new productive workers are not only the technicians and scientists but the organizational managers. The rest of society is a chain of execution that can be easily transformed into a series of cybernetic systems. Such an analysis also deals with new sources of social conflict, like the counterculture, which represents alternative uses and sources of information.

Alan Gartner and Frank Riessman in a very provocative book have given the leftist version of this analysis of the transformation of the structural roots of U.S. society. Let us quote one crucial point of their analysis:

> There is considerable overlap between Bell's formulation and ours. . . . We are suggesting that the functions that Bell focuses upon are those of a neocapitalist system in whose womb, a new service society is growing. The new service society is not developing in a vacuum; it is emerging in a neocapitalist industrial context. . . .
> . . . We believe that it is possible to formulate the concomi-

---

TABLE 27, *continued*

Source:
  1920: U.S. Bureau of the Census, *14th Census of the United States, 1920*, vol. IV, Table 2.
  1930: U.S. Bureau of the Census, *U.S. Census of Population, 1930*, vol. V, General Report on Occupations, chap. 7, Table 1.
  1940: U.S. Bureau of the Census, *U.S. Census of Population, 1940*, vol. III, part 1, Table 74.
  1950 U.S. Bureau of the Census, *U.S. Census of Population, 1950*, vol. IV—Special Reports, part 1, chap. D, "Industrial Characteristics," Table 1.
  1960: U.S. Bureau of the Census, *U.S. Census of Population, 1960*, Subject Reports, Industrial Characteristics," Final Report PC (2)-7F, Table 2.
  1970: I/100 Public Use Sample of U.S. Census of Population, 1970.

TABLE 28. PERCENTAGE DISTRIBUTION OF SELECTED OCCUPATION GROUPS, 1900-1968, PROJECTED TO 1980

	1900	1910	1920	1930	1940	1950	1960	1968	1980
Professional and technical	4.3	4.7	5.4	6.8	7.5	8.6	10.8	13.6	16.3
Managers, officials, and proprietors	5.8	6.6	6.6	7.4	7.3	8.7	10.2	10.0	10.0
Clerical	3.0	5.3	8.0	8.9	9.6	12.3	14.5	16.9	18.2
Operatives	12.8	14.6	15.6	15.8	18.4	20.4	18.6	18.4	16.2

Source: Figures computed from U.S. Department of Labor, *The U.S. Economy in 1980.*

TABLE 29. EVOLUTION OF SOCIETIES ACCORDING TO "POSTINDUSTRIAL IDEOLOGY"

	Industrial	*Postindustrial*	*Service Society*
Regions	Western Europe Soviet Union Japan	United States	United States
Economic sector	Secondary	Tertiary, quaternary, and quinary	Quinary Health, education, and government
Occupational slope	Semiskilled workers Engineers	Professional and technical Scientists	Human-service professionals (education, health, social services)
Technology	Energy	Information	Relational
Design	People/fabricated nature	People/ideas	People/people
Axial principle	Economic growth	Theoretical knowledge	Consumer values

Source: Alan Gartner and Frank Riessman, *The Service Society and the Consumer Vanguard*, New York: Harper & Row, 1974, p. 31. Copyright © 1974 by Alan Gartner and Frank Riessman. Reprinted by permission of Harper & Row, Publishers, Inc.

tant and overlapping existence of three strata within our overall society. On the one hand, there is the old industrial sector composed largely of upper-working-class and middle-class people, many of whom live in middle America, and whose cultural traditions emphasize authority, respect, puritanism, old-style individualism, nationalism, security and so on.

Then there is the neo-industrial group referred to by Bell and the post-industrialists. These are the higher-level technicians, managers, engineers, scientists, and research specialists, who are critical of the development of advanced modern capitalism.

For the most part, they have been well coopted for capitalist goals of productivity, accumulation, profit expansion, growth, power. . . .

. . . The third group, we believe, derives from the consumer-service base that is emerging in our society, from the new importance of the consumer and the significance of the services, particularly the human services. The groups involved here are by no means homogeneous—they include the women, students, minorities, service workers, some of the educated affluents, particularly those involved in or related to the professions but less involved in industry, management, research, engineering, and science.

. . . In our definition there are two outstanding characteristics of the human services: one is that these services are intended to produce benefit or well-being for the recipient either affectively or cognitively; and two, the character of these services is essentially relational, interpersonal, a "hands on" approach.

In essence, the service society derives its character not only from the tremendous expansion of paid and unpaid service work and service consumption but from the powerful multiplier impacts deriving from its very relational character, its labor intensivity (it uses more labor per unit of production), the special significance of education, the role of the media and the fact that large numbers of its workers have direct impact on many other people.[41]

Summarizing this perspective, we find two basic propositions: services are a source of productivity because they generate information; their social creativity comes from the relational character of most human services. In both cases we have new sources of value and new sources of contradictions, which are expressed in different ways. This trend indicates a shift in the key processes of human activity from the traditional forms of production to information and consumption.

Similar theses have been strongly criticized by authors like Braverman and Levison because such arguments suggest that the working conditions of service workers and technicians have improved and that a large percentage of the society still works in the traditional sectors. Both criticisms are right, but insufficient. It is important to remember that people's experiences with the "service economy" show them that the system is still exploitative: they have to put up with increased workloads and impersonal and arbitrary authority in the organization of the labor process. However, this point does not answer the major question about the new relationships between the development of services and the new sources of production of value. What we call the "populist" critique is perfectly justified in denouncing the technocratic approach to the evolution of work and the social division of labor. Gartner and Riessman would agree with this criticism and would take a similar position. They would argue, however, that economic development depends more and more on human services, and that, therefore, the axis of the new social dynamics has shifted to the relationship between the managerial elite controlling the services and the consumers' vanguard. The nature of this relationship is the real question we have to consider.

S. M. Miller treats this question in a very insightful article on neocapitalism. He gives to the problem its exact dimensions:

> The expansion of Riessman-Gartner's service depends on governmental actions to expand health, education and welfare.
>
> Education was the growth industry of the sixties in the United States, and is clearly levelling off. Health is likely to be the growth field of the services in the seventies; how much expansion is clearly a contentious political issue. Day-care could be a growth field later in the seventies. Welfare, if it continues to expand, will likely be growing as a cash program rather than as a service program, providing health and case work to recipients.
>
> I see no inexorable tendency toward an increase in human services. The technological shift within manufacturing to white-collar employment has no counterpart in the human services. The decisions will be almost completely political, affected by public attitudes about helping the poor, taxation levies, and appropriate employment, rather than straight extrapolations of Engels' law that non-subsistence items grow with increased incomes. Expenditures from private disposable income (consumer's expenditures) on services may not be increasing; thus, the overwhelming burden of growth in services

will be on the government, for such recreation expenditures as a percentage of national income have not been increasing.

The services are losing their attractiveness as low-cost sectors. Costs have been rising more rapidly (at least until 1972) than in other fields, e.g. hospital costs. If education and health costs grow more rapidly than post-tax income, they must draw resources away from other activities to maintain their current volume. Wages in service fields have been low; the exploited worker, frequently Black, economically marginal subsidized the services field. But service wages will be under increasing pressure to rise. This is very obviously visible in the salaries of local government employees, especially those in the uniformed services. What may happen is similar to union leaders Harry Bridges' and John L. Lewis' responses to technological advance: less employment but much higher wages for those who are employed. The relative wage gain in the public and service sector is a positive indication of the improvement in the situation of once marginal workers. But such gains may result in limiting expansion of these sectors.

The issue is two-fold: the relative significance of public versus private expenditures, and the direction of public spending. Services compete with say, housing subsidies, within the public sector. On the first issue of public versus private choice, some way of connecting the zeal for cash (and the feeling of independence that goes with it) with the expansion of services is necessary if the latter is to get effective political support.

The provision of services in itself is not redistributive. It can be if concentrated on the low-income in a non-stigmatizing and high quality way. But I think the direction will be toward a universalism benefiting the middle-classes, as perhaps in public child-care with middle-class women benefiting at least as much as poorer women. This is not inevitably an argument against the universalization of child-care or any other service, but a warning to recognize that services have to be structured deliberately to be redistributive. Redistribution is seldom an accidental by-product.[42]

Thus, the expansion of services is economically uncertain, socially unproductive, and politically decided. Services, even human services, are not by themselves productive or redistributive. They can be used to absorb surplus population, they can be used as pork-barrel policies by local governments, or they can be the consequence of successful pressure from the grassroots. In terms of new jobs and more services, they can be the response to demands of scientific and technological development or a political trend toward a welfare state. In short, the development of human services (which seems to be the hard core of the theory of development through services) is a *social* process, and its evolution and characteristics will be the result of *political* conflicts within the political economy of the United States.

This is a major point that must be emphasized. The problem still remains regarding the relationship of these social trends, which underlie the expansion of services and human services, to the development of productive forces and the social organization of economic growth and appropriation of products. Two researchers from the Berkeley Institute of Urban and Regional Development, Larry Hirschhorn and Stephen Cohen, have developed in separate papers some important analyses of the relationships between services, productivity, and social relationships.[43]

The basic argument starts with the econometric discovery, by Robert Solow[44] and others, that statistical analysis of the sources of increased productivity in the United States since 1920 shows that this increase does not come from an increase in capital or labor but from an unidentified "residual factor." This leads to the interpretation that this factor is the particular way in which capital and labor are combined, not only in terms of management but also as a particular arrangement of the production and circulation of information and knowledge. As Hirschhorn writes:

> All this suggests two overlapping ways in which we can understand how services, particularly the fast growing services, might be linked to the sources of productivity. To say that the new sources of productivity are mediated through qualitatively upgraded labor is to argue that the human services, particularly the health and education complexes, become the social loci for the developmental possibilities of society. To say that society's social networks, both informational and organizational, are the keys to the new requirements for flexibility and

adaptability, is to argue for the centrality of the public services, particularly of the administrative, welfare, and planning varieties. Taken together, both arguments suggest that the full development of the forces of production abstractly conceived, rest ultimately on the development and elaboration of the public and human services, of precisely those services that have fueled the emergence of the service society.[45]

The perspective Hirschhorn develops here relies on a more global analysis by Radovan Richta.[46] It points toward a contradictory social relationship between the development of these new productive forces and the particular organizational structures in which these forces rise, namely, the bureaucratic apparatus of the public services. Furthermore, this contradiction between innovation and bureaucracy is the expression of a deeper contradiction in the economic policies that capitalist rules impose on the social services. Because there is a tendency toward stagnation and surplus population, the Keynesian policies applied since 1935 have used the human-service sector as a channel to create jobs and distribute income. This approach has caused low-productivity, which has created inflationary pressures (because of deficit financing of public spending) and has stalled the development of services designed to increase social productivity at the level of the whole society. The struggle is not only between consumers and technocrats, but between human productivity and human services on one side and Keynesian capitalism and bureaucratic routine on the other.

This interpretation is quite closely related to the recent Marxist analyses of the "scientific and technical revolution" as a new stage in the development of productive forces in contradiction with capitalist *and* bureaucratic social relationships. Again, it implies the need for a differential analysis of services with respect not only to the types of activity but also to the different functions accomplished in the processes of production, management, distribution, and social control. For instance, the university is at the same time an instrument of production and distribution of knowledge, an ideological apparatus, and a key institution in the reproduction of the social order. It has different types of contradictions and conflicts linked to each of these dimensions.

However, the analyses suggested by Hirschhorn and Cohen have two major problems. First they deny the labor theory of value on the basis of econometric analyses whose theoretical categories are subject to dispute. It is still possible to say that value is produced by labor, but add that the productivity of labor is increasingly dependent on scientific development. To sustain the metaphysics of the "residual factor" is to open the door to all kinds of idealistic interpretations about the sources of value and the path of development of productive forces in advanced societies such as the one developed by Bell. Second, any perspective of class-struggle analysis disappears in this interpretation, which adopts a somewhat revised version of modernization theory: new factors of production are struggling against old factors of bureaucratic routine in which they are embedded. Nevertheless, the process is different. The contradiction is an expression of several specific contradictions and conflicts between capital and labor: the process of uneven development, which requires increasingly high productivity in the monopoly sector and creates surplus population that has to be absorbed for social and economic reasons (Hirschhorn's analysis refers only to contradictions that are internal to capital); the pressure from the grassroots to ask for more and better services and more and better jobs; the contradiction between the need for the expansion of services and the fact that most of these services are unprofitable for capital; the contradiction between the increasing socialization of consumption and the private direction of the whole economic process as expressed by the increasing socialization of costs and privatization of profits; the differential use and distribution of human services in terms of the class structure and of class practices; the need for dysfunctional aspects of the services (bureaucratic rules, repressive means, etc.) in order to reproduce the social order underlying capitalist social relationships.

Any interpretation focusing on the services first and then trying to build up a general theory of society looks suspiciously like some new kind of prophetic metaphysics. A serious analysis of the different types of services and their role in the process of development and transformation of the social structure should proceed in the opposite direction. That is, we must start from the observation of major trends of evolution in advanced capitalism and show the impact of these trends on the development of the very different activities called "services." Although we cannot develop such an analysis here, we can at least point out some facts that will help us understand the economic crisis, since it would appear that the transformation of "services" is going to be at the core of the policies dealing with the crisis.

Our argument is that the specific pattern of capital accumulation in the United States and its consequences for the evolution of the public sector and for the development of the class struggle have produced, through a set of interactive effects, the growth of the different types of activities and jobs considered as services. In order not to repeat arguments already expressed about the characteristics of the dynamics of U.S. capitalism, we will adopt a highly schematic style to present what seem to be the most important connections between economic and social evolution and the growth of jobs in the service sector.

1. The evolution of *capital accumulation*:*

Results in uneven development, increasing productivity, and surplus population → Research and training

→ Increasing number of technicians and professionals and increasing unemployment and underemployment disguised as new types of unskilled jobs

Increases the number of large-scale corporations ——→ More clerks

Brings development of the functions of control and management over the society and over the economy (real estate, finance, trade, social control, information) ——→ Drawing more women in the labor force, which requires expansion of new "service activities" formerly accomplished in the family

Produces the need for "sales effort" ——→ New "service workers"

2. The evolution of *class struggle* in this particular context:

Requires more services, especially in the field of collective comsumption ——→ Expansion of education, health, housing, and collective means of consumption

* The use of the arrows is equivalent to saying "leading to."

Requires more jobs to ————▶ Expansion of control on the
counteract the surplus   jobs in the public sector
population produced by   through the political process
the monopoly sector

Attempts to have an impact ——▶ Creation of more public jobs,
on the functioning of the   especially at the local level,
state in the interest of   and tendency to reduce
the people   discrimination and to open
                                    access to public jobs for
                                    everybody

Forces a smoothing of the ——▶ Expansion of welfare and
contradictions by   social security
maintaining an increase in
services at a given level
even outside of the market
mechanisms

3. The evolution of *state intervention* for the purpose of accumulation of capital and the legitimization of the social order under pressure from the grassroots:

Creates jobs to absorb   Increasing government
surplus population   employment at the state
                                      and local levels

Creates outlets for capital   Subordination of productivity
                                      requirements to requirements in
                                      terms of employment and outlets

Assumes functions of
maintaining social order
in the United States
and at the world level

Assumes productivity   Bureaucratic functioning of
functions (education,   these service organizations
research, technological
progress)

Assumes social consumption   Increasing tension between
expenditures as well as   pursuing particular interests
social expenses (education,   and performing tasks on behalf
health, social security, etc.)   of the general interest of the
                                      prevailing order (because it is
                                      a political apparatus)

These trends show clearly the differential status of each type of service and the roots of the crisis in the service economy, which in turn is at the center of the current economic crisis. The crisis of the service economy expresses an interrelated set of basic structural contradictions: between the development of productive forces through science and technology and the capitalist *and* bureaucratic social relationships establishing the organization of the production and distribution of knowledge; between the need for maximum flexibility in organizations and the increased social division of labor and "white-collar proletarianization," which includes hard discipline and piecemeal work; between the need for jobs and services for people and the necessity of making a profit; between the expanding unemployment and underemployment and the requirements for increasing productivity in the public sector; between the expanding public services and the narrowing public resources; between the increasing proletarianization, organization, and struggle of the public workers and the increasing inability of the public sector to cope with demands for new and better services and for more and better jobs; between the local constituencies of the state at the political level and the grassroots demands.

Actually, the service sector represents the most extreme contradictions of the model of accumulation. The crisis has developed particularly at the local level where public authorities are responsible for social services and the absorption of unemployment. The structure of "services" has had a large impact on the economic crisis, for the rate of growth of nonproductive activities has been much higher than the ability to generate new value through the development of productive forces because the services are frozen in bureaucratic patterns and dedicated to vested capitalist interests. The impact of the crisis on services has led to an emphasis on improvements in productivity and a reduction in the delivery of public services and the creation of jobs.

The crisis of the big cities is a clear expression of this process. The immediate impact is a dramatic reduction in employment and in nonprofitable (but not necessarily unproductive) services. It is doubtful that this trend will lead to stressing the productive role of services. We must not confuse the productivity of workers (as measured by the relationship between the amount of work obtained in exchange for wages) and the productivity of services (as measured by the qualitative transformation of the production and distribution of information). Rationalization of these services is directed mostly at improving the effectiveness of the organization, overcoming the resistance to routine practices, and opposing the workers' struggle against increased exploitation. To develop service activity along productive lines, it would be necessary to overcome the capitalist social structure. For instance, how do you develop a health-care system based on the progress of medical research without attacking the drug companies and the vested interests of elite doctors and private clinics?[47]

The impact of the present crisis on the service economy will depend on the social structure, which will determine the policies aimed to overcome the crisis. Although it is clear that a major transformation will take place, it is not clear whether it will be a rationalization of services required by corporate capital or the development of productivity and delivery of human services imposed by the grassroots. In either case, however, the present ambiguity of the service economy will be clarified.

This will, to some extent, mark the end of a particular historical period of development of American capitalism. Braverman reminds us that, between 1950 and 1970, two occupational positions have expanded at a similar rate and reached a similar size: engineers and janitors.[48] It appears increasingly evident that the American economy will not be able to afford a continued parallel expansion necessary if engineers are to produce and janitors to keep up and protect engineers' residences and offices.

5. THE TENDENCY TOWARD A SURPLUS
   POPULATION: UNEMPLOYMENT AND
   UNDEREMPLOYMENT IN U.S.
   DEVELOPMENT

One of the most contradictory effects of the pattern of capitalist development that increases the technical composition of capital is the fact that more and more backward forms of production are destroyed and transformed, yet the labor power freed in this process is not required in the expanding sectors at the same rate as it is expelled from the depressed sectors.[49]

The major paradox of the U.S. economy is the persistence of a high level of *unemployment* and the development and deepening of *underemployment*. By unemployment we mean a situation in which labor power that is normally integrated into the labor force remains idle without being remunerated by capital. "Normally integrated" refers to the fact that each particular historical stage of a society establishes the movement and the characteristics of the people who are incorporated into the labor force. Table 30 gives an overview of the evolution of the official rate of unemployment in the United States, which is dramatically higher than in any other advanced country in the same period. The level of unemployment is actually much higher. An important analysis of U.S. unemployment by the editors of *Monthly Review*[50] shows that official statistics underestimate unemployment. The statistics, in fact, consider all employed workers as full-time paid employed workers—not a very realistic assumption in view of the following facts.

In 1972 there were 1.7 million workers employed in part-time jobs. The calculation of employment rates has also not taken into account the number of people who worked at some time during the year. It is concerned only with the percentage of unemployed people out of the total population who worked the entire year. However, Table 31 shows that in several economic sectors a significant portion of people do not work all year round. Another underestimated group is unpaid family workers who are counted as employed. This represents 700,000 people in the agricultural sector alone and another 900,000 in nonagricultural activities. Finally, people who have never been in the labor force are not counted. This study probably gives a more accurate rate of unemployment for 1973 by adding to the officially reported figure of 8.2 million the 3.1 million people who wanted a job and were unable to find one and the 1.7 million who were employed in part-time jobs. The addition of these people to the labor force would give us a total labor force of 100.2 million. Then, the 13 million actually unemployed would give us a real unemployment rate of 13.6 percent. Actually, unemployment affects certain groups, such as nonwhites, women, and youth, much more than others (see Table 30). The actual rate of unemployment for black youth

TABLE 30. UNEMPLOYED AND UNEMPLOYMENT INSURANCE, 1960-1976

	1960	1965	1970	1971	1972	1973	1974	1975	1976 (Jan.-April average)
Total unemployed—1,000	3,852	3,365	4,088	4,994	4,840	4,304	5,076	7,830	7,656
Labor force time lost (percent)	6.7	5.0	5.4	6.4	6.0	5.2	6.1	9.1	8.8
Unemployment rate (percent):									
All workers	5.5	4.5	4.9	5.9	5.6	4.9	5.6	8.5	8.3
White	4.9	4.1	4.5	5.4	5.0	4.3	5.0	7.8	7.5
Male	4.8	3.6	4.0	4.9	4.5	3.7	4.3	7.2	7.3
Female	5.3	5.0	5.4	6.3	5.9	5.3	6.1	8.6	8.0
Negro and other	10.2	8.1	8.2	9.9	10.0	8.9	9.9	13.0	13.6
Male	10.7	7.4	7.3	9.1	8.9	7.6	9.1	13.7	13.8
Female	9.4	9.2	9.3	10.8	11.3	10.5	10.7	14.0	13.3
Ratio, Negro and other to White	2.1	2.0	1.8	1.8	2.0	2.1	2.0	1.8	1.8
Men, 20 years old and over	4.7	3.2	3.5	4.4	4.0	3.2	3.8	6.7	6.8
Women, 20 years old and over	5.1	4.5	4.8	5.7	5.4	4.8	5.5	8.0	7.6
Household heads	n.a.	2.7	2.9	3.6	3.3	2.9	3.3	5.7	5.9
Married men, wife present	3.7	2.4	2.6	3.2	2.8	2.3	2.7	5.1	5.1
White	3.3	2.2	2.4	3.0	2.6	2.1	2.5	4.8	4.8
Negro and others	7.9	4.4	3.9	5.0	4.5	3.8	4.3	8.3	8.2
Teenagers	14.7	14.8	15.3	16.9	16.2	14.5	16.0	19.9	20.1
Male Vietnam veterans, 30-34 years old	n.a.	n.a	6.6	8.2	6.7	5.0	5.3	9.3	9.1
Blue collar workers	7.8	5.3	6.2	7.4	6.5	5.3	6.7	11.7	11.2
White collar workers	2.7	2.3	2.8	3.5	3.4	2.9	3.3	4.7	4.7
Experienced wage and salary workers	5.7	4.3	4.8	5.7	5.3	4.5	5.3	8.2	8.1
Parents without work for									
4 weeks or less	44.6	48.4	52.3	44.7	45.9	51.0	50.6	37.0	34.3
5-10 weeks	21.4	21.0	23.4	22.9	22.5	22.4	22.7	22.2	10.6
11-14 weeks	9.2	8.2	8.1	8.7	7.6	7.7	8.2	9.1	9.3
15-26 weeks	13.0	12.0	10.4	13.3	12.3	11.0	11.1	16.5	16.4
Over 26 weeks	11.8	10.4	5.8	10.4	11.6	7.8	7.3	15.2	2.4
Average duration of unemployment (weeks)	12.8	11.8	8.8	11.4	12.1	10.0	9.7	14.1	17.1
Unemployment insurance Weekly insured unemployed, avg.—1,000	1,908	1,328	1,805	2,150	1,848	1,632	2,260	3,992	n.a.
Percent of covered employment	4.8	3.0	3.4	4.1	3.5	2.7	3.5	6.0	n.a.
Initial claims (weekly average)—1,000	331	232	296	295	261	247	363	478	n.a.
Claimants exhausting benefits—1,000	1,603	1,086	1,295	2,007	1,809	1,495	1,925	4,194	n.a.
Percent of first payment recipients	26.1	21.5	24.4	30.1	29.6	27.7	30.9	37.8	n.a.
Average actual duration of benefits (weeks)	12.7	12.2	12.3	14.4	14.2	13.4	12.7	15.7	n.a.

in the inner cities of metropolitan areas reached as high as 60 to 70 percent in the spring of 1975.

The decreasing capacity of the system to transform labor power into labor force is also expressed in underemployment. Underemployment refers to the impact on the labor force of the process of uneven development and the existence of the so-called irregular economy, which is characterized by the combination of marginal capital and an overexploited nonpermanent labor force. Certain markets are abandoned by monopoly capital because they are nonprofitable, and part of the labor power is not used. However, some of these businesses, which could not operate on the fringes of the monopoly sector, can develop and make a profit if they can control specialized markets. This sector could expand under certain conditions, but it often becomes directly related to the monopoly sector, which appropriates a share of the profit through channels that can only work because of the irregular economy.[51]

Particularly in U.S. capitalism the causes of unemployment and underemployment are based on the process of uneven development. Barry Bluestone analyzes this articulation in one of the best interpretations of the process:

> The dynamics of the American economy are best described by the law of uneven development. Those who control capital resources in the economy will tend over time to reinvest in those particular product lines, machinery, geographical areas, and workers which promise the highest return on dollar investment. Conversely, investment will tend to decline in segments of the economy where potential expected profit is relatively low. The outcome is continuous growth and relative prosperity in the former sector and relative stagnation and impoverishment in the latter. The gap between the rich and the poor grows over time.

TABLE 30, *continued*

n.a.: not available.

Note: Persons 16 years old and over. See also *Historical Statistics, Colonial Times to 1970*, Series D 87-101.

Source: U.S. Bureau of Labor Statistics, *Handbook of Labor Statistics*, annual, and *Employment and Earnings*, monthly; *Statistical Abstract of the U.S., 1976*.

TABLE 31. PERCENTAGE EMPLOYED IN FULL-TIME JOBS IN SELECTED INDUSTRIES

	Percentage of wage earners working year round at full-time jobs in 1973
Agriculture	46.8
Construction	51.1
Manufacturing	68.9
Transportation and public utilities	73.0
Retail trade	38.9
Finance and services	62.1

Note: The usual figures for number employed are too high because they include those with part-time jobs (1.7 million) and unpaid family workers (700,000 in agriculture, 900,000 in nonagriculture). The usual figures for the unemployed are too low because they do not include those who only worked part of the year.
Source: *Manpower Report of the President*, April 1975, p. 275.

There is an inherent tendency in the economy towards a dichotomization between the haves and have-nots. This occurs for two reasons, first, investment in a dynamic economy tends not only to increase the capital-intensity of the product or factor of production in question, but also changes the quality of the factor so as to make further investments profitable.

The second reason for a dichotomization within society derives from the potential redistributive effect of any given private investment. While it may be true that continued investment runs into diminishing marginal returns, owners of private capital will tend to link profitability and distribution criteria in reinvestment decisions. Private investors will reinvest their capital in areas which promise the highest economic returns only if such investment does not tend to alter the long-run income distribution in such a way as to reduce their own relative standing.

The effect of uneven development can also be seen by tracing industry wage histories since World War II. When this is done, it is found that the wage differential between "high-wage" and "low-wage" industries has increased secularly. In 1947 the set of industries with lowest wages paid straight-time hourly wages which averaged seventy-five percent of the average wages prevailing in the highest wage industries in the nation. Regardless of slight cyclical variation in wage increases during the ensuing period, the wage ratio between these two sets of industries fell to 60% by 1966. The low-wage industries granted smaller wage increases (in percentage as well as in absolute terms) in all but four years during the two-decade period.

Econometric evidence indicates that no matter the level of employment or the state of the economy, the secular deterioration of wage rates between industries cannot be reversed. Reinvestment in the more capital-intensive, monopolized, and more profitable industries follows precisely from the profit maximization rule. Conversely, relatively less investment is undertaken in the less profitable, less monopolized industries. Over time capital intensity of the two sets of industries dichotomizes, productivity levels dichotomize, and finally wage terms deteriorate. Data on United States industries indicate that the correlation between monopolization ("concentration"), capital-intensity, and average wage rates is extremely high. The zero-order correlations are:

	Concentration	Capital-Intensity	Average Hourly Earnings
Concentration	1.000	.492	.502
Capital-Intensity		1.000	.433
Average Hourly Earnings			1.000

The result of the uneven development between industries has been the creation of an extensive working poor population. In 1968 over ten million workers—one in five private non-supervisory employees—earned less than $1.60 an hour in the United States. Today the working poor make up well over half the poor in the nation according to Department of Commerce figures. Naturally they are concentrated in those industries which have been disadvantaged in capital-intensity, concentration, profits and wage levels.

But uneven development is not restricted to industrial dichotomization alone. The same pattern of secular deterioration is clearly evident in the investment decisions regarding the schooling, training and health of the nation.

An economic system based on private investment decisions thus tends to promote a dual economy both in the structure of industries and in the structure of the labor force.[52]

Although this subject is well covered in the literature,[53] we should recall the major links between the dynamics of U.S. capitalism and the factors that lead to the expansion of unemployment and underemployment.

The need to increase relative surplus value through technological development leads to increasing mechanization and automation ⟶	Suppression of large numbers of unskilled jobs in all sectors

The enhancement of the rate of exploitation is accomplished by:

Flow of capital abroad ⟶	Suppression of jobs in the United States

The requirements that cause division among workers in order to overexploit them ⟶	Maintenance of a reserve army: unemployment
	Segmentation of the labor market mostly through discrimination

The unplanned nature of development of productive forces and their domination by corporate interests ⟶	Mismatching between skills and jobs that leads both to scarcity and excess of labor power

The development of services for the requirements of productivity, social control, and absorption of surplus population introduces a growing contradiction that leads progressively to the automation and the rationalization of the service sector ⟶	Increasing technological unemployment in the labor-intensive service activities

The expansion of activities ⟶ Decreasing capacity of
and absorption of surplus government sector to
population through the generate jobs
public sector leads to
a fiscal crisis of the state,
especially at the level of
local government

Thus, the continuous growth of unemployment and underemployment is not caused by an accident or a lack of adjustment or an insufficient level of education but by the process of uneven development and the increasing difficulties in the processes of exploitation and realization.[54] The economic crisis has deepened these contradictions, and unemployment and underemployment have jumped to a level without precedent since the Great Depression. The mechanisms necessary to reestablish the rate of profit press more and more toward structural trends that will increase the surplus population because of the rationalization of services, the expansion abroad, and a dramatic reduction of public spending.[55]

In fact, unemployment and underemployment are the most painful consequences of the crisis for the people and the most potentially disruptive contradictions for the system. Following the estimate given by the editors of *Monthly Review*, Table 32 shows 36 million new jobs will be required to keep the system working in the future decade. This means that the estimate in the 1975 Manpower Report of the President of 16.6 million new jobs actually represents only 46 percent of the total required. We can conclude very easily that *the increasing rate of unemployment will become the crucial issue in the relationship between capital and labor in the United States.*

TABLE 32. NUMBER OF NET NEW JOBS NEEDED, 1975-1985

	Millions of jobs
To reduce the rate of unemployment to 5%	8.2
To accommodate population increase with the same unemployment rate of 5%	15.0
To compensate for productivity gains	12.8
Total	36.0

Source: The editors, *Monthly Review*, June 1975, Table 4, p. 13.

6. CLASS, RACE, AND SEX: WHY THE MINORITIES ARE THE MAJORITY

A superficial observer of the social conflicts developing in the United States during recent years would be surprised by our emphasis on the dynamics of social classes. Does reality not show that the most acute conflicts are rooted in the cleavages caused by other sources of discrimination, namely, ethnicity and sex and sometimes age?

Are the minorities the real cause of social transformation, or are they at least the major source of protest in advanced societies? Our analysis starts from the acknowledgment of the specificity of class structure in the United States, and we put a great emphasis on the very important role played by race and sex in this specificity. But we must also link these features to the social relationships of production: the divisions between race and sex are shaped and determined by the specific role they play in the pattern of capital accumulation and the exploitation of labor. Indeed, what we are observing is that racial and sexual oppression are sources of revolt. However, they are sources of revolt that remain isolated and incapable of producing profound social transformation because they are not able to develop along lines that articulate them to the overall historical sources of exploitation in American society. Only a theory that is able to link race and sex to the analysis of class structure in terms of their specific role in the dynamics of U.S. capitalism will be able to foresee their evolution and potential for change beyond the economic crisis.

6.1. The Social Roots of Racial Discrimination[56]

From the very beginning the discrimination and segregation of black Americans has been linked to the requirements of over-exploitation determined by the expansion of capitalism. The slavery system was the major source of primitive accumulation in the Southern plantation economy. The ideological consequences of this association between black skin and slavery remain so persistent because it is still operating at the institutional level. By means of segregated and discriminatory markets and institutions, it is one of the major mechanisms for allocating people to tasks and resources to people.

The persistence and development of this institutionalization of prejudice is due to a great extent to the key role played by discrimination in the process of exploitation and in the reproduction of the social order. The use of racism in the capitalist order has followed two articulated lines known as the "Southern" and "Northern" patterns. The second has become increasingly dominant at the structural level and is one of the major causes of revolt. Racial discrimination in the South was the base of the agricultural economy, and the social relationships of production were only slightly transformed by the change in legal status after the abolition of slavery. Because of the accelerated mechanization of agriculture that occurred after the Depression, the whole infrastructure of social relationships was transformed. The majority of blacks were forced to migrate to the cities in a classic "push-out" migratory movement because they had lost their means of employment and income. Karl Taeuber describes the changed situation:

> By the time the civil rights movement [starting in the 1950's, expanding in the 1960's] was in full swing trying to transform race relations in the traditional deep South, the black population of the United States was already more urbanized and more metropolitan than the white population. At the time of the 1970 census, 71% of the black population lived in metropolitan areas as compared to 64% of the white population. The central cities of metropolitan areas were home for more than one-half (55 percent) of the nation's blacks as compared to a fourth of whites.[57]

Black Americans were the last wave of immigrant workers trying to get into the expanding urban industrial economy. In fact, they never did. They have always been at the bottom of the job market because they lack education, adequate income, decent housing, and other urban services. They have become a major part of the permanent reserve army of the working class because they experience a higher level of unemployment and because they are usually employed in the "irregular economy."

Actually, racial prejudice has been responsible for a number of important trends that were required for capitalist expansion in the United States.[58]

1. Racial prejudice has made it possible to *overexploit** black workers by imposing wages and working conditions on them below the level established by the relations between capital and labor for other workers. This overexploitation has been an additional source of profit for monopoly capital and an indispensable mechanism of survival for "competitive" capital, particularly in the "irregular economy."

2. Racial prejudice has made it possible to maintain a reserve army of unemployed that puts pressure on the working conditions of the entire working class, not just on those of minority workers.[59]

3. Probably the most important use of racial prejudice has been to divide workers along racial lines. This has greatly weakened the labor movement and increased exploitation and the preservation of the capitalist social and political order.

This process is not the result of deliberate manipulation. The same mechanisms that produce capitalist expansion provide the conditions for the structural use of discrimination. At the same time that agricultural mechanization expelled black workers from their jobs, productivity increased in the monopoly sector. Many unskilled jobs were thereby eliminated. These unskilled jobs were the only ones blacks were qualified to do.

Therefore, unskilled and low-paying jobs were maintained primarily in the labor-intensive "competitive" sector. Because of school segregation, which is based largely on the pattern of residential segregation, blacks were not able to obtain the necessary cultural skills that would enable them to qualify for better jobs in the traditional pattern of the division of labor.

Racial prejudice, which is one of the bases of capital accumulation in the United States, is also used indirectly for the benefit of some social groups.[60] For instance, middle-class families often use blacks for cheap domestic help; real-estate interests make money off it in the ghettos, and white workers often use their structural advantages unfairly in competition for jobs (in the way, for instance, some craft unions forbid blacks to enter specific job markets).[61]

---

* By overexploitation we understand the payment (*socially*) to labor power at a price lower than what has been historically established by the capitalist-labor relations at a certain time. This "social price" includes wages, working conditions, and indirect wages.

Thus, from the point of view of the capitalist state, racial discrimination is extremely useful, and there is no reason to change it. Certainly there has been "moral indignation" about racial discrimination, but this has been more or less a handy device to keep some charitable groups busy. The real problem is that racial discrimination represents a source of uncertainty and could possibly result in a revolt against the social order. When blacks were able to develop a mass movement radicalizing their protests and linking this movement to other protest movements, it was necessary for the state to control the protest through the combined action of repression and integration. However, although the legal situation of blacks has improved, most of the sources of discrimination are linked to the social structure and cannot be easily transformed without a major reform of the whole model of accumulation. For instance, residential segregation cannot be abolished without a transformation of the current patterns of urban development.[62] The structural tendency toward segregation and the need for integration by the state have created contradictory consequences because to absorb the black surplus population and improve its situation through increasing services, the state has had to work mainly through the public sector. Black employment and black standards of living have become increasingly linked to public spending and the development of social services. The fiscal crisis of the state and the necessary rationalization of services are major threats to the relative stability achieved in the aftermath of the "hot" sixties.

6.2. The Sexual Division of Labor and the Women's Revolt[63]

It has become clear now that the women's movement is a major factor in the process of social transformation in the United States as well as in all advanced capitalist societies. However, the liberation of women has not always been present in revolutionary processes as some feminists like to assert. Hitherto the mobilization of women and their participation in the process of social change have been mostly the consequences of the general development of the class struggle rather than, as it is now, an autonomous source of revolt.[64] What is new is the massive uprising of women against the social and cultural roots of their individual oppression by the sexual division of labor. Since this oppression is perhaps the oldest in *man*kind's history, it is necessary to explain why at a particular time and in a certain type of society this contradiction has exploded at a level that makes it practically impossible for the system to integrate it in the long-run.[65] We cannot fully develop such an analysis in this book. However, we will not be able to understand the impact of the crisis on the dynamics of American society without referring to the main links between the social-class division of labor and the sexual division of labor. The latter has been historically rooted in the organization of the family as the major apparatus of biological, economic, and ideological reproduction of labor power. Women have always been defined by their tasks in the reproduction process (not only biological, but at all levels) and have been fundamentally subordinate to the process of production and to its agents, mostly men. On this structural basis a particular ideological structure has developed through its own dynamics as a source of prejudice. And sexist ideology has fulfilled different social functions depending on the changing role of women in the overall process of exploitation.

The upsurge of the women's movement in the United States is the result of the interaction between the development of two factors: the general ideological revolt of the sixties; and[66] the transformation of the occupational structure to include increasing numbers of women, including married women, in the labor force.[67]

The participation of women in the labor force jumped from 23 percent in 1920 to 42 percent in 1970. Sixty percent of these women were married as compared to only 30 percent in 1940. Table 33 shows that the most significant increase has been in clerical work and managerial positions; roughly the same proportion has been maintained for white women in professional and technical jobs, but there has been a reduction in those working in farming activities, as well as in personal service for black women. However, participation of women in other occupations including manual labor has not been reduced. What has happened is that the huge expansion of employment in the so-called service areas has been filled by women who had not previously worked outside the home.

The rate of participation of men in the labor force has de-

TABLE 33. CURRENT OCCUPATION OF EMPLOYED PERSONS BY RACE AND SEX, 1970 AND 1960 (IN %)

	White		Black	
	1970	1960	1970	1960
Male				
Professional and technical	14.8	11.6	5.8	3.3
Managerial	15.4	12.2	4.1	1.4
Clerical	7.4	7.7	8.6	6.1
Sales	6.1	7.5	1.6	1.6
Craftsmen	20.6	21.3	14.2	10.0
Operatives	18.9	20.5	30.6	27.0
Nonfarm laborers	5.7	5.6	18.9	24.3
Service workers	6.0	5.5	11.7	15.6
Farm	5.2	8.1	4.5	10.6
Total employed	100.0	100.0	100.0	100.0
Female				
Professional and technical	15.5	14.6	10.0	7.0
Managerial	4.7	4.4	1.4	0.7
Clerical	36.1	34.9	18.9	8.1
Sales	7.3	8.8	2.5	1.3
Craftsmen	1.1	1.4	0.8	0.9
Operatives	14.5	16.7	16.8	14.0
Nonfarm laborers	0.4	0.5	0.9	0.8
Service	18.8	17.2	48.1	63.7
Farm	1.5	1.5	0.5	3.6
Total employed	100.0	100.0	100.0	100.0

Source: U.S. Bureau of the Census, *Current Population Reports*, Series P-23, No. 37, "Social and Economic Characteristics of the Population in Metropolitan and Non-metropolitan Areas: 1970 and 1960," 1971, Table 14, pp. 60-62, as compiled by Charles A. Anderson, *The Political Economy of Social Class*, Englewood Cliffs, N.J.: Prentice-Hall, 1974, p. 147.

creased (from 87 percent in 1960 to 80 percent in 1970), yet unemployment and underemployment have been maintained. Therefore, it is clear that the desire to hire more women is largely due to the fact that they can be exploited more easily through the patterns of prejudice that are linked to the sexual division of labor within the family. Women are paid less even for the same job. They usually get less skilled jobs. They are given proportionally less responsibility in the hierarchy, and they are the last hired and the first fired. This pattern has not been reversed by the protest movement. An important study by David Featherman and Robert Hauser shows that "while the occupational and educational achievement of women (1962-1973) have kept pace with men and indeed exceeded the male means, the ratio of female to male earnings has declined from 0.39 to 0.38 for husbands and wives." What is consistent with the findings is that "discrimination accounts for 85% of the earnings gaps (between sexes) in 1962 and 84% in 1973."[68] This pattern is reinforced by the mistaken idea that women's earnings are simply complementary to their husband's wages. However, existing empirical evidence shows that a substantial number of families, especially in the lower income levels, rely on the women's income for more than 40 percent of their total income.[69]

Discrimination affects not only wages but the type of work and the actual work relationships. The apparently similar profile of women and men in occupational status is a pure artifact originated by the census classifications. For instance, while 14.6 percent of women are employed as "professional and technical," compared to 14.1 percent of men in the same category, these figures represent totally different situations:

1. Only 8.5 percent of physicians are women, but 94 percent of the nurses are women.

2. Only 28.4 percent of college and university professors are women, but 49.1 percent of secondary school teachers and 83.5 percent of elementary school teachers are women.

3. Only 4.8 percent of lawyers and judges are women, but 30.2 percent of writers, artists, and entertainers are women.

It is important to point out that in the development of the job market for women not only has sexual prejudice been used to exploit them but it is also rooted in the ideological pattern of the sexual division of labor developed in the work organizations. Women not only provide cheap labor but are also considered as particularly skilled for certain types of jobs such as secretaries and receptionists and for certain fields such as advertising and public relations where their skills in handling social relationships and their sex appeal can be used to sell products.

Finally, the massive introduction of women into the labor force has created a new and extremely effective cleavage between workers because the big corporations are able to exploit effectively the prejudices of the male-dominated labor organizations.

The absorption of women into the labor market is part of the process of the continuous expansion of capitalism through the destruction of previous forms of social relationships. In order to fill the new jobs created by the development of services, women have been taken out of the family and transformed into workers at an increasing rate. The employment of women has caused a reorganization of family life, and new outlets for capital invest- ment have been developed, such as household appliances to make work "easier." Fast food shops, laundromats, and similar conveniences sprang up to take advantage of these needs. It is important to emphasize that the development of these new serv- ices and the production of these household appliances that were required by the working woman did not precede the *needs* created but that profits were made possible by *some* of these needs. It is interesting to note that day-care centers, which serve one of the most important needs of working mothers, have not proliferated in the same way as other conveniences because they are not profitable and because they create an implicit contradic- tion with the ideology of the family as a major unit for the sociali- zation of children.

In fact, the increasing "white-collar proletarianization" of women and the socialization of some forms of consumption have seriously undermined the economic and social base of family or- ganization and increased the oppression of women. Further- more, since women are now working both at home and outside the family, new contradictions have arisen. Many women are faced with increasing pressure in trying to cope with this new situation without adequate help at home. Male authority within the family appears to have little economic justification since the social division of labor between men/production vs. women/ consumption has been replaced by the men/production vs. women/consumption *and* production. The increasing depend- ence of the family on the woman's income has made it possible for women to revolt against the sexual division of labor, which has lost its "legitimacy" as a form of social cooperation and re- vealed its character as discrimination based on an ideological op- pression enforced by social institutions.

The major contradiction of the system is that by incorporating women into the work force, it destroyed the material basis of their oppression yet it openly appeared as illegitimate oppression. But the system cannot easily allow an adjustment in terms of sexual equality because it must maintain the pattern of discrimination in order to reproduce the social order. The family is a major apparatus of social integration and reproduces the precise ideological factors that make the employment of women advantageous for the capitalist interest. That is, capital can overexploit women and divide workers because there exists an implicit pattern of social discrimination based on sex. Thus, the system uses the sexual division of labor to exploit women. However, in doing so, it creates the possibility of a massive revolt that will threaten the sexual division of labor that is the root of their exploitation. That is why the women's revolt is objectively anticapitalist in the United States.

We are not arguing that the women's movement is an automatic and direct consequence of the participation of women in the labor force. It certainly has expanded from the revolutionary ideas that emerged in the countercultural movements of the 1960s. But the continuing transformation of this radical feminism linking university and other middle-class women into a more popular mass movement could threaten the social order and not just some specific aspects of institutional discrimination caused by changes in the working and living conditions of American women. In this sense, the interaction between the evolution of the class structure and the ideological transformation seems to be the major explanatory factor in this historical process.

This twofold structure of the women's revolt is reflected in the orientation of the women's movement, which is divided into two major trends. One is directed toward improving economic and institutional equality between the sexes, and the other emphasizes the revolt against the ideological roots of a male culture.

This opposition between reformist economism and radical idealism is characteristic of the infancy of all major social movements. The problem is that a deep transformation of the interrelated economic and ideological dimensions of women's oppression requires a major transformation of the social organization, which would be a major political defeat (not necessarily *the* defeat, *the* revolution) for the capitalist class. In this sense, the perspective of the women's movement depends upon its articulation with the political struggles, namely, its capacity to combine economic demands, ideological projects, and political targets. While this is not an appeal for control of the women's movement by a revolutionary party, it is clear that this perspective can only be achieved by a *centralizing* (although not a *centralized*) political organization *that does not concern only women*. Women's movements as social movements *must* be women based for exactly the same reason that working-class unions do not include students. If we recognize the explicit fact of women being oppressed as women, we will also have to recognize the autonomy of their organizations, programs, and tactics. On the other hand, in the same way that unions that are only concerned with business become interest groups rather than forces for social change, the feminist movement if it limits its struggle to women's issues will unconsciously become an instrument of division of progressive forces, a tool for reproducing a social order based on the double exploitation of *man and woman by man and woman*, and of *woman by man*.

6.3. WHY THE MINORITIES ARE THE MAJORITY

There are other "minorities" in the United States for whom the interaction between the deepening contradictions and the emergence of their revolt is following a pattern more and more like that of blacks and women. These include Puerto Ricans and Chicanos, "Latinos" in general, American Indians,[70] youth,[71] and the elderly. We cannot discuss here all the different aspects of this "minority" phenomenon. However, the short analysis of blacks and women ought to provide enough facts to hypothesize about the systematic characteristics that produce this fragmentation, enhance exploitation, and trigger social revolt. Actually, these minorities make up the majority of the population. Why, then, are they socially defined and even self-defined as minorities?

To answer this question we will have to relate the characteristics of the model of accumulation to observed trends. U.S. capitalism has expanded through the continuous destruction of previous forms of production and consumption, including those of the previous capitalist stages and phases. The resources and labor "freed" in this process have been recycled in the new relationships of production, distribution, and management. Therefore, the conditions of production and consumption have been objectively unified for an increasing share of the population at the structural level. In this sense, we can speak of an increasing social homogeneity in contradiction to the appearance of an increasing juxtaposition of piecemeal groups. At the same time, the system has extracted people from different previous positions and equalized their relationship to capital, but it has carefully kept their definition in terms of the old cleavages and distinctions between their former positions in order to overexploit particular segments, to divide all of them, to weaken the opposition, and to be able to exploit everybody.

This process, being systematic, is not necessarily conscious, but it certainly is learned and reproduced as a ruling-class practice. It is characterized by its uneven development and the coexisting expansion of productivity and consumption with surplus population, unemployment, and poverty in certain economic sectors, geographic regions, and cultural-biological statuses. It leads to the establishment of particular segmented channels of employment, consumption, and ways of living that do not build a "dualist society" but apparently a "puzzled one."

People tend to accept this self-definition in terms of particular statuses because it corresponds to their actual experiences of overexploitation, it is reproduced by the functioning of the institutions in the basic mechanisms of the relationship between production and distribution, and it is the dominant ideology in society which tends to be the ideology of the ruling class.

This self-definition is finally assimilated by people through their actual experiences and ultimately leads them to revolt following this perception. That is, if people act so as to reflect their actual experiences, they are not expressing the structural interests. Social revolts are always revolts of the minorities against the prevailing pattern of power in work and daily life—violent minorities against the "silent majority." In other words, once you are not silent, you are not in the majority. However, such a perception is a pure artifact that simply expresses the lack of simultaneous majoritarian "minority revolts." *This pattern of fragmented contradictions and conflict is the major mechanism of social domination by monopoly capital in the United States*. The extraordinary level of contradiction and potential social change that exists in this society is continually frustrated by the process of fragmentation and decentralization of conflicts. To recognize this differential starting point of the contradictions, to unify them progressively in agreement with the structural determinants through a *practice* of increasing political and ideological convergence, seems to be the major challenge for any movement of social change in the United States. Unless a clear political challenge develops along these lines, the deepening of the process of overexploitation by the expanding economic crisis could result in a series of violent explosions that could mobilize the "silent majority" against the revolts: the minorities have to build up a people's majority or they will face, separately, increasing institutional repression.

7. THE DYNAMICS OF SOCIAL RELATIONSHIPS OF DISTRIBUTION: PATTERNS OF INEQUALITY AND POVERTY

The class structure is defined by the social relationships of production. It determines the distribution of the product among groups and individuals, conditioning the way of life and the differential advantages obtained by the holders of every structural position.[72] In a capitalist society the level of income is the clearest indicator of the degree of inequality since income determines, generally, access to goods and services. Table 34 shows

TABLE 34. OCCUPATION OF HEADS BY TOTAL MEDIAN FAMILY INCOME IN 1970

Professional	$14,482
Self-employed	21,096
Salaried	14,135
Managerial	14,014
Self-employed	10,015
Salaried	15,114
Sales	12,325
Clerical	10,471
Craftsmen & foremen	11,294
Operatives	9,602
Service workers	8,562
Laborers	8,118
Farmers & farm managers	6,138
Farm laborers	4,672
Private household workers	3,177

Source: U.S. Bureau of the Census, *Current Population Reports*, Series P-23, No. 37, "Income in 1970," 1971, Table 33, p. 73, as compiled by Charles Anderson, *The Political Economy of Social Class*, Englewood Cliffs, N.J.: Prentice-Hall, 1974, p. 103.

clearly the extent of income inequality in American society. This inequality in income is closely associated with position in the occupational structure, which in turn is closely associated with level of education. The normal path seems to be that the level of education gives access to specific positions in the occupational structure, which allow for a corresponding level of income.[73] But since educational opportunities are largely determined by family background, in terms of income and occupation the structure of inequality is, in fact, largely but not entirely self-reproducing. This fact is confirmed by studies of social mobility, which show very little net intergenerational social mobility.[74] Improvements in standards of living and occupational status have come mainly from changes in the economic structure itself. Little wonder, then, that the extent of relative inequality in income has remained remarkably steady for two decades. The Gini concentration ratio of family personal income between 1929 and 1962 varied as follows: 1929, .49; 1935-1936, .47; 1941, .44; 1944, .39; 1947, .40; 1950, .40; 1954, .39; 1956, .39; 1962, .40.[75] Similar levels of inequality can be observed for the distribution of wealth.[76]

How do these patterns of inequality relate to the dynamics of the model of accumulation? It appears quite clear that the most fundamental factor in the distribution of income is the economic sector rather than the occupation itself. Summarizing recent studies in the United States, S. M. Miller and Martin Rein establish that "variations in earnings within a major occupational category are greater than those between occupational categories. . . . If the average earnings of all occupations in the United States were equalized, earnings inequality would be reduced by only 19%, since variations among the ten occupational categories explain only 19% of the earning variances of men. Earnings inequality would be reduced as much as 40% if the dispersion of earnings within an occupational category were narrowed so that men earned at the average within the occupation."[77]

Barry Bluestone has stressed the significant impact also of the type of activity on the level of income, which is higher than the impact of the level of education.[78] Furthermore, a recent statistical study on interindustrial patterns of social mobility concludes that not only are the differences between economic sectors a major source of income inequality but the system itself is also largely self-reproducing.[79] In that sense, the sources of inequality appear to be linked to both the internal laws of social stratification rooted in the class structure and the dynamics of the model of accumulation.

The equilibrium of this system depends upon its continuous expansion, which means that all the elements, including the distribution of individuals among the new positions generated by the model of accumulation, must maintain the same relative rate of growth. If the educational level accelerates at a faster rate because of continued pressure coming from the need for higher skills, the demographic variations change, there are rising social demands, and there is more surplus population to be absorbed.

It appears that there is an increasing bottleneck in the link between education and occupation. Some occupational positions appear to be filled by people "overeducated" in relation to the level required by capitalist standards.[80]

The dynamics of the inequality, then, will be less a function of internal arrangements (that is, more chances for education or more equal access to certain occupations) than the result of the structural transformation of the internal composition of the GNP and of the general trends of the system. Such is the conclusion reached by Miller and Rein after their thorough study of inequality and redistribution in advanced capitalist societies including the United States.[81]

Nevertheless, given the importance of state intervention in recent years, we could expect some level of income redistribution and reduction of inequality through taxation, collective consumption expenditures, or other public policies. Miller and Rein conclude negatively: "The public policies have not been redistributive by principle but their effects depend upon concrete circumstances and, in any case, they have failed in the last decade in the United States."[82] Also, the study by Friedland, Hicks and Johnson shows that redistribution only occurs in the policies of the American state under strong pressure from the labor movement.[83] That is why it is not astonishing that Miller and Rein could observe the relative worsening of the situation at the bottom of the scale in the United States.[84]

So far we have found that the so-called vicious circle of poverty in the United States is the direct expression of the functioning of the system of social stratification under the conditions of uneven development.[85] Twelve percent of Americans lived in poverty in 1975, and prospects are that the percentage will increase as a consequence of the evolution of unemployment and underemployment and of discrimination by race and sex in a fragmented labor market that is self-reproducing under the pattern of accumulation we have described. The description of the "urban poor" in 1968 in an accurate study by Anthony Downs gives empirical evidence supporting our interpretation.[86]

The increasing contradiction between growth and poverty becomes most evident in the crisis of the inner cities, in the progressive collapse of social services, and in the fiscal crisis of local governments. The limits to the absorption of surplus population combined with the deepening of the structural causes of poverty are transforming the largest U.S. inner cities into what has become the most direct expression of American social decay: the urban crisis.

8. THE CRISIS OF AMERICAN CITIES[87]

The economic crisis is the expression of some fundamental structural contradictions embodied in the pattern of capitalist accumulation in the United States. Therefore, it concerns not only the relationships of production and distribution but also the collective conditions of organization of everyday life. The crisis of public services and urban infrastructure in American cities is perhaps one of the most spectacular manifestations of the larger economic crisis. It reveals in a particularly striking manner the problems resulting from the tendency toward the socialization of costs and the privatization of profits. It expresses also the crisis of the service sector and the state's growing difficulties in supporting capital accumulation and absorbing surplus population while maintaining the current basis of social interests. At the same time, the politicization of collective consumption as a consequence of state intervention in urban services leads to an increase in the protest movements and political dissent that have grown out of the urban crisis.

The urban crisis is the crisis of a particular form of urban structure that plays a major role in the U.S. process of capitalist accumulation, in the organization of socialized consumption, and in the reproduction of the social order. This model of urban structure can be characterized by three major trends: metropolitanization, suburbanization, and institutional fragmentation. The process of *metropolitanization*,[88] namely, the concentration of population and activities in some major areas at an accelerated rate, follows from the process of uneven development and from the concentration (economic, organizational, and spatial) of capital, means of production, labor, means of consumption, and institutions.

The process of *suburbanization*,[89] which is the process of selective decentralization and spatial sprawl of population and activities within metropolitan areas, started on a large scale after World War II. The basic trend is for suburbs to expand through massive construction of single-family dwellings for private ownership. This pattern of suburban growth was made possible by federal housing policy. On the one hand, tax deductions and loans were available to families buying a home *in the suburbs*. On the other hand, a federally backed secondary mortgage market was created, which removed the risk for private capital lending money to all home buyers. Another element in this suburban expansion was the general spread of automobiles as the major means of transportation. Here also the state was decisive in launching the highway program which built the intrametropolitan highway system using up to 90 percent public funds. The urban sprawl that followed led to the decentralization of many industrial plants and businesses. A large portion of the middle-class and skilled workers moved as well. Middle-income groups found better housing conditions in the suburbs and abandoned older buildings in the center cities. These buildings were subdivided into small apartments that were crowded with low-income families, among them black immigrants from the South who had been displaced by labor-saving investments in agriculture. There followed a process of urban dilapidation in these central-city neighborhoods. This could not be stopped by public policies because of the growing gap between fiscal resources, depleted by the outflow of business and well-to-do dwellers, and social needs, aggravated by the unemployment endemic among many inner-city inhabitants. At the same time, the maintenance of highly expensive office concentrations in downtown areas necessitated an increasingly sophisticated urban infrastructure. Preserving the central functions of the large metropolitan areas required the overwhelming part of public resources devoted to urban services.

The *fragmentation of local governments*[90] has allowed suburban communities to avoid any social redistribution of fiscal resources. A relatively high level of collective services is maintained in those neighborhoods already in a better position to obtain goods and services in the private market. Thus, local autonomy becomes a mechanism for perpetuating social segregation and developing income inequality. Since the school system is also organized along the lines of residential segregation,[91] the reproduction of economic and cultural inequality continues across generations.

The wage-earning population is split so that each social position is crystallized in physical and social space, in consumption of services, in organizational networks, and in local government institutions. Future conflicts are channeled toward intracity competition among equally exploited residents for a structurally limited pie. The surburban local governments enforce this situation through all kinds of discriminatory land-use regulations: large-lot zoning, minimum house-size requirements, exclusion of multiple dwellings, obstacles to nonreliable building permits, etc.

At the same time, the suburban model of consumption has had a very clear impact on the reproduction of the dominant social relationships. Because the (legally owned) domestic household was in fact purchased with borrowed money, it could only be kept on the assumption of a stable permanent job. Any major deviation or failure threatened (job-dependent) financial reliability. Mass consumption also meant mass dependence on the economic *and cultural* rules of the financial institutions. Social relationships in the suburban neighborhood expressed the values of individualism, conformism, and social integration, reducing the world to the nuclear family and social desires to the maximization of individual consumption.

Thus, class-based metropolitan inequality is derived from uneven capitalist development. Expressed in the unequal social composition of the urban structure, it is ultimately preserved and reinforced by the state through the institutional arrangement of local governments and the class-determined fragmentation of the metropolitan areas.

The U.S. pattern of urban development individualizes and commodifies profitable consumption while simultaneously deteriorating nonprofitable socialized consumption. At the same time, the institutional mechanisms for the preservation of the social order are structurally provided.

Nevertheless, this model of urban structure depends on some basic structural contradictions: the contradiction between the growing need for public services in a system of socialized consumption and the increasing privatization of profits; the contradiction between the need to maintain some central functions and the urban sprawl of metropolitan areas; the contradiction between the growth of local governments' responsibilities and their inability to deal with the problems, either financially or institutionally; the contradiction between the spatial concentration of surplus population and oppressed ethnic minorities in the ghettos and the lack of mechanisms of integration in the central city. Deepened by economic crisis and expressed by movements of revolt, these contradictions are threatening the very basis of the existing pattern of urban development. Since the mid-fifties, the urban crisis has developed rapidly along three lines: the crisis in the production, distribution, and management of the means of collective consumption; the crisis of social order; and the crisis of local governments.

At the level of the means of collective consumption, the crisis of the postwar pattern of urban development reflects an increasing inability to keep the segregated delivery of urban services functioning smoothly. The most significant examples include housing, transportation, and education.[92]

The crisis of the housing market, particularly acute in the central cities of large metropolitan areas, is revealed in a total failure of the "filtering down" theory, the relative deterioration in the resources of the poor, the rising level of property tax and maintenance costs, and the depreciation of the housing stock caused by the overall decay of the city, overcrowding, and lack of maintenance.

Many landlords faced declining purchasing power and profitability.[93] The incomes of a large portion of central-city families were insufficient to provide landlords with rents that would cover maintenance costs and still leave acceptable profit margins. Thus, many families overcrowded small dwellings, accelerating the rate of deterioration, abandoned housing units in the quest for cheaper housing, or launched rent strikes, in which case either the families were evicted or the landlord abandoned the house to force urban renewal and to obtain a revaluation of his property by public funds.

Many central-city landlords facing increasing costs and property taxes could not obtain higher rents because of the low income of tenants and could not sell because of tenants' resistance and lack of buyers. Therefore, they stopped making repairs and maintaining their buildings. Later on, they stopped paying property taxes, obtaining superprofits during the two or more years before the city could legally take over the house. Since the cost of demolition was high and without profitable purpose, the empty houses were quickly occupied by squatters, often drug addicts or inner-city gangs. Violence, prejudice, actual assaults, and widespread fear contributed to the abandonment of the entire sector by the neighbors, creating a process of contagion that literally produced no man's lands in large parts of the cities. This trend is developing very fast in the United States. Some official figures for 1973 estimated ("conservatively") that 100,000 units were abandoned in New York City, 30,000 in Philadelphia, 12,000 in Baltimore, 10,000 in St. Louis, etc. Abandonment was going on in New York between 1968 and 1975 at a rate of 50,000 housing units each year, which (with corrections for demolition and adding previously abandoned stock) gives an estimate of between 400,000 and 450,000 abandoned apartments in 1975.[94]

The crisis in central-city housing stock is paralleled by a crisis in the mechanisms of production and distribution of suburban housing, reflected in creeping inflation and the instability of financial markets. Financial intermediaries are decisive in the family's ability to purchase a home. The major contradiction is manifested in increasing individual, corporate, and state debt in general, and residential debt in particular. Residential debt as a percentage of total debt rose from 9.5 in 1947 to 23.7 in 1972.

More and more resources have to be devoted to paying the past debt. With the skyrocketing of interest rates and the stagnation of real income, the cost of new surburban housing threatens a financial collapse that could start an explosive chain reaction.[95]

Housing investments are becoming more and more risky, and therefore the leading financial institutions are retreating from the mortgage-holding markets. In the process the federal government has assumed an increasing share of the debt, avoiding a mass of foreclosures in the suburbs and in the central cities. Increasing government debt and thus inflation were crucial for maintaining the demand for housing between 1968 and 1972.

But there are major unresolved contradictions linked to this process. Either interest rates grow faster than inflation and families will be increasingly unable to pay them, or inflation speeds up and financial institutions will refuse to make unprofitable investments. The federal government intervenes but is increasingly unable to stop inflationary expenditures and simultaneously meet other priorities.

The pattern of transportation in the dual model of urbansuburban structure produced several contradictions during the sixties.[96] The most important was the differential speed of residential sprawl and decentralization of activities in the central business district. The undersupported public transportation network became increasingly overcrowded and run down, and the new urban highways were not sufficient to accommodate peakhour traffic. An increasing amount of central land was devoted to parking lots, and downtown streets were more and more submerged by traffic. Federally backed use of the automobile created a permanent financial crisis in public transit and reinforced the downgrading of the service, thus expanding a vicious circle.[97]

Urban crises have been generated by the contradictions inherent in a situation where downtown-redevelopment interests require renewed public support for mass transit to make the facilities they are building more accessible and inner-city residents have problems driving in the city and are disadvantaged in their travels to suburban work places. As a response, the federal government started a new program funding 80 percent of city projects proposing mass-transit development.[98] The most important initiative under this new provision was the BART system in the

San Francisco Bay area. But as several analysts have shown, this experience, as well as the general trend in other current mass-transit programs, has favored middle-class suburban residents commuting to work in the central business district rather than the increasingly isolated city residents or the mass of workers commuting from the working-class suburbs.

But the model came under attack from the suburbs as well. Car maintenance costs increase, and a significant portion of the suburban population cannot drive. Also, measures to protect the environment against pollution have emphasized the damage done by the automobile, mobilizing one dimension of the suburban model (living "within nature") against another (traveling by car).

Ultimately, the oil crisis is producing a major breakdown in the perspectives of unlimited car-based transportation. With the 55 mph speed limit on the highways, commuting time increases substantially, and the absurdity of extra large powerful cars running slowly in twelve-lane express highways is starting to strike many North American minds.

Another key mechanism in the class model of urban structure that is crumbling is the school system. We will not refer here to the whole complex set of contradictions concerning education, but exclusively to its role in the reproduction of the system of urban segregation through the "separate and unequal" rule. The autonomy of the school districts over the functioning of their schools has come under attack from the grassroots and the institutions at the same time. Neighborhood movements, particularly in the minority sectors of the city, have campaigned for community control over the schools, trying to mobilize the parents in order to improve the quality of the service and to break down the differential class logic of the educational bureaucracies in the inner-city schools. Without challenging segregation, this movement opposes the effects of segregation on services, calling into question the structural inequality in the distribution of public resources.[99]

On the other hand, the impact of mass protests and liberal pressure on the institutional system has led to a potentially explosive trend: the busing of school children between different school districts to achieve a racial balance and avoid segregation.[100] Busing is one way to bypass the vicious circle between the social status determined by the quality of education and the quality of education determined, through residential segregation, by social status. In some cities courts have ordered two-way busing to improve integration in the schools. While the upper and middle classes do not care too much, being "protected" in the suburbs or able to send their children to private schools, the white working-class neighborhoods have reacted strongly (rioting and demonstrating in Boston and Louisville, for example) against what they consider a threat to the social chances of their children or even their physical security.

The system of supplying "educational vouchers" to families who can use them in the school of their choice, each school receiving funding proportionate to the demand, is an attempt to make the schools work through market mechanisms. Experiences in California do not seem very encouraging, either in terms of efficiency or equality, since the mechanisms of reciprocal selection by schools and parents work to keep in general the same social recruitment.

What this process of contradiction and conflict over school segregation makes clear is that the U.S. urban model is being shaken not only in its daily functioning but also in its mechanisms of self-reproduction. Similar problems appear in other basic public services, such as health, garbage collection, and welfare. Analysis of these service areas would provide additional evidence about the general breakdown of the organization of the means of collective consumption settled during the expanding period that followed World War II.

The most striking effects of these trends are undoubtedly the growing abandonment and physical destruction of large sectors of the central cities, particularly in the ghettos. Baltimore's Pennsylvania Avenue, Boston's Columbia Point, and St. Louis's Pruitt-Igoe are symbols of the massive destruction that could occur if the current pattern is not reversed. The most famous example is the South Bronx in New York City, where 600,000 people live. The process of abandonment, the deterioration of real estate values, and the loss of control by the system have induced the landlords to encourage the setting of fires in order to get money from their insurance companies. In other cases fires are started just to obtain plumbing and building materials. Landlords pay children three to ten dollars apiece to start the fires. There were 12,300 fires in the South Bronx in 1974, with more than one-third proved intentional—ten every night! And this is not a unique district: Brownsville in Brooklyn, Bushwick, and others are also burning. Zones of New York appear as if they had been bombed.

But the most direct and most disruptive expression of the urban crisis was a series of different phenomena that suddenly and radically disrupted the reproduction of the social order. The breakdown, which had its roots in the central-city social order, occurred in the social structure of exploitation and the political and ideological experiences of oppression. Since the central city was, on the one hand, a material apparatus for the managerial functions of the economy and of the society and, on the other hand, a form of organization of the labor power in the stagnant economic sector, the revolt of the overexploited against the symbols and practice of the rulers was expressed through the material base and organizational supports of the inner city's everyday life.

This major disruption of the dominant social order took several different forms, but they all expressed the rejection of a given situation and produced a similar impact on the functioning and structure of the central city. The most important forms of breakdowns of social control were the following:

There was a rapid increase of so-called crime and particularly of "crime in the streets," which was clearly linked to an individual reaction against structural oppression in the absence of a stable mass-based political alternative.[101] "Crime" is not explained by "deprivation" alone. For example, in the depression of the 1930s, crime rates actually went down and only went up again in the late fifties and early sixties. In the current depression crime rates are higher still (up 20 percent in 1975 over what they were in 1974). This comparison implies that the collective movement that during the thirties forced the government to launch the New Deal was viewed by many urban dwellers as an adequate response and a hopeful trend. Today the structurally unemployed are concentrated in the inner cities and lack an effective channel for collective action. But we also observe that the most rapid increase in the crime rate occurred during the sixties, when in fact, until 1966, the economic situation was improving on the average. It seems, therefore, that the major factor has been the collapse of the system of social control by the family, the school, or the southern communities from which many inner-city dwellers came. Not only was urban crime a challenge to the social order, but it became a way of life, economically and culturally, for a large sector of inner-ghetto youth who had no chance outside the irregular economy to which some forms of crime are structurally connected.

Another source of challenge to the established social and spatial division of labor and consumption was the development of community organizations and urban protest movements that defied the logic of the functioning and delivery of specific services as well as the legitimacy of traditional local authorities.[102] The most widespread urban movements were mobilizations against urban renewal to protect a neighborhood from demolition or obtain adequate help and money for relocating. Given urban renewal's direct threat, it was relatively easy to mobilize neighborhoods, but these movements were defensive and limited in scope. After several years of experience, however, the movements progressively shifted toward demands for comprehensive neighborhood planning forcing a new approach to urban redevelopment.

Rent strikes, particularly in New York, St. Louis, Philadelphia, and Chicago, ushered in a new period, in which the "filtering down" process was blocked by insistence on adequate repairs and by demands that rents be controlled according to some public standards instead of at the landlord's will.[103] All social services (health and education in particular) as well as social welfare were subject to assault by central-city residents. Frances Piven and Richard Cloward have shown how, in fact, the spectacular increase in the welfare rolls during the sixties was not due to increasing needs (these already existed) but to increasing demands.[104] Thus, urban protest was not the effect of urbanization, but the grassroots attempt to overcome the segregated model of collective consumption, an expression of the loss of social control caused by the combined impact of the internal contradictions of urban services and generalized unrest in American society.

The poor and black mobilizations were paralleled by Alinsky-type community organizations trying to develop middle-class citizens' participation and control over local governments and social services. Robert Bailey has shown how this very moderate populist approach developed mostly where middle-class groups found "poor people types of problems," that is, where the inner-city crisis struck the remaining middle-class dwellers.[105] Thus, in spite of their ideological conservatism and pragmatic approach, the Alinsky-type movements were a real threat to the social order (contrary to what Bailey thinks), since they were channeling toward protests groups that were generally supportive of local institutions. Certainly, their localism and economicism kept them within the mainstream of the consumer movement, but their growing influence was a factor pushing in the direction of a multiclass movement that could have been developed on a more conflictual base in a different political context. In summary, while limited, localistic and strictly economic, the urban movements during the sixties clearly limited the overexploitation implicit in the pattern of urban development that had until then been predominant.

The most significant factor in the breakdown of the social order in the cities during the sixties was the riots, which took place mostly in the black ghettos. After the explosions of Harlem (1964) and Watts (1965) they were generalized in the famous hot summer of 1967 and as a mass response to the murder of Martin Luther King in 1968. There followed, in 1969, 1970, and 1971, an important number of less publicized riots.[106] Certainly, the riots were not "urban movements" in the sense that they were not exclusively linked to a protest related to the living conditions in the inner city. They were a form of general protest and struggle of the black people against the general conditions of their oppression. There had been much debate and empirical research on the riots, but the best systematic statistical analysis, carried out by Seymour Spilerman, shows that the only variables significantly correlated with the occurrence and intensity of riots were the size of the black population in the city (the larger the black population, the more riots) and the region (the northern cities are more likely to have riots).[107] Statistically speaking, the riots were strongly linked to the large inner-city ghettos of the largest metropolitan areas. This fact can be interpreted either in organizational terms (the largest possible base for sustained mass organization) or in terms of the specific effects of the segregated organization of work, services, and everyday life, as expressed in the largest ghettos. The hypotheses are complementary. The riots were mass protests against the racist society, including one of its dimensions, the specific pattern of racial segregation in the ghetto and its effects on the delivery of services and jobs.[108]

If the black movement, in its different expressions, could not overcome its isolation and if its vast radical component was destroyed by repression, the struggles of the sixties at least forced the state at the federal and local level to a major reexamination of the use of central cities as a reservation for ethnic minorities. Blacks increasingly gained access to local governments and state agencies, more and better services were distributed (at least for a period), and more public jobs were made available for inner-city residents. Often this amelioration was part of a process of cooptation of the community leaders intended to disorganize the grassroots, but nevertheless the overall effects produced a decisive breach in the social logic dominating the urban services and local governments. Thus, the protest from the grassroots obtained tangible social benefits, challenged the structural logic, and eventually precipitated the urban fiscal crisis.

The crisis of urban services and the breakdown of the social order at the individual and at the collective level had a major impact on the management of the urban system itself, striking deeply the state apparatus and its internal operations: this is what emerged openly as the urban crisis of the seventies.

The most visible effect of the impact of the urban contradictions and conflict on the state apparatus is the fiscal crisis of the central cities.[109] This is the direct expression of the articulation of the different processes I have described. The fiscal crisis of the central cities is a particularly acute expression of the fiscal crisis of the state: the increasing gap between expenditures and revenues brought on by the socialization of costs and privatization of profits. The crisis is even more acute in the local governments of large central cities because they express the contradictory expansion of the "service sector."[110]

On the one hand, corporate capital must build managerial function centers which require a concentration of service workers and public facilities. On the other hand, in order to maintain the social order, the state must absorb the surplus population and provide welfare and public services to the large fraction of structurally exploited population, mostly concentrated in the inner cities. During the fifties, accumulation requirements had top priority, and local finance started to recover. During the sixties the mass protests in the inner cities forced some redistribution through social expenditures as well as through the provision of jobs.

The increase in the number of municipal workers triggered a process of escalating demands and economic struggles that were favored by the absence of established bargaining patterns in the public sector. Teachers, municipal service workers, public health workers, sanitation workers, fireman, and policemen have been among the most militant strikers and union-organizing sectors of American labor. They have improved their position substantially even if their wages are still below those in the private monopoly sector. The entire set of labor relationships has been disrupted in the local public sector, creating inflationary trends in the cost of labor-intensive services. The city did not react by levying new taxes on the corporations, which were the most expensive municipal-service consumers, but by raising taxes on central-city residents and trying to oppose between them taxpayers, the welfare-consuming poor, and municipal workers. In spite of renewed fiscal effort and higher public service charges, the city had to increase public debt and count on expected future revenues in order to balance the budget. This is what happened to New York City in 1975-1976, provoking a world famous fiscal crisis.

During the 1950s the New York City budget expanded at an annual rate of approximately 6 percent. Since 1965, the year pressure from communities and workers started, the budget has increased at an annual rate of 15 percent. One-eighth of New Yorkers are on welfare. New York maintains the largest system of public hospitals, subsidized mass transit, welfare payments, tuition-free universities, and cultural facilities in the United States. Nevertheless, the "bankruptcy" of New York City is not a consequence of the distribution of "excessive" services and jobs, as the elite circles have tried to argue. It is the combined result of corporate rejection of increased taxes that could pay for the social services and, even more important, the decision of the financial community to impose discipline on New York City's social-welfare policy.

The case of New York City is perhaps the most extreme example of the tendencies implicit in the whole evolution of urban contradictions, but most central cities face similar problems. In 1975, in Cleveland, the city's debt service represented 17.9 percent of its current budget expenditures, even higher than New York. In Milwaukee, this figure (indicator of potential imbalance) was 15.2 percent in spite of very high local taxes. Detroit also had a structural deficit and laid off 15 percent of its municipal workers in 1975. Buffalo had a debt-service-to-operating-budget ratio of $17 million to $229 million. Boston reduced its municipal work force by 10 percent in 1975, particularly in the health sector. San Francisco in September 1975 faced a strike of firemen and policemen that forced the mayor to keep their jobs and raise their salaries, provoking the indignation of the financial community and subjecting the mayor to embittered accusations that he was on the path to a very serious fiscal crisis.

The potential consequences of the urban fiscal crisis are very serious because they could threaten the already unstable political legitimacy of local governments. Let us explain this important point.

The municipal reformers of the thirties replaced the pork-barrel and patronage policies of the political machines with the urban-development schemes of the city managers. They risked the loss of the person-to-person ties that had founded machine control of inner-city neighborhoods. The pressures from the grassroots during the sixties forced local bureaucracies open to the poor and the ethnic minorities. If "all-out business" policies predominate, the local governments of the largest cities are going to be increasingly isolated from the different conflicting social interests and are going to lose all their past sources of legitimacy, whether in terms of clientele, in terms of management, or in terms of specific interests being served. First line in the revision of the social policies of the sixties, the cities are actually caught in the crossfire of the business interests calling for restraint and the workers and consumers refusing to carry the burden of a crisis that is not theirs. Thus, the status apparatus in the central cities, besides supporting increasing contradictions at the level of fiscal policies and being shaken by demands for services, jobs, and wages, is also losing political control over the social conflicts growing out of urban issues.

The postwar pattern of urban development itself is now at stake. The converging trends of the social conflicts, the crisis of services, and the economic and political breakdown of local governments have put into question the urban-suburban structure that emerged as a powerful factor in the process of capitalist accumulation and segregated commodity consumption. Actually, even the trend of metropolitanization is now being reversed. For the first time in U.S. urban history, between 1970 and 1973 five of the eight major metropolitan areas decreased instead of increased in size. The New York metropolitan area had a net decrease of 305,000 inhabitants. The decrease in Chicago was 124,000; in Philadelphia 75,000; in Detroit 114,000. Los Angeles in 1972-1973 showed a net outmigration of 119,000. Boston (up 0.4 percent) and San Francisco (up 0.5 percent) remained stable after having grown during the sixties. Only Washington grew, by 1 percent, largely because of federal government employment.

A new and major contradiction arises. If the flight of activities and residences toward the nonmetropolitan areas continues (these areas gained 4.2 percent population between 1970 and 1973), the deterioration of the large cities will accelerate. But the large metropolitan areas remain organizational forms for major economic and political interests of the ruling class, as well as the dwelling place for a large portion of the American people. The new urban form arising from the current crisis will be largely a function of urban social movements and political conflicts. A similar argument could be used for other dimensions of the economic crisis as well as for its impact on American society.

Thus, the social order emerging from the transformations triggered by the economic crisis will be shaped primarily by the policies implemented to overcome the crisis. And these policies will be the result of class conflicts and political strategies within the framework of constraints and tendencies of the American social structure, as presented in this chapter.

4

■■

Class Interests, Policies for the
Crisis, and the Political Process

W E HAVE SEEN that the "economic crisis" is, in fact, a social process. Therefore, its treatment will also be a social process. Each month economists look at "leading indicators" as if they were meteorologists trying to predict the weather for the weekend or a natural storm of uncontrollable origin. In fact, the evolution of the crisis and its impact on the social structure and the dynamics of U.S. society will depend on the interaction between the structural social contradictions it reveals and the policies used to counteract the effects of the crisis. By policies we mean a series of articulated decisions made by the two major centers of economic and social power—the large corporations and the state. These policies are obviously not neutral or scientific. They are embedded in particular social interests; other interests will be opposed and, if necessary, sacrificed.

Their orientation, plausibility, and final effects of these policies will be mostly a function of the social conflicts expressed at both the grassroots level and the level of the political process related to the state. Thus, to understand the economic crisis, we must systematize and define the major orientations of the state policies used in the United States over the past fifteen years to try to control the increasing contradictions of the process of accumulation. In fact, the current crisis is also a political crisis in the sense that the political system has been seriously shaken by the failure of economic policies and by the triggering of new political contradictions generated by those policies. Today it has become indispensable at all levels (economic, political, ideological) to organize a new departure for the system as a whole, in the United States as well as in the rest of the world. To outline the set of interactions between the current crisis and the political implications on the different policies designed to deal with it will be the final outcome of our analysis. We will treat successively: the relationship of the crisis to the interests of different classes and groups; the background of the policies used during the 1960s, namely, the contradictory combination of integration and repression; the requirements for new domestic economic policies and their social implications; the international dimensions of the economic policies and their impact on U.S. foreign policy; the consequences for the political process in the United States.

1. THE RELATIONSHIP OF THE CRISIS TO CLASS INTERESTS

From the analysis we have developed up to this point, it appears to be clear that the development of the economic crisis is a consequence of the contradictions of the pattern of capital accumulation and of the transformation of the class structure, which are complementary aspects of a single historical process. In this sense, the economic crisis is not external to the class structure. It is not an event from the outside world that suddenly affects the social classes. What we find is that at a certain time specific trends of the economic crisis will have a particular differential impact on the classes, defined both as positions at the production and distribution levels *and* as sociopolitical actors. To understand the precise impact of these trends on U.S. society is a central point in the interpretation of the crisis and its significance in the dynamics of world capitalism. We have enough facts to develop some hypotheses about the relationship between the two processes that we have already analyzed: the economic crisis and the transformation of the class structure.

We will consider three different sources of effects on the interests of social classes: the components of the current crisis; the major economic countertendencies previously introduced by capitalist policies, which led to the crisis, as described in chapter 2; and the probable trends of economic measures that will be undertaken to overcome the current crisis. Also, we should consider at least two different levels of interests of the social classes: the economic interests and the political-ideological interests.

To avoid excessive complexity in developing this theoretical framework, we will condense our analysis into some brief, necessarily schematic, remarks.

The immediate effects of the crisis are, as we know, unemployment, recession, and inflation. How do they affect different social positions?

Unemployment is concentrated in certain categories. It affects mostly workers in the so-called irregular economy. Manual workers, especially those in the construction, automotive, and transportation industries are also seriously affected either by layoffs or by a reduction in working hours.

The recession means not only a reduction in the number of jobs, but a reduction of real income. This, obviously, affects everybody. But it has a significant differential impact on different social categories. We do not have accurate data concerning these differentials in the current crisis, but there is a study that tried to measure the distributional impact on income of the 1970 recession; the results should be similar to the current crisis, but on a much smaller scale. For each group, expected income calculated on the basis of previous income is compared with actual income. The old and the new working classes (artisans and mechanics, craftsmen, professional and technical workers in that order) are the occupational categories most seriously affected by the recession. However, considering the impact by level of income, "the burden (measured as a proportional income loss) increased with family income up to $15,000 or $20,000 and then decreased slightly for families with incomes up to $25,000. Above this level, the data reveals no generalizable patterns."[1] This is consistent with the findings concerning the impact on the majority of workers, manual and professional.

What appears to happen is that the recession affects workers in different sectors of the economy through different channels. Workers in the irregular economy and unskilled workers are hurt by increasing unemployment; skilled workers in the monopoly sector are affected by a proportionally larger reduction in real income.

Concerning the impact of inflation, we have an excellent study by Hollister and Palmer on the differential effect of inflation by level of income in respect to expenditure patterns. Although these cover the period from 1940 to 1967, they can still help us discuss current trends. The most important finding is that price increases hurt the poor less than the nonpoor.

In looking at expenditure patterns, we construct a Poor Price Index (PPI) and compare its movements with those of the Consumer Price Index. The comparison suggests that price rises have hurt the poor *less* than the non-poor. On the income side, several types of evidence suggest that the benefits of the tight labor markets which normally accompany inflationary pressures are very important to the poor. Simple regressions relating the incidence of poverty to unemployment, median family income and price rises indicate that the gains to the poor from tight labor markets go beyond those strictly related to lower employment. It seems that the poor gain relatively *more* than other groups probably because of increases in hours worked and narrowing of wage differentials. Public transfer payments, second only to wages and salaries as income sources for the poor, are found to have risen more than enough to offset the rise in the Consumer Price Index—though the position of Social Security benefits is somewhat unclear. The assets of the poor are found to be small in total value and of the total a very small proportion is vulnerable to inflation. Thus negative wealth effects of inflation are extremely small.

One might conjecture that the idea that the poor are hurt by inflation has gained credence because of a tendency to generalize from piecemeal considerations and isolated cases. If the money incomes of the poor are fixed then price rises will cause a deterioration in their economic well-being, but one must go the next step and consider whether the same process which generates the rise in prices is not likely to generate rises in the income of the poor as great or greater than the rise in prices. Similarly though there are some poor families living on incomes from fixed value assets or pensions vulnerable to inflation it should not be concluded that the majority of the poor are in this circumstance.[2]

These findings must be qualified. Otherwise, they could be misleading. The poor are seriously hurt by inflation as are all wage earners and people living on social benefits. Their savings are more likely to be in cash than in fixed-value assets and are therefore extremely vulnerable to inflation. Also, even if we accept that they are relatively less hurt by inflation than middle-income groups, the absolute loss represents for them a more serious burden added to their already existing difficulties. And even more fundamental criticism can be addressed to this widely cited study: it relies on observations made at a time when inflation was associated with economic expansion and when social pressures generated by mass protests of the poor were able to bring about increases in social welfare that kept up with inflation. In fact, these two arguments are implicit in Hollister and Palmer's explanation of the relative improvement of poor people's incomes. But this means that the impact of inflation on the poor cannot be generalized from these data. When inflation is combined with recession and the protests of the poor are curbed by the state, their vulnerable assets will be increasingly unable to escape erosion by inflation. What can be argued is that inflation was less damaging for the poor during the sixties because they were able to organize, imposing social-welfare policies and improving their situation. In that sense, they forced capital either to cut its profits or to increase inflation even more to finance the new social costs. The resultant widespread inflation hurt the mainstream of society and seriously threatened the mechanisms of the functioning of financial capital. Then, because of the social inability of capital to pass off the effects of inflation on workers and poor people, an accelerating rate of inflation seems to be the greatest enemy of capital corporate interests and of the middle and upper strata that are the main bases of social support for those corporate interests.

Turning now to the impact of the countertendencies underlying the crisis, we find the following:

1. The internationalization of capital has seriously affected the level of employment, the standard of living, and the bargaining power of the workers in the monopoly sector.

2. The expansion of credit and of the debt economy has provided a great number of jobs for service workers and enlarged consumption for most workers.

3. Increased state intervention in the economy has favored many people: manual workers in the monopoly sector whose jobs are largely dependent on public spending; unskilled workers and

minority workers who are absorbed into less discriminatory public jobs; the poor who are subsidized by the development of public services and social welfare; a large portion of the population who make a profit from all kinds of public services (education, health, urban services, etc.). These relationships are very important because they are going to be differentially transformed by the management of crisis.

Let us consider now the potential impact of anticrisis policies. To correct the immediate effects of the crisis, two different measures can be used. Either steps will be taken to stimulate the economy and fight the recession (through new public spending or tax rebates to increase private consumption or both), or stronger measures will be undertaken to stop inflation. From our previous analysis, it would seem that inflation hurts corporations the most. Unemployment hurts especially the most exploited sectors of the working class. And recession cuts the income of middle-level workers. Thus, the most damaging policy for the working population would be a set of antiinflationary measures because, in the private sector, they would stop credit, reducing jobs for the service workers who depend on the continuous expansion of consumption.

Even more important, antiinflationary measures in the public sector means that nondiscriminatory jobs will be reduced, cutting down the absorption of surplus population (which will affect mostly women and minority workers), public workers will be laid off, there will be a freeze on wages of public workers that will seriously affect service workers, many of whom are low-level professionals, welfare payments will be reduced, and social services will be curtailed, affecting almost everyone, but especially the poor and elderly.

Since social classes are defined not only by their economic interests but also by their political-ideological stands as historical actors, it is important to consider the effect the economic crisis would have at the political-ideological level. We are referring not only to the potential historical interests of the classes but to their immediate interests that depend upon their special situation and commitments in the crisis of the 1970s.

The political-ideological self-definition of classes depends on their actual performance, which is generally determined by the level, rhythms, and orientations of the class struggle.[3] In this sense, what strongly characterizes U.S. society is the absence of a politically oriented class-conscious labor movement. By this we do not necessarily mean the "classical" model of a large union led by a Marxist party. We refer to the lack of a social-democratic oriented militant labor movement of the British or Scandinavian type. The reason for this situation is not merely economic (the high level of capitalist development in the United States). We have observed the contradictory unevenness of this development. Furthermore, there is not an automatic relationship between the level of economic development and the orientations of the working class. For instance, in Italy the acceleration of capitalist development and improvement in the standard of living in the 1960s have considerably reinforced the leftist strength among workers in the industrialized north. The same pattern appears in Spain. Without rejecting the influence of the concentration of a large share of world surplus value in the United States or the possibility of partial integration through economic gains of the working-class movement into the monopoly sector, we believe that the most important reasons are historical, linked to the particular pattern of capitalist development in the United States.[4] *The absence of feudalism and of an aristocracy-based ancien regime of social privileges, the open-frontier pattern of labor mobility and the corresponding workers' ideology, the early franchise in the political system, the fragmentation and decentralization of the state, and, above all, the successive ethnic and social segmentation of a working class built up by waves of immigration from very different backward areas seem to be factors important enough to explain the split between the sharpness and violence of class struggle in the United States[5] and the weakness of a class-conscious labor movement.*[6]

In addition, specific political factors seem to have played a major role in the frustration of the left-oriented wing of the labor movement that emerged during the thirties. The Communist party was a victim of the Cold War and its own political mistakes (such as the systematic alignment with the Soviet Union).[7] Its isolation, repression, and destruction in the forties and early fifties eliminated the main political challenge from the Left and opened the way to the repression of all other left-wing political forces.

As a result, the labor movement became increasingly de-

politicized. This does not mean that workers are more conservative than other social groups, however. Hamilton and Levison
have presented evidence contradicting this bourgeois myth.[8]
Even the labor movement, including the AFL-CIO and other important independent unions (for instance, the powerful United
Auto Workers), is clearly placed to the left *within the system*, as
far as domestic policies are concerned.[9] Levison gives very convincing evidence of the progressive stand of the labor unions in
the laws they supported in Congress. At the same time, it is clear
that the AFL-CIO national leadership has a strong anticom-
munist and antileft position. In international affairs it is sometimes even more conservative than the U.S. government. Actually, most of the old labor "leaders" won their position by "purging
the Communists," and they (and their line) can only survive by
preventing the end of international tension, which has been so
effective in scaring American workers.

Thus, the labor movement and the working class in general*
have been historically self-defined in the United States as an "interest group" trying to get as much as possible from capital
within the rules of the game but being committed at the same
time to reproducing the rules that keep the game going. This attitude implies that although there are some common interests for
all workers, such as the fight against unemployment, hostility to
the freezing of wages, the development of social services, and the
reduction of taxes, there is separation and even competition between different unions fighting for their own specific interests.

This pattern of self-definition as an interest group that has developed in the American working-class movement has characterized all the social movements that emerged during the sixties,
including those of the blacks, the minorities, students, and
women, as well as ecological movements and the counterculture.
In all these cases the axis for the mobilization was some specific
demand. The demands were not generalized, nor did these
movements develop any strategies for building broader alliances.

Under these conditions, the political-ideological interests of

---

* We do *not* equate the labor movement with the working class. It is clear that
new expressions of working-class historical interests are being formed at the
grassroots level. Nevertheless, while these tendencies are crucial for future development, they are too small and fragmented to change the observed pattern in
the current crisis.

the "majority," including the unions and community groups, have been equivalent to their economic interests. Their political perspectives have been centered on the improvement of their bargaining capacities in relation to the distribution of the product.

From this point of view, we have seen that the current crisis has hurt significantly, but in different ways, the majority of manual and nonmanual workers and the workers in the irregular economy. This has happened because of the dramatic reduction in public services, which affects all sectors of the population in terms of jobs and levels of consumption. By centering the treatment of the crisis on antiinflationary policies (as required by the corporations), the state can increase the communality of economic interests for most people, and for the majority of the population these economic interests are still identified with their political goals.

In this sense, it is going to be very difficult, for a society that has always based a substantial part of its legitimacy on the improvement in living standards, to reverse that pattern for the sake of national salvation. And only if facts verify that there is no other way out of the crisis than to follow the corporate policies will the "majority"* resign its autonomy again in the hope of better times.

The main goals of the "minorities,"** especially women and ethnic minorities, at the political-ideological level have been to improve equality and end discrimination. However, if dealing with the crisis requires stricter policies of employment and exploitation with greater control over the ideological roots of social order, this will provoke a *tendency* to stop the shift toward equality or to channel it through segregated forms of existence, such as black capitalist cooperatives in the ghettos or self-help movements for women. In this sense, the strategy of self-reliance is extremely ambiguous when it is separated from broader movements against the social roots of discrimination. Also, family life must be strengthened to reproduce social order: blacks should be kept in their ghettos and women in their kitchens to avoid increasing official unemployment.

* "Majority" is here equivalent to the mainstream of the working population of the monopoly sector, actually a statistical minority of workers.

** Remember: "minorities" are, statistically, the majority.

Since the margin for maneuvering in this field is very narrow, the present crisis will probably sharpen sexist and racist patterns, creating the structural conditions for new major uprisings.*

The relationship of the counterculture movements to the crisis is extremely ambiguous. These movements, which are defined at the ideological level, were to a degree linked to the student revolt, which has largely disappeared from major American campuses.** The new ideology of austerity and the reinforcement of the social order around the old virtues of family and tradition are needed to rationalize the coming hard times. The appeals to "community," "family," and "nation" strike a serious blow to the hedonism, individual freedom, and self-affirmation of the libertarian ideologies that emerged during the sixties. However, the "back to nature" movement calling for abandonment of the "consumption society" and adherence to "the simple life" should be perfectly functional to a system that is asking for a reduction in standards of living and social services. Thus, the contradiction is that the need for overexploitation curbs the antiwork culture while the need for decreasing consumption fits perfectly with the drop-out effect of the ecological culture. Therefore, the actual impact will depend ultimately on the class position of the people in the counterculture. So, while the "Lordstown young worker" type will probably be increasingly disciplined and repressed, the "utopian-communities-student-based" types will probably be encouraged to continue as a convenient, cheap channel for absorbing the "overeducated" surplus population.

Thus, the effects of the crisis at the political-ideological level will depend ultimately upon the interaction between the trends we have exposed: the impact on the structurally defined eco-

---

* Witness, for example, the campaign against the ERA, or the cut in federal funds for abortion.

** In fact, the student movement has not disappeared in the seventies. Rather, it has been clearly *transformed*. While it is largely absent from the campuses of the leading universities, it is spreading very fast in the working-class colleges of inner cities. The linkage between workers' issues and students' protests becomes more direct. The movement's lack of visibility comes mostly from a media blackout and from the fact that the ruling elite is satisfied with keeping under control the training institutions necessary to reproduce itself and to produce knowledge. This important trend of American social dynamics has been called to my attention by James Cockcroft.

nomic interests; the impact on the historical structurally defined political-ideological interests; and the interaction of the political-ideological *process* through which the classes deal with the current crisis from their differential standpoints.

What this implies is that the ultimate outcome of the crisis, from the point of view of the historical process, will depend on the interaction between the policies of the crisis and the political conflicts. Therefore, we should now turn to an analysis of the recent evolution of state policies.

2. INTEGRATION AND REPRESSION IN
   U.S. GOVERNMENTAL POLICIES: FROM
   THE GREAT SOCIETY DREAMS TO THE
   WATERGATE NIGHTMARES

It was in the late 1950s that the first signs of weakness appeared in the "American miracle." The serious economic crisis of 1957-1958 to some degree affected the productivity agreement reached between monopoly capital and organized labor, triggering a new wave of strikes. The Soviet sputniks appeared in the until then clear skies that had up to then been decorated with stars and stripes. Internally, it had become clear that economic growth was not great enough to close the gap between the "mainstream" and the "underdogs." Unemployment, underemployment, and poverty were recognized as structural trends. Racial discrimination was continuing and, more seriously, a black mass movement was spreading under the theme of civil rights. People started new fights for freedom and life. Class struggle was intensifying.

These hidden dangers in American society were more than failures of the for-export model of economic achievement through corporate capitalism. They were potential sources of social disruption, individual violence, political challenge, and autonomous mass organizations. After talking about crime and thinking about political and social stability, one fraction of the ruling class conceived a vast project of institutional reform and social integration in order to improve the productivity of the system through a massive expansion of education and research, and to develop new channels of integration through a program of social organization and public welfare. This could be done fairly easily because at this time the challenges to the political and ideological hegemony of monopoly capital, while potentially powerful, were scattered and hardly politically conscious. Internally, the labor movement had been repressed, purged, controlled, and, finally, integrated. The leftists had been persecuted, and the liberals had been disorganized and coopted individually by the Establishment. Externally, peaceful coexistence had been accepted, and the empire seemed to be under control after the successful intervention in 1954 in Guatemala and in 1958 in Lebanon. There were some difficulties in the 1960 election, but the fraction of the ruling class organized around Kennedy did win the political battle against short-sighted conservatism. Subsequently, under pressure from the grassroots, a series of reformist policies were put into effect, directed at rationalizing and stabilizing the uneven capitalist development of the United States. Kennedy's New Frontier policies and Johnson's Great Society programs were backed by a much more active state.[10] The pro-Keynesian coalition finally assumed the hegemony of the state apparatus. Under its rule U.S. corporations spread all over the world, especially in Western Europe, and economic growth reached the highest level of the postwar period. Economically and technologically this offensive was a complete success from the point of view of corporate capital. Advances in productivity allowed U.S. corporations to gain control of the world economy. However, this move led to the contradictions we have analyzed, which have surfaced again in the current economic crisis, particularly creeping inflation and its effect on the international monetary system.

The most important shortcoming of this strategy was not economic, but political and social. The international social order began to deteriorate rapidly. Cuba successfully resisted U.S. intervention, and this example encouraged other antiimperialistic revolts in Latin America. Liberation movements grew stronger in the Third World, while Western Europe became more economically challenging and politically independent. China entered the nuclear club. The Soviet Union was able to develop enough military power to make excessively costly any direct attack from the United States: the "terror equilibrium" was reached. But, above all, the Vietnam War, considered a crucial test of the ability to restore order over the empire, became a military and political catastrophe.[11]

Also, the programs designed to improve social integration in American society became a major cause of social disruption.[12] The dramatic expansion of educational programs combined with the ideological breakdown of conservatism and the effects of the Vietnam War resulted in unprecedented unrest on the campuses that threatened the core of the apparatus for the production of knowledge and reproduction of social legitimacy.[13]

More important, however, the poverty programs and the community-action programs designed to integrate blacks and the poor clearly failed in their purpose.[14] On the contrary, the grass-roots movements subverted most of the agencies and resources and used them to put pressure on the local authorities to strengthen their organizations. The black movement expanded through partially spontaneous revolts in the ghettos.[15] The welfare-rights movement,[16] the tenants movement,[17] and the health-care movement[18] spread their influence and transformed what had been presented as a big American family into a permanent source of turmoil.

Even if "needs" were no greater than in the past, demands and social expectations skyrocketed. Obviously, the problem was not that the people wanted too much, but that the ruling elite had tried to provide a limited amount of social reform without altering the major mechanisms that caused inequality, poverty, and discrimination. The urban programs of the Great Society did not really change the material conditions of the "bottom society." Indeed, by opening some channels of organization and mobilization and thereby legitimizing the protests, these "urban programs" accelerated, instead of integrating, the revolt.

In 1968 the ruling class in the United States found itself in a very serious situation. Internationally, the Vietnam War was rapidly becoming a military catastrophe after the Tet offensive by the National Liberation Front. New upheavals of class struggle and student revolts were under way in Western Europe and Japan. The Soviet Union considered itself strong enough to reestablish control over its own empire by invading Czechoslovakia. Above all, the international monetary crisis had begun to reveal the deterioration of the economic mechanisms that had insured world hegemony for the United States.

Internally, the social order was continuously threatened by waves of ghetto revolts during the summer of 1967. The mass response by blacks to Martin Luther King's assassination in 1968 profoundly impressed the ruling class. Furthermore, a political challenge was emerging from the student movement, which was building up a nationwide organization, and from the Black Panthers and other black radical groups, which were in a process of renewal and reinforcement. Clearly, a major realignment and a tough policy were needed to restore world hegemony and control the internal social unrest.

Three options were theoretically possible to deal with the structural contradictions and conjunctural problems.[19]

The first strategy was to continue the existing pattern, centered on the so-called warfare-welfare state, with some modification, but principally to increase repression and exercise stricter control over institutions of social reform, which essentially was the only policy of the majority of the Democratic party.[20]

The second strategy, which was backed by the left of the Democratic party and by the progressive sectors of labor, was to implement some major structural social reforms in the direction previously followed by European social democracies. This strategy had a major obstacle to overcome—the strong opposition of corporate interests. They worked hard to avoid the establishment in the United States of a welfare state of the European type, with its costly burden of social services and its effect of improving the bargaining position of labor through the development of social security. In fact, the mere possibility of this happening reinforced the mobilization of the corporate interests in favor of the third strategy.

The remaining strategy was to reverse completely the policies followed during the sixties, especially in domestic social affairs and international economic policies. This included dismantling the social programs, energetically repressing mass revolts and radical movements, restoring labor discipline, fighting inflation, defending the empire, and reestablishing world hegemony, economically and politically. The magnitude of the political rectifications necessary to implement this strategy was so potentially dramatic that the political ruling class did not accept them entirely, and the 1968 election was hotly contested. Nevertheless, this strategy won, and Nixon came to power to implement it.

The program had two stages. In the first one, three major axes were emphasized: enforcing law and order; reorganizing the defense line in foreign policy, to try and disengage American troops and develop the autonomy of dependent capitalist states with a less costly and more sophisticated method of keeping control; and reversing the international monetary crisis by deevaluating the dollar and opening a commercial war with Europe and Japan.

The second stage was designed to dismantle the social programs, especially the federally funded, locally based institutions that had become the organizational base of social reform and the political tool of the reformist wing of the ruling class. This policy was not just negative, it was also preparation for a new pattern of accumulation. In fact, the corporate interests could no longer afford the luxury of integrating people and absorbing the surplus population. The uneven development at the world scale had to be recognized, the social unrest controlled, and the political challenge repressed. However, in order to switch from the Great Society to this new puritan repressive model, major changes had to be made not only in the policies but also in the political system and in the machinery of the state. Nixon was able to begin using this strategy after his huge victory over the reformist coalition around McGovern in 1972, which clearly demonstrated that not only the corporate interests but the ideologically mobilized "middle classes" also had been convinced that new authority must be restored in the name of capitalist domination.

The application of this political strategy implied dismantling federal agencies and bypassing Congress and the political parties, including the Republicans, in order to build up a new concentrated and uncontrolled apparatus directly linked to the executive. This highly concentrated leadership would be supported by a "silent majority" manipulated ideologically through mobilization "against" the enemies of the "system" assimilating all possible opposition to an almost criminal violent unrest.

These strategies led to many conflicts during and after the 1972 election. Once this apparatus was built, it tried to destroy not only the external but also the internal enemies who were an obstacle in its path toward total autonomy from the system of institutional representation. The methods designed to repress the "outside world" and the American radical movements eventually were used against opponents within the ruling class. It was in this sense that Nixon broke the rules of the game. Although the situation was serious, it was not threatening enough to justify the "state of emergency" in the institutions of the American state.[21]

Watergate was a symbol of a dangerous tendency to break away from the formal and informal institutional rules of political behavior within the ruling class. Power was concentrated more and more in the hands of a small group of Nixon's personal advisors.[22] Despite the actual achievements of the Nixon policies on behalf of the ruling class, the use by the political elite of the same methods against the Democrats that were being used against the blacks and radicals was found to be unacceptable. It appeared that Nixon was using his personal power *dangerously*, and the existing problems were not serious enough to require such action.

The political leaders of the ruling class decided to discipline Nixon. When he resisted by cover-up and sharpened the opposition by firing the institutions' legitimate appointees in the Saturday Night Massacre, they decided to sacrifice Nixon in order to preserve the legitimacy of the whole system. For this purpose, the ruling class used its absolute weapon: the mass media. After this step was taken, Nixon's resistance served only to prolong his agony. In fact, the ruling class could do this without regret because Nixon's policies had been successful in fulfilling nearly all their requirements. Order had been restored, the black movement had been largely repressed or coopted, the student movement had largely disappeared, the European countries had been recalled to solidarity within the system, Latin America was pretty much under control, and all serious internal political challenges had been dispersed after McGovern's defeat. The serious problems now were the increasing economic difficulties and the fact that some of the Nixon political strategies were creating turmoil and fear within the ranks of the political institutions at a time when unity and confidence were necessary.

Therefore, the ruling class decided that a "good guy" was needed. They fired the bad guys, Agnew first, then Nixon, and appointed a "good guy." The mechanisms were cleaned up, the legitimacy of the system was restored, the belief of the American people in their democratic institutions was strengthened. Nevertheless, the process did reveal a danger for the ideological roots of political domination in the United States. Once people learn to distrust their leaders, even though they trust the system, they may no longer believe in the arguments they have been offered by those in control of the political process.

The Watergate crisis showed the contradictions implicit in all processes of political repression. The Great Society programs were an example of the limits of social reform. To legitimize change and to organize people for it without making the structural changes required for the reform to really work led to extreme pressure on the process from the grassroots. But giving almost full powers to a president, Nixon in this case, in order to restore order and reestablish the capitalist interests over the grassroots movements and the rebellion of the world's people led to a process of concentration of power that finally threatened the political ruling class itself. This very serious crisis of the American political system created a situation of extreme weakness and confusion in the American state in 1973-1974. And this situation occurred at the same time that the economic crisis was raging, the Vietnam War was being lost, and the Middle East tinderbox was threatening to explode. Thus, the attempt to develop policies to handle the economic and social contradictions linked to the particular patterns of U.S. capitalist development caused a new set of contradictions at the political level. The American government was almost paralyzed by its internal contradictions at a decisive time. To some extent, the slowness of the reactions to the economic crisis can be explained by the time required for the recovery of a highly destabilized political system.

Although some people stress the remarkable stability of a system that can survive such a continuous series of deep contradictions, there is no mystery. It is impossible to have a political vacuum in any society. All systems can survive, in spite of their weaknesses, as long as there is no concrete political alternative. In this sense, the Nixon policies, by repressing, disorganizing, and delegitimizing the emerging leftist alternative, had done their job well. However, by developing additional conflicts on a higher level and delegitimizing the ruling political elites, the Watergate crisis undermined in the long term the political hegemony of the U.S. ruling class. And this happened at a decisive time when new policies had to be implemented to deal with a major structural crisis.

3. ECONOMIC POLICIES: CONJUNCTURAL OR STRUCTURAL?

To handle the problems presented by the crisis, it is necessary to try to stop inflation and avoid stagnation, reduce unemployment and stimulate new demand simultaneously. It soon became evident that both problems could not be solved at the same time *within the established economic parameters*. If all policies had to be compatible at least formally, it would appear that the most dramatic choice was selecting the top priority. Without this initial choice it would be impossible to set up any coherent program of measures to alleviate the crisis. In this sense, the evidence seems to indicate that the most important priority for corporate interests was to fight inflation. The threat of financial collapse coming from the astronomical self-cumulative debt, combined with spiraling prices and their impact on costs, was warming up an already overheated economy, pushing up wages, spreading instability, and causing a lack of confidence in investment, credit, and anticipated consumption.

The major requirement set by corporate capital was to clean up the economy by reducing costs and debts (mostly public), freezing wages, and preventing the undue escalation of prices in order to restore a minimum level of performance and planned investment. The policies followed by President Ford in 1974 and 1975 were conceived within these priorities. They were aimed at controlling inflation, but they were also intended to keep the economy working in the sectors profitable for monopoly capital. To have this effect, the Ford strategy combined several initiatives and lack of initiatives.[23]

The most important step was to reduce dramatically all public spending that was not profitable for monopoly capital. Otherwise, this public expenditure could have been used to reduce the disciplinary effects of the recession on labor demands. Ford vetoed several "social bills" passed by Congress in the early months of 1975. These included a housing bill, which would have provided help primarily in the middle-class market, a bill that would have provided additional public jobs to absorb part of the unemployment, one developing health-care services, and one designed to improve educational services. In addition, he severely cut all social services in the 1975 and 1976 budgets. He also tried to raise the price of food stamps (which directly affected the poor and the elderly) and tried to prevent an increase in social-security payments. However, he maintained the high level of public spending directly required by monopoly capital and the political interests of U.S. hegemony, which was essentially military expenditures.

Also, the government had to reestablish the U.S. balance of payments in order to recover control of the international mechanisms favoring U.S. capital expansion. To do this without hurting Europe (whose delicate situation had to be considered in order not to worsen the world crisis), two major mechanisms were intended to be used: a high price for oil, by proposing to tax imported oil and decontrolling the price for domestic oil, which could reduce oil consumption because of the cost, stimulate exploration for domestic oil, and discourage the importation of foreign oil; and a massive sale of grain and other agricultural products to the Soviet Union.

These mechanisms would seem to introduce a contradiction into the policies because they are both inflationary. But, again, inflation has to be socially qualified. To generate inflation through increases in food prices resulting from the export of crops affects mostly the consumer. If the increase in food prices is not covered by increases in wages, the inflationary movement is stopped, and the people pay the difference.

The next step was essentially to freeze real wages. This was accomplished directly through the wage and job policies followed in the public sector, indirectly through the reduction in money supply, credit, and public spending. The government also asked private firms to follow its example, that is, to reduce costs as much as possible and shift as much as possible of the burden to the workers.

Next, tax rebates to individuals were used to stimulate the

economy. This mechanism of giving money back to the people in the hope of stimulating demand and restarting the economy does not have the effect of increasing demand but of changing its character. Instead of spending public money through social services, the state cuts its own spending and gives the money back to the individual. It is hoped that the money will be spent to buy goods produced by private business at the cost of public jobs and services.

To manipulate public opinion, economic recovery was repeatedly announced while the recession was being deliberately maintained. The Ford strategy was clearly designed to restore social order, keep inflation under control, and maintain a high rate of unemployment for an extended time. This would help further reduce wages and increase the rate of profit; at the same time, it would stop the upward spiral of prices and wages by stabilizing the economy at a high level of prices and a low level of wages.

This policy was challenged by other fractions of the political elite in the Democratic party (and the populist left). These groups prefer to use a "fine tuning" of Keynesian policies to stimulate the economy through the provision of public jobs and services, controlling inflation through price controls (especially on oil and food) and cuts in the federal budget. This opposition to the conjunctural policies for dealing with the crisis was at the center of the continuous struggle between Ford and the Democratic Congress. Ford was forced to negotiate a series of measures (such as the tax on imported oil) with Congress. However, the division in the Democratic party gave him a great advantage.

In fact, these are two opposing policies within the accepted parameters of the capitalist system that can be used to overcome the crisis and preserve corporate interests. One uses the recession to restore profit and control inflation; the other tries to find ways out of the recession by stimulating public spending and economic intervention, fighting inflation, and controlling prices. One is the pure expression of monopoly capital, the other is mediated by the political needs of popular social legitimatization and by the maintenance of the alliance with organized labor.

Nevertheless, *both policies are purely conjunctural: they do not affect the major structural trends underlying the crisis*. If the crisis deepens, if it becomes evident that all attempts to restart the economy trigger new inflationary processes, if the short-term strategies are not able to solve the problems at the world level where the system operates, then a major structural reorganization will be required. The model of accumulation itself will have to be transformed. Some consciousness of this potential need began to emerge in the American ruling class. For instance, President Ford himself asserted: "We have gone through a long process at least during my time in the Congress, where we have come up with short-range solutions that have serious long-range liabilities, and they look good right now but they only complicate the problems down the road. I think that the time has come in this country to make sure we have a long-range solution so we don't go through these peaks and valleys and up and down escalation which by any standing does not help the less well-off."[24]

What are these long-range solutions? From the point of view of corporate capital, the policies that will be necessary to restabilize structurally the model of accumulation will have to enhance the rate of profit, provide opportunities for its realization (markets), and be able to do this without introducing mechanisms that will generate inflation.

There is only one way to do all this *under these particular historical circumstances without altering the structure of capital*, and that is by increasing dramatically the amount of surplus value under the same conditions of production. This means substantially increasing the rate of exploitation by an absolute and relative reduction of wages, an increase in productivity, and a reduction in corporate taxes. To achieve this end, capital will have to discipline labor by maintaining a high level of unemployment, by eliminating channels for the absorption of surplus population, and by reducing social services. Reducing social services means a reduction in jobs and in the distribution of the social product to the workers through indirect wages. It makes unemployment and underemployment harder because of the lack of an adequate welfare system and forces workers to accept lower wages and less desirable working conditions.

This strategy is directed not only at the traditional working class but also at the new working class, which consists mostly of service workers. The rationalization of the service sector, which will require reduced employment, an increase in the division of labor, and an increase in the amount of work performed by each worker, is one of the main targets in the reorganization of the economy as foreseen by corporate capital.

This strategy has two complementary goals: to increase exploitation by exporting more capital to other countries where these conditions of exploitation can be met; and to increase exploitation of American workers by dramatically changing the power relationship in favor of capital.

At the level of pure economic coherence, this policy has an internal contradiction. The dramatic increase in the rate of exploitation will considerably reduce the workers' demand for goods. While this outcome reduces inflation, it will also endanger the realization of profit through the selling of commodities. That is why *this strategy is inseparable from the expansion of outlets at the international level.* The restoration of the rate of profit through increased exploitation implies, then, a new acceleration of the process of internationalization of American capitalism, both at the level of the productive process and at the level of the market.

This strategy is not yet clear in U.S. policies except for the deliberately maintained high level of unemployment. But these are mostly conjunctural policies of austerity that have to be dramatically developed in order to affect structurally the overall rate of exploitation. Nevertheless, an attempt to perfect that strategy is expressed by the austerity policy implemented in New York City, under the direct control of international financial capital, to solve the fiscal crisis, which was directly provoked by the combined action of the financial markets, the Ford administration, and the New York State Assembly controlled by the GOP. This case is the clearest example of what could be a systematic policy to restore exploitation: massive layoffs, drastic reduction of services, increasing public rates, wage freezes, less hiring, rationalization of services, acceleration of workloads, attacks on the unions, and repression of the militants. Disciplining New York City will be like gaining a foothold in the hard battle capital is preparing against labor.

Nevertheless, this strategy could cause serious problems for capital. It implies a major defeat of the U.S. labor movement, which may threaten the social peace gained through years of economic bargaining and ideological consensus. Also, it would mean that social unrest caused by unemployment, minorities, welfare recipients, urban consumers, and so on would have to be kept under control. The extent of social unrest and political conflict will be the factor that will decide if this structural strategy will be feasible or not in the United States in the coming years. We will discuss some of the implications in our analysis of the relationship between economic policies and the political process.

If the crisis continues and this strategy becomes impossible because of massive popular opposition, an alternative structural reform will become necessary, one that does not depend on increases in absolute exploitation. The alternative then would be to increase the productivity of the system by using the expansion of human services as human capital investment in a strategy that has become known as the building of the social-industrial complex. This strategy would not imply a new increase in the organic composition of capital: by increasing the productivity and capability of human labor, it would create additional value, thus restoring the rate of profit in the long term without increasing the absolute rate of exploitation and without harming people's living and working conditions. The obstacle to this policy is that even if it is a capitalist reform, it would imply a reduction in the rate of profit for the corporations in the short term in order to finance the huge public investments required in a noninflationary way, through taxation of corporate profits and, perhaps, some public enterprises. This policy of developing productivity in the human services certainly would require some kind of planning. In fact, it would seem that some form of centralized capitalist planning is absolutely necessary in all of the policies directed at major structural changes in the pattern of accumulation.[25]

What is decisive in the tentative analysis we have developed is the major distinction between conjunctural and structural policies, on the one hand, and policies of austerity and repression (directly linked to capital) and reform and integration (mediated politically by the capitalist reformist forces), on the other. On the basis of these distinctions we have composed a typology of possible policies for the crisis.

| | | Scope of Intervention | |
		Conjunctural	Structural
Policy's *Orientation*	Austerity and repression	Antiinflationary measures through reduction of public services	Overexploitation
	Reform and integration	Neo-Keynesian policies: controlled public spending	Social reform and increasing productivity

Which policy will be implemented will depend essentially on the evolution of the crisis at the international level and on the domestic development of class struggle and political conflicts.

4. ROOTS OF WAR AND BRANCHES OF PEACE: POLICIES FOR THE CRISIS AND AMERICAN FOREIGN POLICY

The economic crisis is worldwide. So is the scope of American policies. That is why the development of the crisis in the United States and its political impact directly concern all people in the world. In this sense, a new situation has been created for U.S. foreign policy because new arrangements are required by the world capitalist economy in the aftermath of the Vietnam War and in the middle of a major economic crisis.

This situation is characterized by the need to find conjunctural and structural solutions to a set of interrelated problems, old and new. The basic problems are:

1. *To reestablish U.S. world political and military hegemony*, which is the basis for reproducing the social relationships that make possible the smooth functioning and adjustment of the requirements of capital, both at the economic level and as a historical social order. This problem has become very serious since the major defeat in Indochina and because of the increasing number of antiimperialist movements in Africa, Asia, and the Middle East and the shift toward the left in Western Europe.

2. *To stabilize the level and conditions of the supply of basic raw materials*, especially sources of energy, oil in the short term, nuclear power (uranium) in the future. This means overcoming

the challenge presented by the OPEC countries and the threat of an increasingly united front of raw-material producers throughout the world.

3. *To stabilize the international circulation of capital*, in terms of financial markets and the international monetary system.

4. *To introduce and emphasize mechanisms of internationalization of capital* that would help overcome the major problems of U.S. corporate interests, reverse the falling rate of profit, and ease the process of realization. New means will be used to expand exploitation at the international level and develop new markets for U.S. based commodities.

To handle these major problems, several initiatives have been taken. More will be taken, some of them relative to the present crisis, others directed at the structural pattern of world accumulation of capital. All these policies are taking into consideration the fact that the *United States can no longer afford to pay the cost, economically or politically, of a new revolutionary war of the Vietnam type.** This is explicit in the statements of U.S. political and military leaders. The decisive role played by the Vietnam War in making the crisis much more severe could explain why. However, this fact, which is fundamental for our understanding of this new period of U.S. foreign policy, could have two opposite effects. One could lead toward war, and the other could lead to an improvement in peace. What happens will depend on a complex set of circumstances, which we will try to outline.

The application of this problem-solving strategy to the situation as described will determine several *conjunctural* policies. One would be *to reestablish U.S. security in some areas of the world where there is a great deal of tension*, such as the Middle East, the Mediterranean, and Africa. The new policy, which has been devised since Vietnam, is to show the determination of the United States to forestall any major moves that could lead to a new disintegration of the empire. A second policy would be *to control the supply and price of oil for the United States and Western Europe* because the oil crisis could be very damaging to the whole system. This has become a top priority, because of the increasing tendency of the United States and other advanced

---

* The experiences in Angola and Nicaragua clearly support this statement.

capitalist countries to become more dependent on imported oil. Several measures have been designed to counteract this tendency: *for the long term*, to increase the production of domestic oil, to explore for new oil fields in the more "secure" zones, especially in Alaska and the North Atlantic, and to develop alternative energy sources, especially nuclear power; *for the short term*, to negotiate with the OPEC countries to avoid sudden increases in oil prices. This implies maintaining political support to Israel, but moderating Israeli expansionism to keep the status quo in the Middle East and using all possible means to obtain an alliance with the moderate Arab states. These objectives could lead to a peaceful settlement, but there are two potential obstacles: the Palestinians might react strongly against any attempt to stall their liberation struggle; and Israel could launch a new war to avoid increasing political isolation. If either of these developments occur, we could not exclude the possibility of U.S. intervention to occupy the oil fields to prevent any new use of oil by the Arabs. But this would not happen unless the United States finds itself in an almost desperate situation.

A third conjunctural measure would be *to stabilize the international monetary system* in order to stop the deterioration of the dollar and reestablish its stability in the financial markets. To do this, three major initiatives will probably have to be taken: stabilizing the Special Drawing Rights as the reserve currency, which implies negotiations with the Common Market and Japan; using petrodollars in a plan of controlled investments, which reinforces the perspective of a closer relationship with the Arabs; reestablishing equilibrium in the balance of payments by taxing imported oil and inaugurating a massive development of U.S. exports, like the huge sale of grain to the Soviet Union, which would be done even though both measures are inflationary.

If we take into consideration the relationship between the required *structural* economic policies and their implications for foreign policy, we observe the following. *The tendency to increase the rate of exploitation will accelerate and extend the flow of capital toward more profitable areas.* There will be increasing activity in Western Europe. The countries of the new developing periphery (Mexico, Brazil, Iran, Malaysia, Taiwan, Korea) will be industrialized but will still have to develop a more complex technological environment in order to be real alternatives for the transnationals. It is important to consider the *timing* of this trend. It will begin only after a recovery in the European and American economies, which will provide new markets for the products manufactured under the advantageous conditions of the new international division of labor.

One major consequence of this trend for U.S. foreign policy will be an increasing interdependence of U.S. capital and Western European economies through the transnational corporations. In this sense, the "isolationist" syndrome of the United States is purely ideological. Western Europe becomes more and more the lung of the United States and the United States more and more the nerve center of Western European capitalism. Since European societies are largely autonomous at the political level, this does not imply dependence but interdependence. In any case, American and European social and political evolution will be increasingly related. Another trend in the overexploited dependent societies will be increasing internal differentiation between the countries committed to the new peripheral industrialization and the countries used mostly as reservoirs of raw materials and agricultural products, the former becoming potentially subcenters of the dominant system. The relationship of this evolution to U.S. foreign policy is twofold. For the countries that will become subcenters of the system, the relationship will be increasingly closer in all dimensions; for the peripheral countries, domination will be exercised mostly in terms of political control over the empire.

The second major structural trend in the development of U.S. capitalism at the international level is the absolute need of the system to expand its potential outlets, especially to compensate for the decrease in demand caused by the austerity policies developed in the advanced capitalist countries to overexploit the workers. However, the problem is where to find new markets willing and able to absorb the commodities of the capitalist corporations.

Of course, the industrialization of the countries on the periphery will provide some outlets because new equipment will be required and new demands will be generated. This trend will reinforce the interdependence already created within the new "core" of the periphery countries in terms of industrial investment. On the other hand, the most important future expanding market would seem to be the socialist countries, especially the Soviet

Union. The implications of this major trend are obvious. The economic foundations will require peaceful coexistence and the progressive relaxation of the tension between the two blocs.

This transformation of the requirements of the system at the political level is expressed and therefore reinforced by the attitudes of Americans and of the American elite toward U.S. foreign policy. An important public opinion survey of a national sample carried out in December 1974 by the prestigious Chicago Council on Foreign Relations gives us some significant insights into these attitudes.[26] The "public" and a national sample of "leaders" representing the top elite in politics, business circles, the mass media, and academic and scientific institutions were surveyed separately. On the basis of the findings of this study, several points should be emphasized.

1. There is a moderate trend toward avoiding deep involvement in international affairs. This reaction seems to have been caused by the Vietnam War, which traumatized Americans and many of their leaders. In December 1974, 87 percent of the leaders were opposed to any new involvement in Vietnam despite the fact that there was a direct threat to Saigon. The attitude of Congress in the spring of 1975 confirmed this pattern, which helped to accelerate the liberation of Indochina.

2. The attitudes of the leaders are particularly revealing with respect to the shift in the emphasis on particular regions. Clearly, good relations with Western Europe, Japan, and the Soviet Union are valued strongly. There is less interest in the traditional zones under the influence of imperialism. Also, the leaders are less opposed than the "public" to intervening militarily in Europe and more opposed to doing it in other areas.

3. Finally, there is a great deal of resistance to any new military involvement, even in a "dramatic" situation, and a great deal of reluctance to support CIA activities, especially among the leaders.

Certainly, it is not "public" opinion that makes foreign policy in the United States, as the people who were interviewed knew, but these data are significant for three reasons: because the survey was made during a period when the President was searching for new legitimacy and could not totally ignore public opinion; because public opinion largely reflects the ideological patterns of the mass media, which express the major orientations of ruling elites; and because the attitudes of the "leaders" reflect greater awareness than those of the "public" and resemble closely the structural trends we have outlined concerning the international needs of the system and their implications for foreign policy.

Most of the trends we have outlined point quite clearly toward a reinforcement of peaceful coexistence in spite of the defeat in Vietnam or, perhaps, because of it. Some of the factors leading toward an increasing internatonial detente are the internal economic difficulties, the danger of massive social unrest in case of another war, the opposition of most Americans to new foreign involvement, the necessity of negotiating with the countries that produce oil and raw materials, the interdependence with Western Europe, and the need to develop new markets in the socialist countries. This trend was clearly shown in the 1975 European peace conference in Helsinki and in the agreement signed there and followed up in 1977 in Belgrade.

In this sense, *the economic crisis does not lead to war but to the strengthening of peace.* Some of the analyses linking the "economic catastrophes" to war are totally outdated. We are not in 1933, the crisis is different, and so are the international power relationships. U.S. capitalism will try to overcome its difficulties along the lines we have described, and to carry out these recovery plans, it *needs* detente.

Nevertheless, we must take into consideration two other trends that are pushing in the opposite direction—toward an increase in tension and the danger of war.

1. The military-industrial complex in the U.S. economy requires some tension to justify the arms race. But this does not seem to be a decisive factor since the development of military expenditures can be made intensively rather than extensively, that is, through increasing the potential for destruction by replacing obsolete weapons. The arms race can be integrated as an element of a stabilized "terror equilibrium." Also, the sale of arms to belligerent Third World countries will increase.[27]

2. Even more important is the fact that the United States has suffered several major defeats in the last few years, and with economic and political weakness increasing within the system, it cannot afford any further deterioration of its position. The violent

reaction against the Portuguese revolution was a clear example of this need to protect its position, as the concern over the developments in France, and Italy.

Thus, the dominant trend will be toward peace as long as there are no new major assaults that threaten the increasingly fragile position of world capitalism. However, even though the status quo can be accepted by the socialist countries, it is less clear whether the Left in Europe and the liberation movements in Asia, Africa, and Latin America will accept a permanent situation of exploitation and oppression.

How is the United States going to handle the contradictions between the economic and political impossibility of new military involvement and the need to reestablish world hegemony in its search for new markets for monopoly capital? One possible solution is to increase the level of indirect intervention through the initiative of allied dependent states, through alliances with internal political forces in different countries, and through "CIA-type" operations. There seems to be significant evidence that this type of operation is currently being developed. Military action might be considered in case of a serious defeat, but it would not be likely to be of the Vietnam War type. The new strategy of the Pentagon would probably be to use the technological superiority of U.S. weapons as a method of intimidation. The first clear expression of this trend was a series of successive statements in 1975 by the then Secretary of Defense Schlesinger: that the United States would use nuclear weapons against North Korea in case of an "invasion" of the South, that the United States was developing new tactical nuclear weapons to use against limited targets within a particular area, and that the United States, if a dangerous situation warranted it, would initiate the use of nuclear weapons against "the enemy" (namely, the Soviet Union).

These statements were considered unnecessarily strong, and Schlesinger was ousted some months later. Nevertheless, although Carter's public discourses have been far more conciliatory, military policy continues to move along the same path. The decision to develop the neutron bomb dramatically illustrates this tendency: production of "clean" nuclear weapons (that is, weapons that "only" kill people) is the first step toward the possibility of actually using them.

The dramatic increase in defense expenditures in 1974-1977

and the general support of the political establishment for a "tough" new international policy lead to the conclusion that detente within the status quo is inseparable from a more aggressive and uneasy military policy in the case of a serious emergency. This means that the margin between the edge separating the liberation of the world's peoples and a local nuclear war becomes increasingly narrow.

5. FROM CRISIS TO CONFLICT: CLASS STRUGGLE, POLITICS, AND POLICIES

People make their own history, but they do so within the framework of given social conditions. We have outlined the major structural determinants that characterize the economic crisis of the seventies as well as the historical specificity of U.S. society. But the evolution of the crisis and its impact on the American people (and, hence, on the people in the rest of the world) will depend on the dynamics of the class struggle and its expression at the political level.

Unfortunately, we cannot fully develop such an analysis here. But we can show what the implications of the trends outlined are for the economic crisis and for the class struggle in respect to the political process. We will adopt again a highly schematic style to emphasize and make clear the main points.

The political consequences of the current crisis will develop through the interaction of its effects on two related levels of the social process: on the one hand, the economic class struggle and grassroots mobilization; on the other, the mediation of social protest and structurally dominant interests by the political system.

5.1. THE CRISIS AND THE GRASSROOTS

Perhaps the major problem in managing the crisis with a policy based on imposing sustained economic austerity will be how to control potential social unrest with an actual rate of unemployment of 8 percent and at the same time reduce the level of wages and social services. One of the "mysteries" that constantly intrigues observers is the relative calm of the unemployed, the absence of mass riots in the ghettos, and the absence of major working-class struggles even when there are massive layoffs and wages are frozen. How has the system managed to keep the social unrest under control for such a long time?

The contracts signed in 1975, the worst period of the crisis, represented a significant defeat for most workers. They oscillated between a 5- and a 10-percent increase, which means real wages fell because of the increases in consumer prices. The average wage earner in 1975 was 6.5 percent below the peak level reached in October 1972 in real take-home pay. Willie Usery, chief federal mediator of the Department of Labor coming back to Washington from an international conference on industrial relations in Paris in June 1975, declared: "There is much more discord around the world than we have here. Our system's flexibility is once again proving to be a tremendous national asset."[28] U.S. capital was obviously very happy about the fact that railroad and airline workers had accepted voluntary wage reductions, that police officers in Detroit had agreed to take fourteen days off in unpaid vacation, and that workers trying to strike had suffered major defeats at the McDonald Douglas Aircraft plant.

Why this pattern? Because the discontent among workers—and it did exist in 1975—did not lead to mass action and protest because of the lack of consciousness and organization, which are closely linked. The unions, including the AFL-CIO, represent a minority of the working class. They must handle their leadership carefully so that they can preserve the system of industrial relations because they are closely tied to corporate capital. The control of union leadership on the workers has become so relaxed after increasing militancy in the rank and file that any attempt to radicalize and centralize the protest against economic policies could have led to a situation similar to what triggered the emergence of the CIO in the thirties. An example of this situation was the leaders' disregard of the symbolic march on Washington on April 26, 1975. Tens of thousands of workers had come from all over the country and gathered in the J. F. Kennedy Stadium at the invitation of the AFL-CIO. However, the workers interrupted the speeches of the leaders by shouting their own slogans and finally walked out of the stadium and marched through the streets of Washington. After this demonstration, the unions decided not to call any more national mass meetings. Thus, workers, lacking any kind of organized centralized initiative, could only voice their discontent without being able to translate it into mass action. In the absence of any serious challenge to the leadership of the conservative officials, the American workers watched their position deteriorate little by little without much significant collective reaction, with the exception of the public workers and the coal miners. It remains to be seen whether the factory-level unions will continue to follow the general pattern of the top officials of AFL-CIO or will be able to develop an opposition front to the most reactionary policies if the crisis worsens and the austerity policies become tougher.

But what about the unemployed? Why do they not react? Several myths have been used to account for their inaction. One is that because of unemployment insurance (three-fourths of the officially unemployed are covered) no one is really suffering from hard times. It is true that the existence of some level of unemployment compensation for the majority of workers does create a situation different from that of the 1930s. However, this compensation only lasts for fifty-two weeks. This is the reason Congress voted supplementary funds to extend unemployment benefits. Also, some families have two wage earners, and others take part-time work. Yet a careful analysis by Eileen Shanahan of the data from a survey of the U.S. Department of Labor on the situation of the unemployed seriously questions the apparent tranquillity of the currently unemployed. After reviewing the different arguments in the light of the data collected by the survey, she concluded: "In sum, what the available statistics show is that the calm in the nation in the face of high unemployment cannot be explained on the grounds that most of the unemployed are not suffering any serious deprivations. Compared to their former standards of living, most of the unemployed certainly are suffering, even if they are not hungry or out in the street."[29]

The economistic interpretation is not valid. Clearly, the reasons for the "calm" of Americans in the face of the crisis is not to be found in the fact that "things are not so bad," but in the capacity of the system to develop mechanisms of social control, integration, and repression.

The stand taken by the union leadership appears decisive for the majority of workers. For instance, the spontaneous reaction of the rank-and-file members of the New York municipal unions was to strike against the layoffs. However, their isolation from other unions weakened their position, and the union leaders negotiated "realistic" agreements. One of these realistic agreements was to pay from the union treasury part of the wages of the workers if the city was not successful in its economic initiatives. Also, the mechanisms that fragment and divide the workers, which we have previously described, are actively at work. To be sure, the localistic and fragmented approach to the crisis could be defeated if there were a large coordinated initiative. However, this has been prevented by the cooptation and repression of the potential leaders.

The paradox is even more striking in the ghettos. Why is it that these "volatile zones" where there is an unemployment rate as high as 70 percent among the youth do not become sources of revolt? The *New York Times* consulted several informed experts on the subject in August 1975, and three major themes appeared.

1. Police repression is brutal and effective. Massive expenditures on weapons, manpower, and training during the Nixon administration produced a real change. Blacks know that any attempt to revolt could lead to a massacre, and they have learned to appreciate this power relationship since the political impasse in the aftermath of the 1967-1968 riots. The indoctrination and training of "special police" forces in addition to the regular police trained in riot control are a major threat to any community that might wish to express massive discontent in the future. Ben Holman, director of the Community Relations Service of the Department of Justice, stated that he was disturbed by the attitude of some police officials, which he described as: "We are ready for them, so let them come." An observer, far from being a radical, has written: "The police have been ready for five years, but they are ready for the wrong thing." A civil rights figure commented: "Not only that, blacks are not stupid. We know that they are ready with their tanks and bazookas, so blacks are not about to go up against them."

2. There is an absence of any immediate political perspective for blacks and the poor because their linkage to radical and militant groups has nearly disappeared. The grassroots-organized groups know now that the violent mass revolts in the ghettos led to disorganization when they could not be pushed forward at the political level. Although community groups are expanding and the political foundations for a mass movement are being established, there is still little communication between the active polit-

ical groups and the increasingly angry masses of the inner cities.

3. This leads to what seems to be the most important mechanism of control and channeling of spontaneous revolt at this time: the transformation of collective protest into individual violence. The rate of "crime" has increased dramatically in the United States since the beginning of the crisis, accentuating a marked twenty-year pattern. The "gang" culture controls large areas of the inner cities. The drug industry is flourishing, particularly among inner-city dwellers. The police seem deliberately to maintain the status quo by making arrangements with the gangs in order to keep the violence within the ghettos. This channels the revolts into paths that are extremely easy to delegitimize and isolate.

Sometimes this form of individual violence expresses social protest in a much clearer way, but under the cover of unjustifiable personalized violence. One of the most revealing events happened in July 1975 in Washington, D.C. Once a year the city organizes a "Human Kindness Day," which supposedly tries to improve the quality of human relations at the interpersonal level. A crowd of 125,000 people gathered on the grounds of the Washington Monument "to be nice to each other." It turned out to be "the day of the locust": more than five hundred whites were injured by random attacks by blacks, sometimes in bands, sometimes alone. In the East New York section of Brooklyn the "Tomahawks" govern. The police know this, but it is better to keep the people in the ghetto busy with their own people. Busy? "An old man walks toward his apartment in the early afternoon, carrying a small bag of groceries. He is stopped by two youths who throw him to the ground and demand money. The old man says that he has none and begs for mercy. The youth then stomp on his legs, saying, 'You will never walk again, Whitey.' "[30]

Oppressed by persistent discrimination, overexploited or unemployed, repressed and disorganized, the ghetto minorities are given few opportunities except to blow themselves up. The economic crisis makes the situation worse. The police and the gangs close the exits, and the South Bronx continues to burn. The smog is increasingly dark over American inner cities.*

* A striking verification of this analysis was provided by the mass looting during the New York blackout in July 1977. Police arrested and sent to court almost

5.2 THE MANAGEMENT OF THE CRISIS AND THE POLITICAL PROCESS

With the grassroots largely under control, either by integration, repression, or delegitimization of protest, the political effects of the crisis in the United States *in the short term* will be expressed essentially through the institutional system. This increasing responsibility comes at a time when the two American parties are, *for very different reasons*, relatively divided and disorganized. The Republican party has not yet recovered from the catastrophe provoked by Watergate and from Nixon's maneuvers to bypass the GOP machinery. Despite several efforts to start anew by adapting the old conservatism to a new style, the Republicans survived only through their control of the presidency and the policies Ford developed in the interests of the ruling class. Nevertheless, since the party is extremely weak, some conservatives have been building up a new, more distinctly reactionary political force around the leadership of Ronald Reagan. The functioning of American institutions makes bypassing the two-party system in the presidential elections extremely hazardous. Therefore, it is highly unlikely that such an initiative will be developed outside the Republican party. In fact, the organization of a new conservative group is a symptom of the division of the Republicans and of the hesitation of the political elite in facing up to the crisis. As long as Reagan can use the Republican party, the fight will be channeled within the partisan structure.

The situation in the Democratic party is even more paradoxical. Despite the fact that the Republicans have been greatly discredited by the public, despite the Democratic victories in the Congressional elections of 1974 and the presidential election of 1976, despite Carter's renewed leadership, the Democratic party is seriously divided internally in several informal tendencies. The conservative-populist Southern wing still maintains its position around the legacy of George Wallace. The mainstream of the party is trying to rebuild a neo-Keynesian coalition supported by the business circles and the national leaders of the AFL-CIO. The reformist establishment elite decided to re-enter the battle,

---

4,000 people. In fact, for the people it was a great happening, according to most witnesses. But the local press called that night "the night of the animals."

supporting Edward Kennedy. The new populists like Jerry Brown are trying to begin new paths within the party. The social-democrats are represented by Harrington or by the Black Democratic Caucus. And even radicals like Tom Hayden and Bill Domhoff were relatively successful in their California campaign.

This division and increasing diversification of the Democratic party is not purely a matter of group interest and personal quarrels. It is caused by two major factors. After the collapse of the Republicans following Watergate, the Democrats became the most viable political instrument for almost all fractions of the ruling class, and this situation produced a rush to the party and as a consequence accentuated its internal diversity. Despite the fact that it is the party "to the left of the system," the Democratic party is a capitalist party as its *policies* clearly show. At the same time, the Democratic party has become the ambiguous expression of new social unrest that cannot express itself through any other political means.

It is important to remember that it is entirely false to say the the two American parties are exactly the same. There is a right (the Republicans) and a left (the Democrats) *in the system*. Traditionally, there is a tendency for the oppressed and exploited (including women during the sixties, after the development of the women's movement) to vote for the Democrats in larger proportions. Thus, we have a situation in which the Democratic party must speak for the electoral interests of the majority of people *and* for the ruling class at the same time that the development of the crisis has sharpened the opposition, reinforcing the differences between immediate class interests. As a consequence, the Democrats are divided and can be paralyzed by the conflicting demands from the different sectors of society.

There are also two rapidly growing populist trends, one from the left and one from the right. The trend from the left is manifested increasingly at the level of local government. This is a more accessible way to satisfy the economic interests of the grassroots in the near future. It is our hypothesis that this trend is the most likely way the mass mobilization developing in the United States will become connected to the political system. The trend from the right, composed of racist Southerners and small-business and working-class people reacting against "the big ones," is extremely dangerous and could form the basis of a fascist movement if the crisis deteriorates.

In 1975 and 1976 the conflict between the President and the Congress over the management of the crisis was based mostly on their different positions. Ford could rely mostly on direct expressions of interests by corporate capital. The Democrats, operating within the framework of those supreme interests that have to be preserved, also had to be somewhat responsive to grassroots pressure. This conflict was eased considerably by the fact that the policies being discussed were essentially conjunctural.

However, if the debate should reach the level of major structural transformation of the model of accumulation, the political lines would become openly contradictory and could produce new trends in political leadership. Actually, the political hegemony within the American ruling class will depend on the *policies* the situation will require and on the interaction between the evolution of the economic crisis and the development of social protest from the grassroots. In a highly schematic way we could present the hypothetical evolution of the relationship between the economic crisis, the class struggle, the policies implemented by the ruling class, and their translation in terms of political groups, in the following chart.

		Intensity of the Economic Crisis	
		−	+
Intensity of the class struggle	−	Conjunctural policy of economic austerity: (Ford line)	Structural policy of overexploitation: (Reagan line)
	+	Conjunctural neo-Keynesian policy: (AFL-CIO line)	Need for structural reform of the pattern of accumulation: social reform and increased productivity (Edward Kennedy line)
			↓ (Could provoke a fascist-populist reaction)

Each one of these lines was present (under the names cited) in the presidential campaign of 1976, with the major exception of Edward Kennedy. The situation did not require, at that time, a costly major structural reform. The capital of public legitimacy held by the last of the Kennedys had to be cautiously preserved in case of a political emergency, which eventually happened in 1979.

Nevertheless, interestingly enough, *the political process in 1976, showed, at the same time, its dependence on the structural alternatives we have described and its relative autonomy in relation to economic constraints.* That is, the election was won by an outsider who became a political leader by giving a major emphasis to the restoration of political and ideological hegemony of the system. The discussion over economic policies, which were a central issue, was subordinated to the basic goal of repairing the legitimacy undermined by Watergate and the continuous deterioration of living standards. The Carter campaign was in this sense a model of winning general consensus by avoiding any precise policy line and by stressing above all moral and ideological issues. It was a line of moderate populism that progressively absorbed all other elements of the Democratic party by concessions at the economic, symbolic, and institutional levels. The major point was the pact reached with organized labor, which saw most of its policies adopted by Carter; thus organized labor became once again one of the crucial supports of the new Democratic party legitimacy. In 1977 the AFL-CIO was rewarded by obtaining increasing legal facilities to organize workers. Thus, Carter's ability to restore political legitimacy among some popular sectors was combined with an emphasis on more jobs and the preservation of welfare services. It was clearly understood that a further step in the tough line adopted by Ford could lead to a mounting social protest. But, at the same time, the structural trends toward inflation still operated in the absence of any major structural change. Thus, Carter's policies combined elements of a neo-Keynesian approach, backed by labor, with cautious rectifications of the state's initiatives at the first sign of new inflationary trends. To some extent, it was the institutionalization of a "stop-and-go" economic policy. Such a policy becomes increasingly vulnerable to any sudden event that can trigger another spiraling process of inflation and recession because the structural causes are not under control. Carter's approach was electorally successful because he clearly realized that the social base for any policy dealing with the crisis was first to restore the ideological and political hegemony of American capital, seriously undermined after the economic and political failures of recent years. But by promising jobs and services to win popular support, by reorganizing the institutional channels of integration (community groups, for instance), and by directly appealing to people's consciousness, Carter was playing with fire.

People took seriously these promises and appeals. When the system will be forced to tighten its policies in the aftermath of the deepening of the latent crisis, the new ideals of morality and social concern can become obstacles for the legitimacy of the capitalist state. Thus, the contradictions triggered by the economic crisis may lead to a major transformation of American political processes, characterized by a renewed appeal to people's participation, followed by an attempt of popular control over corporate interests in the decision of public policies.

We should like to say that the process will, therefore, be increasingly shaped by people's actions and consciousness. But it would be too easy and too comfortable to conclude by this statement, forgetting the situation of repression and manipulation we have observed. Like other peoples of the world, the American people will be the makers of their own history. But the profile of such a historical practice still remains to be discovered.

■■

Twilight of American Capitalism?

T HE ECONOMIC crisis has produced profound effects on American society and has altered the social relationships that gave
rise to it. Are we at a historical turning point? Is the crisis of the
seventies the beginning of American decline, as the 1929-1933
crisis sounded the knell for the hegemony of British capital? Do
we find ourselves at the threshold of a new world? Which one?
And through what processes will it be shaped?

During these last few years many observers have insisted, as
we have done ourselves, that American hegemony has been deteriorating at the economic as well as the political level. The
growing competition of Western Europe and Japan, the deficit in
the U.S. balance of payments, the dollar crisis, the relative parity
of Soviet military power, the defeats suffered by several imperialist enterprises, the mounting resistance of oppressed
peoples all over the world, the partial loss of social control over
the American people, are all signs of a putting into question of
the absolute supremacy held by American capital and its state
since the Second World War.

Nevertheless, James Petras is apparently right to remind us:

> Rather than seeing a decline of power in the U.S., it would
> be more exact to consider the U.S. as a power that is regaining
> the surface. The periodic modifications in the relations be-
> tween capitalist countries, the relative commercial decline, the
> victory of this or that revolutionary power suggest possible
> changes, but do not indicate by themselves a weakening of the
> U.S.'s fundamental capacities. The processes by which the ap-
> parent setbacks are transformed into positive advantages, the
> defeats in reconcentration of power, and temporary com-
> promises in break-through tactics stress just to what point it is
> important to study the structures and historic relations that
> facilitate the assumption of global powers.[1]

Petras underlines several fundamental facts: the political and economic dependence on the United States of the "new rich" of the Third World, the nearly absolute control that the United States has over international economic institutions, the reestablished stability of the internal political system after the shock of Watergate, the new big-stick policy exercised with impunity with regard to Latin America, the reversal of alliances—in their favor—with the Middle Eastern countries, increased exchanges—with mutual benefit—with the socialist countries, the "big silence of the American workers' movement," the consolidation of the transnational corporations as the main power in the world economy, the relative weakening of Western Europe after the crisis. There is no doubt that in the second half of the decade American capital and the American government were regaining control, in general, of the capitalist world as a whole. Without this hegemony being inexorable, as is shown by the outcome of the liberation struggle in Angola, it seemed more clearly affirmed in 1979 than at the moment of the triggering of the economic crisis in 1974.

What, then, can one conclude? Is this merely an episode without major historical consequences? Is this or is this not the first stage in the decline of the American empire?

Actually, the question thus formulated simplifies to the extreme a much more complex reality. This question can be the object of various interpretations, therefore giving rise to several answers concerning the nature of historical evolution.

One possible interpretation is that U.S. hegemony might be replaced by that of another power within the capitalist system. On this point we must be clear: the capitalist system, as it is now constituted on the world level, can only exist if it is centered in the United States—on both the political and the economic levels. Economically, the concentration of capital and management has taken place at the world level through the transnational corporations. These, as we know, are for the most part based on American capital. And even when, legally or economically, they have other origins, such as Germany, England, Switzerland, or France, they are completely interdependent. At the heart of the network the financial gears, the research units, and the decisionmaking processes are centralized in the United States. In this sense, the European economy is strongly dominated by the American-based transnational firms. Moreover, in an economy internationalized to such a degree, what is the meaning of "being American"? If it refers to the social networks of training and decisionmaking, these are concentrated more and more in the United States or in institutions elsewhere built on the same principles as American institutions. If it concerns the circulation of capital, production, markets, and labor, these are fragmented and interconnected more and more on a worldwide level. In a certain sense, the transnational corporation largely blur the national lines of capital on the economic level. In fact, "being American" has mostly political and social meaning, namely, that different units of economic power refer to a center of political domination and regulation capable of taking the necessary initiatives for the expansion of the system as a whole. In this sense, the crucial political instrument of the transnational corporations (and not only those based on American capital) is the U.S. government. This does not mean that capital does not have ties to particular nation-states. But to achieve equilibrium in the system beyond particular states, a state capable of intervention at the same level as that of the economic system is required, namely, an imperial state, which today can only be the United States of America. Thus, the apparent new German economic hegemony is one of the most persistent myths of recent years. Not only is German hegemony largely fictive since it depends mainly on American capital and on the American market, but it is also usually expressed by the high rate of exchange of the mark, which is in fact a mechanism imposed by the dollar to avoid its devaluation. Finally, political hegemony being inseparable from military hegemony, the German Federal Republic is on this level a society for the most part still under American protection and deprived of the instruments of world power that within the capitalist system remain the exclusive privilege of the United States. The fact that the American state is an imperial state makes the American society and economy (this time defined by institutional boundaries) the center of the capitalist system. Indeed, to the extent that the state expresses the class relationships in American society, its rhythms and initiatives depend on both the requirements of capital at the global level and on the internal dynamics of U.S. society. The American people thus find themselves, objectively and subjectively, at the heart of the historical evolution of capitalism. On seeing the question from this angle, we certainly cannot speak about American decline. There is no transfer of hegemony. American decline is indissoluble from the decline of the whole capitalist system.

We must then examine the question at this second level. Does the economic crisis represent the beginning of the end of American *and* world capitalism and its replacement by socialism? Are we witnessing, not the decline of America, but the decline of the capitalist empire as a whole? It is certain that this crisis expresses structural contradictions whose historical perspective demands a radical transformation of class relationships and thus, in a manner, the transition to socialism, in all the vagueness of the word. But the transformation of a mode of production does not arise only from its crisis, and even less from a potential catastrophic collapse: it emerges from a historical process shaped and directed by social classes and political agents. Thus, whatever the difficulties of capitalism might be now, the transition to socialism depends upon social and political conditions determining the issues of class struggles caused by the economic crisis. Now, what do we observe on this level?

From the point of view of power relationships at the international level, the "balance of terror" continues to maintain the peaceful coexistence of the two blocs, which are becoming more and more interdependent economically. The shaking of American domination in certain zones (Indochina, Africa) is compensated for by the intensified hold over other regions (Latin America, Middle East). The effects of the crisis tend, rather, toward an acceleration of capitalist expansion on the global level, and the unequal development of antiimperialist struggles makes the collapse of the system, under the impact of national-liberation struggles, a very long-term possibility. The new national-dependent states constitute more sophisticated apparatuses for the reproduction of the fundamental mechanisms of the system.

From the point of view of the internal development of class struggles in the United States, the chances for a socialist alternative seem even weaker on a short- or mid-term basis. On the one hand, there are no political agents capable of advancing such a perspective; on the other, the social-control mechanisms in America continue to be most effective, particularly over the working-class movement, which explains in large part why new socialist political forces did not arise from the mass revolts of the 1960s. Finally, this "socialist perspective" is extremely vague and oscillates between petty-bourgeois ideological myths (like those of the conservation of nature or the liberation of the individual) and outdated doctrines that provoke only revulsion on the part of the American people (as, for example, insistence on the purity of a Stalinist system, even though the reality of Stalinism has been execrated by whole generations of workers in America and elsewhere). As long as the perspective of overcoming capitalism is not accompanied by proposals for an alternative social model (which we may call socialist if we like), a model adapted to the current desires of the American people and contrary to the interests of capital, the crisis will only bring about a reorganization within the system. As long as the left is not capable in the United States (as well as in other societies) of offering new concrete historical perspectives superior to those of capitalism, the crisis will only aggravate living conditions without leading toward social transformation.

Thus, we reach a first conclusion: there is no fundamental loss of American hegemony within the capitalist system; there is no foreseeable collapse of the capitalist system of which the United States is the center. Let us assume this. But, in fact, the current structural transformations at stake cannot really be revealed by the kind of questions we asked—which are the questions generally debated. We must realize that the economic crisis, even if it does not produce a total transformation of the mode of production (because the necessary social and political conditions are lacking), will compel, nevertheless, a halt and modification of the model of accumulation characteristic of the capitalist system in general, and of American capitalism in particular, during the last thirty years. In fact, all our analyses tend toward this idea: *the crisis of the 1970s reveals structural contradictions that make the continuation of world capitalist accumulation (with its center in the United States) impossible without a fundamental restructuring of processes of production, circulation, and distribution of surplus value.*

We witness, then, the decline of a specific model of development. As for the capitalist system itself, the current processes of reorganization can just as well lead to a reinforcement of the system as to the effective beginning of the decline. That will depend, above all, on the class struggles triggered by the reorientation of the system. We will try to analyze, schematically, what this reorientation consists of, what the possible options are, and how we can anticipate the immediate historical evolution.

Remembering our analysis of the structural causes of the economic crisis (explained in Chapter 1), and our analysis of its development in the United States (presented in Chapter 2), we can summarize the structural requirements for rectification of the model of capitalist accumulation in the following manner. To overcome its crisis, American capitalism should increase the amount and the rate of surplus value and broaden outlets in order to make the realization of profit possible, in such a way that the measures taken for these purposes would not have a significant impact on a new increase in the organic composition of capital or a new process of accelerated inflation. On the other hand, it is necessary that there be internal coherence among the different measures taken to restructure the model of accumulation.

From the point of view of outlets, this analysis implies the limitation of the expansion of consumption founded on household and firm indebtedness and its replacement by the search for and conquest of new markets and a reorientation of domestic demand in advanced capitalist countries. On the first point we have seen that the only new markets, in a way outside the system, are the dependent capitalist countries engaged in the new peripheral industrialization (on a long-term basis, because such a process still offers only weak outlets, the big stock of petrodollars being reinvested in the dominant economies) and the socialist countries (on a short- and mid-term basis). The reorganization of domestic demand would be mostly in the direction of developing collective consumption goods, the need for which becomes more and more pressing for the whole system. The expansion of this demand, however, stumbles over the obstacle represented by its lack of solvency, which requires massive state intervention. This risks being inflationary, except in the conditions we shall point out.

Within a capitalist framework, there are two possible strategies for increasing the rate of surplus value, without reintroducing inflation (these are, in a certain sense, contradictory at the scale of the same society):

1. Increase surplus value without raising the organic composition of capital by raising the rate of exploitation, either through intensification of the direct exploitation of workers (by speeding up work or lowering wages) or through the brutal reduction of nonproductive jobs, particularly in the public sector. This tendency can operate on both the workers of central countries and the new masses of productive workers in the peripheral countries. We will call this policy overexploitation.

2. Increase surplus value without raising the organic composition of capital by increasing the productivity of labor power by a substantial enhancing of human creative capacities. This would be accomplished by massive public investment in the social services and by the reorganization of these services so that they could play a dynamic role in developing social productivity.[2] Obstacles to such a formula arise from the following facts. It implies a liberation of the workers' creative capacities that can only happen with a concomitant transformation of the social relationships in the work process, in the sense of an increase in the workers' control over the means of production. In order not to trigger a new inflationary process, this transformation can only be done by public investment obtained from the existing surplus value. Now since all deductions from wages would reduce internal demand even more and would attack the living conditions of the workers, whose assistance is indispensable for the general reorganization of the system, the new investments (whose effects on productivity, and thus on profits, would not be felt in the short run) could only be financed by a levy on profits. This means that such a strategy requires that monopoly capital pay the expenses of a reorientation of the model of accumulation accepting, in the short term at least, a further reduction in the rate of profit. Therefore, such a strategy can only be realized if there is a major political defeat of monopoly capital by the popular and socialist political forces. That is what provides all the interest in this strategy for dealing with the crisis. If the present political and social conditions (in the capitalist world as a whole) do not permit the immediate success of a socialist alternative, they may instead permit a partial victory, followed by a compromise capable of imposing the most favorable issue of the crisis from the workers'

point of view. Such a formula would open a double breach in the logic of the capitalist system: on the one hand, it would deepen the contradiction between the socialization of the production of value and the privatization of its orientation by means of capitalist profit; on the other hand, it would rely on a decisive political defeat of monopoly capital, which would open the way to political hegemony for the working class and popular classes. Thus, the transition to socialism would begin on a political level instead of engaging in the immediate destruction of capitalism, which could provoke considerable ideological resistance until the socialist alternative becomes sufficiently precise.

What are we to think, then, of the evolution of the United States in the light of these strategic alternatives, in which the issue would depend on political class struggles?

It seems quite clear that the hegemony of corporate capital is total on the American political scene and that the labor movement is entirely under control. Under these conditions, the policy of overexploitation has many chances to develop in the United States, leading to an increase in internal demand centered on the stimulation of the middle classes and a reduction in social services and public employment. Also, the control maintained by the United States over large sectors of the world permits an increase in accumulation by means of increased exploitation on a worldwide scale. Combined with the opening of new markets, this policy should allow breathing space for the present accumulation model, although it will always be threatened by inflationary slips, given the continuation of some mechanisms potentially leading to inflation.

Nevertheless, the possibility of reorganizing the model of accumulation will not depend on the American economy alone. We live in a worldwide economic system. Thus, the readjustment in favor of capital can only be effective if it works efficiently in the system as a whole. And it is here that decisive elements of rupture can appear at the heart of the model of accumulation we have known. On the one hand, by being forced to industrialize the periphery of the system, the transnational corporations reproduce the phenomenon of proletarianization, and hence the formation, organization, and radicalization of a working class and a new petty bourgeoisie who are becoming more and more crucial historical actors—in other words, the living alternatives to the capitalist model of accumulation. On the other hand, and mainly because in Western Europe, presently the key piece of American capital, the bourgeois political hegemony is wavering, the pressure from the left and from the workers' movement in Italy, England, Spain, France, and elsewhere carries with it a probable outcome of the crisis. This outcome will bear a form similar to that of the alternative to overexploitation. That is to say, in the first phase the outcome will remain within the capitalist system, but at the same time it will increase the state's control of the economy and the workers' control of the state. The functioning in the short term of an important part of the European economy along these lines will render impossible, in the end, the reproduction of the model of accumulation in the system as a whole, including the United States—which will call again, in a much more dramatic way, for the restructuring of the system. At the same time, such a process thus launched will be likely to produce important changes in the social struggles and political conflicts in the United States. Indeed, the increasing of internal exploitation, the shunning of productive investments, the maintenance of unemployment, the reduction of social services, the continuation of inflation, and the political repression implicit in this model will probably radicalize the tensions, sharpen the consciousness, and consolidate and unify the present embryos of alternative organization of the American people. Furthermore, the progress in Europe of a concrete alternative for the crisis and the development of a new socialist strategy and of a humanistic model of society closer to the needs of the American people will facilitate and stimulate the transition from social revolts to political projects. Then, perhaps, the decline of the model of accumulation characteristic of American capitalism since World War II will actually begin. Thus, there is a complex and largely open process of class struggles and political conflicts that leads from the crisis begun in 1974 to the historical supersession of structural contradictions it reveals.

It is in this precise manner that the twilight of the American Empire looms on the horizon—and, with it, the rebirth of America.

NOTES

■■■

NOTES TO CHAPTER 1

1. Karl Marx, *Capital, A Critique of Political Economy*, New York: International Publishers, 1967, Vol. III, Part III.
2. There is much discussion of the correct formula for representing the organic composition of capital. Erik Wright argues convincingly for a new formula: $Q = c/v+s$. While this certainly changes the calculation of the empirical trend toward a rising organic composition of capital (by making it more difficult for Q to rise), the basic theoretical argument is not altered. We prefer to keep the formula as it was presented by Marx himself (c/v) and to introduce changes in the *general theory* after discussing the different steps of the argument.
3. Paul Boccara et al., *Etudes sur le capitalisme monopoliste d'Etat*, Paris: Editions Sociales, 1973.
4. *Ibid.*
5. Journal published by Maspero in Paris.
6. "Some Problems in the Theory of Capital Accumulation," *Monthly Review* 26, no. 1, 1975, p. 47.
7. Paul Mattick, *Marx and Keynes: The Limits of the Mixed Economy*, Boston: Porter Sargent, 1973; Mario Cogoy, "Les theories neo-Marxistes, Marx et l'accumulation du capital," *Les Temps Modernes*, Sept.-Oct. 1972; David Yaffee, "The Marxian Theory of Crisis, Capital and the State," *Economy and Society* 2, 1973.
8. Geoff Hodgson, "The Theory of the Falling Rate of Profit," *New Left Review*, no. 84, 1974.
9. London: New Left Books, 1975.
10. Bob Rowthorn, "Late Capitalism," *New Left Review*, no. 98, 1976.
11. *Late Capitalism*, pp. 202-203.
12. Michael A. Lebowitz, "Marx's Falling Rate of Profit: A Dialectical View," *The Canadian Journal of Economics* 9, 1976, p. 247.
13. *Ibid.*, pp. 248-49.
14. Paul A. Baran and Paul M. Sweezy, *Monopoly Capital*, New York: Monthly Review Press, 1966.
15. "Class Conflict and Macro-policy: The Political Business Cycle," *Review of Radical Political Economics* 7, no. 1, 1975.
16. *British Capitalism, Workers and the Profit Squeeze*, London: Penguin Books, 1972.
17. "Marxist Theory, Class Struggle and the Crisis of Capitalism," in Jesse Schwartz, ed., *The Subtle Anatomy of Capitalism*, Santa Monica, Calif.: Goodyear, 1977.
18. *Capital in the American Economy*, Princeton, N.J.: Princeton University Press, 1961.
19. *Late Capitalism*, p. 201.
20. *Structural Change in the American Economy*, Cambridge, Mass.: Harvard

University Press, 1970. Quotations following are from pp. 150, 151, 187, and 218.

21. *Investment Demand and U.S. Economic Growth*, Washington, D.C.: The Brookings Institution, 1965.

22. *Fresque historique du système productif*, Collections de l'INSEE, series E, no. 27, Oct. 1974; Michel Bénard, "Rendement économique et productivité du capital fixe de 1959 à 1972," *Economie et Statistique* 60, Oct. 1976, pp. 7-17; Christian Sautter, "L'efficacité et la rentabilité de l'économie française de 1954 à 1976," *Economie et Statistique* 68, p. 7.

23. *The Falling Rate of Profit: Marx's Law and Its Significance to Twentieth Century Capitalism*, London: Dennis Dobson, 1957.

24. "The Law of the Falling Tendency of the Rate of Profit," Ph.D. diss., Columbia University, 1963 (available on microfilm).

25. Hodgson calculates the data from his own formula for the organic composition of capital: $q = k/x+v$ (where k is fixed capital). Mage's data are *already* computed under this formula. Gillman's data as presented in Table 2 are recalculated by Hodgson on the basis of this formula.

26. *Regulation et crises du capitalisme: L'experience des Ètats-Unis*, Paris: Calmann-Levy, 1976.

27. Gillman, *The Falling Rate of Profit*, pp. 82, 83, 85.

28. Some of these trends are compatible in the line of the findings of the economic studies done by Solow on the factors determining productivity increases in the American economy. See Robert M. Solow, "Contribution to the Theory of Economic Growth," *Quarterly Journal of Economics* 70, Feb. 1956.

29. Samir Amin, *L'accumulation à l'échelle mondiale*, Paris: Anthropos, 1970.

30. "Some Problems in the Theory of Capital Accumulation," p. 51.

31. Manuel Castells and Emilio de Ipola, "Epistemological Practice and Social Sciences," *Economy and Society* 5, no. 2, June 1976.

32. *Class, Crisis and the State*, London: New Left Books, 1978.

33. We follow here the very thorough analysis presented by Erik Wright in his chapter on "Alternative Perspectives in Marxist Theory of Accumulation and Crisis" in *Class, Crisis and the State*.

34. On the social conditions for the development of productive forces based on the combination of energy and information, see the book by Jacques Attali, *La parole et l'outil*, Paris: Presses Universitaires de France, 1975.

35. See Lebowitz, "Marx's Falling Rate of Profit," for the theoretical distinction between *barriers* and *limits* in the process of historical development.

36. Jurgen Habermas, *Legitimation and Crisis*, Boston: Beacon Press, 1973.

37. Nicos Poulantzas, ed., *La crise de l'Etat*, Paris: Presses Universitaires de France, 1976.

38. J. L. Dallemagne, *L'inflation capitaliste*, Paris: Maspero, 1972.

39. See Michel Wieworka, *L'Etat, le patronat et les consommateurs*, Paris: Presses Universitaires de France, 1977; Manuel Castells, *City, Class and Power*, London: Macmillan, 1978.

40. Manuel Castells, "Immigrant Workers and Class Struggle," *Politics and Society*, no. 1, 1975.

41. See Aglietta, *Regulation et crises du capitalisme*, p. 89.

42. John K. Galbraith, *The New Industrial State*, Boston: Houghton Mifflin, 1967.

43. J. P. Delilez, *Les Monopoles*, Paris: Editions Sociales, 1972.

44. For an analysis of state expenditures, see, for France, the very important statistical study: C. André, R. Delormé and A. Kouevi, "Etude Analytique de l'evolution des depenses et recettes publiques françaises, 1870-1970," mimeographed, Paris: Cepremap, 1976.

45. Philip Herzog, *Politique économique et planification en regime capitaliste*, Paris: Editions Sociales, 1972.

46. J. L. Dallemagne, "Inflation et crises ou le mythe de la stagflation," *Critiques de l'économie politique*, April-Sept. 1973.

47. See "Il Marxismo e lo Stato," *Mondoperaio*, Rome, special issue, May 1976.

48. James O'Connor, *The Fiscal Crisis of the State*, New York: St. Martin's Press, 1973.

49. See Christian Palloix, *L'internationalisation du capital*, Paris: Maspero, 1973.

50. Paolo Leon, *Congiuntura e crisi strutturale nei rapporti tra economie capitalistiche*, Padua: Marsilio, 1973.

51. See Nicos Poulantzas, *Social Classes in Contemporary Capitalism*, London: New Left Books, 1975, chap. 1.

52. Charles Levinson, *Inflation and the Multinationals*, London: George Allen & Unwin, 1971.

53. On the monetary crisis, see Jacques Kahn, *Pour comprendre les crises monétaires*, Paris: Editions Sociales, 1972.

NOTES TO CHAPTER 2

1. For a summary of the basic data on the economic crisis, see David Mermelstein, *The Economic Crisis Reader*, New York: Vintage Books, 1975; Union of Radical Political Economics, *Radical Perspectives on the Economic Crisis of Monopoly Capitalism*, New York: URPE-PEA, 1975; David Gordon, "Recession is Capitalism as Usual," *New York Times Magazine*, April 27, 1975. For a well-documented interpretation of the whole historical process, see Douglas F. Dowd, "Accumulation and Crisis: 1919-29 and 1955-75," unpublished when we consulted it.

2. Boddy and Crotty, "Class Conflict and Macro-policy," and "Class Conflict, Keynesian Policies and the Business Cycle," *Monthly Review*, Oct. 1974.

3. It would appear there is a contradiction between the deterioration of the ratio between profits and wages and the fact that the rate of exploitation increased. In truth, there is no contradiction at all. Exploitation increased because of the differential appropriation of productivity gains. The rate of profits to wages deteriorated because the workers got important increases in nominal wages and resisted the speeding up of work in the monopoly sector; real wages remained *on the average* at the same level because of the differences in the increases between economic sectors and because of the accelerated rate of inflation.

4. See Arthur MacEwan, "Changes in World Capitalism and the Current Crisis of the U.S. Economy," in URPE, *Radical Perspectives*; also Joyce Kolko, *America and the Crisis of World Capitalism*, Boston, Mass.: Beacon Press, 1974.

5. See the important analysis by Paul M. Sweezy and Harry Magdoff, *The Dynamics of U.S. Capitalism, Corporate Structure, Inflation, Credit, Gold and the Dollar*, New York: Monthly Review Press, 1972.

6. We have followed the analysis by Leonard A. Rapping, "The Current Crisis

of U.S. Capitalism," paper presented at the Union of Radical Political Economics, San Francisco, Dec. 28, 1974.

7. On the oil crisis, see Dankwart A. Rustow, "Petroleum Politics 1951-1976: A Five-act Drama Reconstructed," *Dissent*, Spring 1974; Pierre Pean, *Petrole: la troisième guerre mondiale*, Paris: Calmann-Levy, 1974; Michael Tanzer, *The Energy Crisis*, New York: Monthly Review Press, 1975.

8. See Rustow, "Petroleum Politics."

9. Such arguments have been expressed, for instance, by Andre Farhi, "Comment imposer à l'Europe la volonté de Washington," *Le Monde Diplomatique*, Paris, Nov. 1974.

10. We have used extensively: U.S. Department of Labor, *The Structure of the U.S. Economy in 1980 and 1985*, Bureau of Labor Statistics, Bulletin 1831, Washington, D.C., 1975; Victor Perlo, *The Unstable Economy: Booms and Recessions in the U.S. since 1945*, New York: International Publishers, 1973; and S. M. Rosen, ed., *Economic Power Failure: The Current American Crisis*, New York: McGraw-Hill, 1975. For a description of the American economy before the crisis, see Emma S. Woytinsky, *Profile of the U.S. Economy*, New York: Frederick A. Praeger, 1967; and Clopper Almon, *The American Economy to 1975*, New York: Harper & Row, 1966.

11. Albert E. Burger, "Relative Movements in Wages and Profits," *Federal Reserve Bank of St. Louis*, Feb. 1973.

12. D. C. Bock and J. T. Dunlop, *Labor and the American Community*, Englewood Cliffs, N.J.: Prentice-Hall, 1970.

13. See the very important paper by David Gold, "The Rise and Decline of the Keynesian Coalition," *Kapitalistate*, no. 6, 1977.

14. J. David Greenstone, *Labor in American Politics*, Chicago: University of Chicago Press, 1977.

15. James Weinstein, *Ambiguous Legacy*, New York: Franklin Watts, 1975.

16. See "Monopoly and Inflation: Why Prices Never Go Down," *Dollars and Sense*, Dec. 1974.

17. *Monopoly Capital*, New York: Monthly Review Press, 1966, chap. 4.

18. We do not want to enter here into a critique of the underconsumptionist perspective implicit in Baran and Sweezy's *Monopoly Capital*, which considerably limits the generalization of the book's theses to the functioning of the whole capitalist system. We subscribe to the criticisms of James O'Connor, "Monopoly Capital," *New Left Review*, no. 40, Nov.-Dec. 1966, and J. P. Delilez, *Les monopoles*, Paris: Editions Sociales, 1971.

19. Paul M. Sweezy and Harry Magdoff, "Economic Stagnation and Stagnation of Economics," *Monthly Review*, April 1971.

20. *Monopoly Capital*, statistical appendix.

21. William Nordhaus, "The Falling Share of Profits," *Brookings Papers on Economic Activity*, 1974.

22. Barry Bluestone, "Economic Crises and the Law of Uneven Development," *Politics and Society*, no. 3, 1972.

23. *The Modern World System: Capitalist Agriculture and the Origins of the European World Economy in the Sixteenth Century*, New York: Academic Press, 1974.

24. Michael Barratt Brown, *The Economics of Imperialism*, Harmondsworth, Middlesex: Penguin Books, 1974.

25. David P. Calleo and Benjamin M. Rowland, *America and the World Political*

Economy: Atlantic Dreams and National Realities, Bloomington: Indiana University Press, 1973.

26. Ernest Mandel, *Europe vs. America: The Socialist Alternative to the American Challenges*, London: New Left Books, 1967.

27. Levinson, *Inflation and the Multinationals*.

28. Joseph D. Collins, "Transnationales americaines et USA. Retour à l'envoyeur," *Politique aujourd'hui*, Jan.-Feb. 1975, pp. 25-54.

29. Perlo, *The Unstable Economy*.

30. Ernest Mandel, *Decline of the Dollar*, New York: Monad Press, 1972.

31. Paul M. Sweezy and Harry Magdoff, "The End of U.S. Hegemony," *Monthly Review*, Oct. 1971.

32. C. Fred Bergsten, "The Dollar's $200-Billion Handicap Abroad," *New York Times*, June 22, 1975.

33. *Monopoly Capital*, chap. 5.

34. *Economics and the Public Purpose*, New York: Signet Books, 1975.

35. For the data, see the important special issue of *Business Week*, Oct. 12, 1974, "The Debt Economy." For a general analysis, see Harry Magdoff and Paul M. Sweezy, "Keynesian Chickens Come Home to Roost," *Monthly Review*, April 1974.

36. The editors, "Banks: Skating on Thin Ice," *Monthly Review*, Feb. 1975.

37. *Ibid.*, pp. 4-8. Copyright © 1975 by Monthly Review Inc. Reprinted by permission of Monthly Review Press.

38. S. M. Rosen, "The End of the Keynesian Era," in *Economic Power Failure*, pp. 71-72.

39. Mattick, *Marx and Keynes*.

40. *Fiscal Crisis*; see also his *Corporations and the State*, New York: Harper & Row, 1974.

41. Manuel Castells, "Neo-capitalism, Collective Consumption and Urban Contradictions," in L. Lindberg, ed., *Stress and Contradictions in Advanced Capitalist Societies*, Lexington, Mass.: Heath, 1976.

42. James Cypher, "Capitalist Planning and Military Expenditures," *The Review of Radical Political Economics* 6, no. 3, 1974.

43. Rosen, "The End of the Keynesian Era."

NOTES TO CHAPTER 3

1. See O'Connor, *Fiscal Crisis*; Galbraith, *Economics and the Public Purpose*; Baran and Sweezy, *Monopoly Capital*; Nathan Rosenberg, *Technology and American Growth*, New York: Harper and Row, 1972; Harry Magdoff, "Problems of U.S. Capitalism," *Socialist Register*, New York: Monthly Review Press, 1965; Ernest Mandel, "Where is America Going?" *New Left Review*, no. 54, March-April 1969.

2. From the point of view of the reproduction of the system, integration and repression are complementary policies of capital toward labor. From the point of view of the living conditions of the workers and their opportunities to improve their political position, they represent entirely different situations. We believe that repression is the most serious problem that workers can experience.

3. See Richard Meier, *Science and Economic Development*, Cambridge, Mass.:

MIT Press, 1956; Denis Gabor, *Innovations: Scientific, Technological and Social, American Design*, New York: Oxford University Press, 1970.

4. We cannot develop here a complex discussion that would state more explicitly the theoretical assumptions of our theory of social class. By social class we understand, following Lenin, "large groups of people characterized by their position in a historically given system of social production, by their relationship (generally fixed by law) to the means of production, by their role in the social organization of labor, and, therefore, by the means of appropriation and the share of wealth they can have. The classes are groups of people that can appropriate others' work as a consequence of the place they hold in a given social system." (Lenin, "The Great Initiative," *Selected Works*, New York: International Publishing Co., and Moscow: *Editions du Progrès*, 1966.) My conception of classes relies heavily on the continuous discussions I have had these last few years with Nicos Poulantzas, Erik O. Wright, and Maurice Zeitlin. I have tried to use this theoretical model in my understanding of the Chilean process. See Manuel Castells, *La lucha de clases en Chile*, Buenos Aires: Siglo XXI, 1974. A crucial recent theoretical discussion on the subject appears in the article by Erik O. Wright. "Class Boundaries in Advanced Capitalist Societies," *New Left Review*, no. 98, July-Aug. 1976, pp. 3-11. For the United States see Charles A. Anderson, *The Political Economy of the Social Class*, Englewood Cliffs, N.J.: Prentice-Hall, 1974.

5. For a more accurate characterization, see Boccara et al., *Etudes sur le capitalisme monopoliste d'Etat*, Paris: Editions Sociales, 1973; Mandel, *Late Capitalism*.

6. Particularly useful on this point have been my discussions with Alain Touraine in Paris and Maurice Zeitlin in Madison.

7. *The Political Economy of the Social Class.*

8. *American Society, Inc.*, Chicago: Markham, 1970, esp. pp. 3-85.

9. See James O'Connor, "Who Rules the Corporations? The Ruling Class?" *Socialist Revolution* 2, no. 1, Jan.-Feb. 1971.

10. *The Modern Corporation and Private Property*, New York: Macmillan, 1932.

11. *The New Industrial State.*

12. Victor Perlo, *The Empire of High Finance*, New York: International Publishers, 1957; S. Menshikov, *Millionaires and Managers*, Moscow: Progress Publishers, 1969.

13. "Corporate Ownership and Control: The Large Corporation and the Capitalist Class," *American Journal of Sociology*, vol. 79, no. 5, March 1974, pp. 1073-1119. Copyright © 1974 by the University of Chicago. Reprinted by permission.

14. *Ibid.*, pp. 1100-1104.

15. "Who Rules the Corporations," *Socialist Revolution* 1, nos. 4, 5, 6, July-Aug., Sept.-Oct., Nov.-Dec. 1970.

16. O'Connor, *Corporations and the State.*

17. *Management Control and the Large Corporations*, Cambridge, Mass.: Harvard University Press, 1970.

18. *Fiscal Crisis.*

19. *Who Rules America?* Englewood Cliffs, N.J.: Prentice-Hall, 1967; *The Higher Circles: The Governing Class in America*, New York: Random House, 1970.

20. For several analyses of the theory of the state in advanced capitalism, see Poulantzas, ed., *La crise de l'Etat*.

21. Roger Friedland, Alexander Hicks, and Edwin Johnson, "The Political Economy of Redistribution in the American States: National Corporate Capital, Organized Labor and Electoral Politics," paper delivered at the meeting of the American Sociological Association, San Francisco, Aug. 1975.

22. Vicente Navarro, "Social Policy Issues: An Explanation of the Composition, Nature and Functions of the Present Health Sector of the U.S.," *Bulletin of the New York Academy of Medicine*, Jan. 1975; Robert F. Alford, *Health Care Politics: Ideological and Interest Group Barriers to Reform*, Chicago: University of Chicago Press, 1975.

23. Robert R. Alford and Nancy DiTomaso, "Interest Groups and the Potential Consequences of Federal Housing Subsidies to the States," mimeographed, Department of Sociology, University of Wisconsin, Madison, 1973; Juliet Z. Saltman, *Open Housing as a Social Movement*, Lexington, Mass.: Heath, 1971.

24. Barbara Koeppel, "The Big Social Security Rip-Off," *The Progressive*, Aug. 1975.

25. I have relied on the first phase of the research done by Glenn Yago, "State Policy, Corporate Planning and Transportation Needs: The Development of the U.S. Urban Ground Transportation System," mimeographed, Department of Sociology, University of Wisconsin, Madison, Dec. 1974.

26. *Regulating the Poor: The Functions of Public Relief*, New York: Pantheon, 1971.

27. The underlying theoretical model consists of a combination of two distinctions concerning class interests: (a) immediate and historical interests and (b) interests at three different levels: economic, political and ideological. For a justification and definition of this perspective, see the background on the theory of social classes quoted in footnote 4 *supra*.

28. For a good example of the explicit demands of corporate capital, see the article by the chairman of FMC, Robert H. Malott, "Encouraging Capital Formation," *New York Times*, June 21, 1975.

29. See the article by Albert Szymanski, "Trends in American Class Structure," *Socialist Revolution* 3, no. 4, July-Aug. 1972.

30. *The Working-Class Majority*, New York: Coward, McCann and Geoghegan, 1974.

31. *Class and Politics in the United States*, New York: John Wiley, 1972.

32. Harry Braverman, *Labor and Monopoly Capital*, New York: Monthly Review Press, 1974, p. 293.

33. See the summary of research on this issue by Ronald M. Pavalko, *Sociology of Occupations and Professions*, Itasca, Ill.: F. E. Peacock, 1971, esp. chap. 6.

34. For a theoretical analysis of this point, we have used chapter 2, "Productive and Unproductive Labor," of James O'Connor's forthcoming book, *The Class Struggle*.

35. *Labor and Monopoly Capital*, p. 423.

36. On the definition of class capacities, see Wright, "Class Boundaries in Advanced Capitalist Societies."

37. See Anderson, *The Political Economy of the Social Class*.

38. *The Transformation of Industry: From Agriculture to Service Employment*, Beverly Hills, Calif.: Sage Publications, 1977.

39. See Alain Touraine, *The Post-Industrial Society*, New York: Random House, 1973.

40. *The Coming of the Post-Industrial Society: A Venture in Social Forecasting*, New York: Basic Books, 1973.

41. *The Service Society and the Consumer Vanguard*, New York: Harper and Row, 1974, pp. 30, 31, 32, 34.

42. "Notes on Neo-capitalism," *Theory and Society*, no. 1, 1975, pp. 18-22.

43. Hirschhorn, "Towards a Political Economy of the Service Society," working paper 229, Institute of Urban and Regional Development, University of California, Berkeley, Feb. 1974; also, from the same author and institution, "The Social Service Crisis and the New Subjectivity: Social Services in the Post-Industrial Revolution," working paper 244, Dec. 1974; and "A Model of Public Sector Growth," working paper 191, Oct. 1972. An important book on the subject is Victor Fuchs, *The Service Economy*, New York: Columbia University Press, 1969. Also, Stephen Cohen (with Charles Goldfinger), "From Perma-crisis to Real Crisis in French Social Security," Institute of Urban and Regional Development, University of California, Berkeley, working paper 250, March 1975.

44. "Technical Changes and the Aggregate Production Function," *Review of Economics and Statistics*, Aug. 1957.

45. Hirschhorn, "Toward a Political Economy of the Service Society."

46. *La Civilisation au Carrefour*, Paris: Anthropos, 1970.

47. See Vicente Navarro, "The Underdevelopment of Health of Working America: Causes, Consequences and Possible Solution," paper based on a presentation at the 103rd Annual Meeting of the American Public Health Association, on the theme of Health and Work in America, Chicago, Nov. 1975.

48. This is an excellent example of the ambiguity of the evolution toward a "service society." *Labor and Monopoly Capital*, p. 26.

49. See David M. Gordon, ed., *Problems in Political Economy: An Urban Perspective*, Lexington, Mass.: Heath, 1971.

50. See the special issue on unemployment of the *Monthly Review*, June 1975.

51. See William Tabb, *The Political Economy of the Black Ghetto*, New York: W. W. Norton, 1975.

52. "Economic Crises and the Law of Uneven Development," pp. 67-70; and "The Characteristics of Marginal Industries," in Gordon, ed., *Problems in Political Economy*.

53. David M. Gordon, ed., *Theories of Poverty and Underemployment*, Lexington, Mass.: Heath, 1972.

54. Michael J. Piore, "The Dual Labor Market: Theory and Implications," in Gordon, ed., *Theories of Poverty and Underemployment*.

55. Harry Braverman, "Work and Unemployment," *Monthly Review* 27, no. 2, 1975.

56. See the excellent analysis of this topic by Baran and Sweezy in chapter 9 of *Monopoly Capital*; see also Milton Mankoff, ed., *The Poverty of Progress*, New York: Rinehart and Winston, 1972, chap. 5. The best source of data on racism in the United States is still the *Report of the National Advisory Committee on Civil Disorders*, Washington, D.C.: GPO, March 1968.

57. "Social and Demographic Trends: Focus on Race," in Eli Ginsberg, ed., *The Future of the Metropolis: People, Jobs, Income*, Salt Lake City, Utah: Olympus Publishing Co., 1974, p. 33.

58. See Castells, "Immigrant Workers and Class Struggle."

59. Braverman, *Labor and Monopoly Capital*, chap. 17.

60. See Baran and Sweezy, *Monopoly Capital*, chap. 9.

61. See Levinson, *The Working-Class Majority*.

62. See David Harvey, *Social Justice and the City*, Baltimore: Johns Hopkins Press, 1973.

63. See Juliet Mitchell, *Woman's Estate*, New York: Random House, 1977. A mass of literature exists on this subject. I have been stimulated by the following works: an excellent position paper by Elizabeth Fee, "Women and Health: A Comparison of Theories," mimeographed, Johns Hopkins University, Baltimore, Feb. 1975; Dorothe E. Smith, "Women, The Family and Corporate Capitalism," paper presented at the meeting of the Canadian Sociological Association, May 1972; Joan Huber, ed., *Changing Women in a Changing Society*, Chicago: University of Chicago Press, 1973; Sheila Rowbotham, *Woman's Consciousness, Man's World*, London: Penguin Books, 1973; Anne Koedt, Ellen Levine, and Anita Rapone, eds., *Radical Feminism*, New York: Quadrangle, 1973; Nona Glazer-Malbin and Helen Youngelson Waehrer, eds., *Woman in a Man-Made World: A Socioeconomic Handbook*, Chicago: Rand McNally, 1972.

64. See in particular the theory and practice of the Bolshevik leader, Alexandra Kollontai, Judith Stora-Sandor, *Alexandra Kollontai: Marxisme et revolution sexuelle*, Paris: Maspero, 1973.

65. There is obviously an urgent need for a serious Marxist analysis of women's oppression and liberation. There have been some interesting attempts in Italy, particularly in "Il Manifesto," which link capitalism, family, and women's oppression. See Luciana Castellina, ed., *Famiglia e societa capitalistica*, Rome: Alfani Editore, 1974.

66. See Roderick Aya and Norman Miller, eds., *The New American Revolution*, New York: Free Press, 1971.

67. See Elizabeth Waldman, "Change in the Labor Force Activity of Women," *Monthly Labor Review*, June 1970; and James A. Sweet, "Recent Trends in the Employment of American Women," mimeographed, Center for Demography and Ecology, University of Wisconsin, Madison, 1975.

68. "Sexual Inequalities and Socio-Economic Achievement in the U.S. 1962-1973," *American Sociological Review* 41, June 1976, p. 462.

69. For 1973, see "Marital and Family Characteristics of the Labor Force, 1973," U.S. Bureau of Labor Statistics, Special Labor Force Report 164; for 1963, "Marital and Family Characteristics of Workers, 1963," U.S. Bureau of Labor Statistics, Special Labor Force Report 40.

70. See Stuart Levine and Nancy O'Lurie, eds., *The American Indian Today*, Ann Arbor, Mich.: Everett-Edwards, 1971.

71. See the observations on younger workers and their influence in the Lordstown strike in 1972 by Stanley Aronowitz, *False Promises: The Shaping of American Working-Class Consciousness*, New York: McGraw-Hill, 1973.

72. Anderson, *The Political Economy of the Social Class*, chap. 4; Gerald W. Thielbar and Saul D. Feldman, eds., *Issues in Social Inequality*, Boston: Little, Brown, 1972; Thomas E. Weisskopf, "Capitalism and Equality," in Richard G. Edwards, Michael Reich, and Thomas E. Weisskopf, eds., *The Capitalist System*, Englewood Cliffs, N.J.: Prentice-Hall, 1972.

73. See William H. Sewell and Robert M. Hauser, *Education, Occupation and Earnings*, New York: Academic Press, 1975.

74. See the classic study by Peter M. Blau and Otis D. Duncan, *The American Occupational Structure*, New York: John Wiley, 1967.

75. See Edward C. Budd, "Inequality in Income and Taxes," in Zeitlin, ed., *American Society, Inc.*

76. See Robert J. Lampman, *The Share of Top Wealth-holders in National Wealth, 1922-1956*, Princeton, N.J.: Princeton University Press, 1962; and by the same author, *Ends and Means of Reducing Income Property*, Chicago: Markham, 1971.

77. "The Possibility of Income Redistribution," unpublished paper, 1975, pp. 17-18.

78. "Labor Markets, Defense Subsidies and the Working Poor," in Pamela Roby, ed., *The Poverty Establishment*, Englewood Cliffs, N.J.: Prentice-Hall, 1974.

79. See Dennis P. Hogan, "The Situs and Status Dimensions of Social Mobility in the Labor Force: An Examination of Industry and Occupation," mimeographed, Center for Demography and Ecology, University of Wisconsin, Madison, 1975.

80. See Raymond Boudon, *L'inegalité des chances*, Paris: Armand Colin, 1974. The work by Boudon has been severely criticized by Robert M. Hauser, "On Boudon's Model of Social Mobility," Center for Demography and Ecology, University of Wisconsin, Madison, 1975, but the criticism does not deal with this fact.

81. "The Possibility of Income Redistribution."

82. *Ibid.*, pp. 17-18.

83. "The Political Economy of Redistribution in the American States."

84. "The Possibility of Income Redistribution," p. 51.

85. See Hyman Lumer, *Poverty: Its Roots and Its Future*, New York: International Publishers, 1965; also, for more recent data, Sheldon Danziger and Michael Weinstein, "Employment Location and Wage Rates of Poverty-Area Residents," mimeographed, Institute for Research on Poverty, University of Wisconsin, Madison, 1974.

86. *Who Are the Urban Poor?* New York: Committee for Economic Development, 1970.

87. There are a huge number of sources and literature on which we have relied for our understanding of the urban crisis in the United States. Besides the references already quoted, we should mention John Mollenkopf, *Growth Defied: Community Organization and the Struggle over Urban Development in America*, forthcoming book based on a 1973 Harvard University Ph.D. diss.; Stephen Gale and Eric G. Moore, *The Manipulated City*, Chicago: Maaroeja Press, 1975; William K. Tabb and Larry Sawers, eds., *Marxism and the Metropolis*, New York: Oxford University Press, forthcoming; Roger Friedland, *Class Structure, Central City and Urban Crisis*, forthcoming book based on a 1976 University of Wisconsin Ph.D. diss.; and, above all, David Harvey, "The Political Economy of Urbanization in Advanced Capitalist Societies: The Case of the U.S.," *Urban Affairs Annual Review*, Beverly Hills, Calif.: Sage Publications, 1975.

88. For basic information on the characteristic functions and transformation of

metropolitan growth and urban structure in the United States, see Leo Schnore, *The Urban Scene*, Glencoe, Ill.: The Free Press, 1965; Beverly Duncan and Stanley Lieberson, *Metropolis and Region in Transition*, Beverly Hills, Calif.: Sage Publications, 1970; Sylvia F. Fava and Noel P. Gist, *Urban Society*, New York: Thomas Y. Crowell, 1975; Leonard E. Goodall, *The American Metropolis*, Columbus, Ohio: Charles E. Merrill, 1968; Amos H. Hawley and Basil G. Zimmer, *The Metropolitan Community*, Beverly Hills, Calif.: Sage Publications, 1970; Jeffrey K. Hadden and Edgar F. Borgatta, *American Cities: Their Social Characteristics*, Chicago: Rand McNally, 1965. For a well-informed presentation of the historical evolution of American cities, see Charles N. Glaab, *The American City*, Homewood, Ill.: Dorsey Press, 1963.

89. The best source of data, bibliography, and interpretations for the suburbanization process is the reader edited by Louis H. Masotti and Jeffrey K. Hadden, "The Urbanization of the Suburbs," Urban Affairs Annual Review, Beverly Hills, Calif.: Sage Publications, 1973, Elliott Schlar, of Brandeis University, is finishing an important book on the subject. I have benefited from discussing the topic with him as well as from reading the chapter of his book entitled "Levels of Entrapment." For additional references, see Timothy Schilts and William Moffitt, "Inner City Outer City Relationships in Metropolitan Areas: A Bibliographic Essay," *Urban Affairs Quarterly* 7, Sept. 1, 1971; and Leo F. Schnore, *Class and Race in Cities and Suburbs*, Chicago: Markham, 1972.

90. See the now classic analysis of the subject by Norton E. Long, "Political Science and the City," in Leo F. Schnore and Henry Fagin, eds., "Urban Research and Policy Planning," *Urban Affairs Annual Review*, Beverly Hills, Calif.: Sage Publications, 1967; also, an important empirical study by Richard Child Hill, "Separate and Unequal: Goverment Inequality in the Metropolis," *American Political Science Review*, Dec. 1974.

91. See Alan K. Campbell and Philip Meranto, "The Metropolitan Education Dilemma: Matching Resources to Needs," in Marilyn Gittell, ed., *Educating an Urban Population*, Beverly Hills, Calif.: Sage Publications, 1967; and James S. Coleman, *Equality and Educational Opportunity*, Washington, D.C.: GPO, 1966.

92. The best available source of data and references on the problems of the central city in the United States and its social and economic interactions is the study prepared by the Congressional Research Service for the Subcommittee on Housing and Urban Affairs, United States Senate, Washington, D.C.: GPO, 1973. See also William Tabb, *The Economy of the Black Ghetto*, New York: W. W. Norton, 1971.

93. See the insightful study of George Sternlieb and Robert W. Burchell, *Residential Abandonment: The Tenement Landlord Revisited*, center for Urban Policy Research, Rutgers University, New Brunswick, N.J., 1973. The study is centered on Newark, but the analysis has a more general scope.

94. *Housing in the Seventies*, Hearings on Housing and Community Development Legislation, 1973, Part 3, House of Representatives Subcommittee on Banking and Currency, 93rd Cong., 1st Sess., Washington, D.C.: GPO, 1973. This is probably the most important source of data on housing in the United States. Information on New York was gathered personally in 1975 from members of the Metropolitan Housing Council.

95. See David Harvey, *The Political Economy of Urbanization: The Case of the U.S.*, Baltimore: Center for Metropolitan Studies, 1975.

96. K. H. Schaeffer and Elliot Sclar, *Access for All: Transportation and Urban Growth*, Baltimore: Penguin Books, 1975.

97. See Michael N. Danielson, *Federal-Metropolitan Politics and the Commuter Crisis*, New York: Columbia University Press, 1965.

98. See James F. Veatch, "Federal and Local Urban Transportation Policy," *Urban Affairs Quarterly* 10, no. 4, June 1975.

99. See Norman I. Fainstein and Susan S. Fainstein, "The Future of Community Control," mimeographed, Bureau of Applied Social Research, Columbia University, New York, Sept. 1974.

100. I have relied on the very detailed summary research paper done by a working group of graduate students for my seminar on urban politics: Mary A. Evans, Alfonzo Thurman, Anthony Edoh, and Augusto Figueroa, "Busing and Urban Segregation: The Continuing Struggle," Department of Sociology, University of Wisconsin, Madison, Aug. 1975.

101. See Norman I. Fainstein and Susan S. Fainstein, *Urban Political Movements*, Englewood Cliffs, N.J.: Prentice-Hall, 1974; John Mollenkopf, "On the Causes and Consequences of Neighborhood Political Mobilization," paper delivered at the meeting of the American Political Science Association, New Orleans, Sept. 1973.

102. See John Mollenkopf and Jon Pynoos, "Property, Politics and Local Housing Policy," *Politics and Society* 2, no. 4, 1972.

103. See Michael Lipsky, *Protest in City Politics: Rent Strikes, Housing and the Power of the Poor*, Chicago: Rand McNally, 1970.

104. *Regulating the Poor*.

105. *Radicals in Urban Politics: The Alinsky Approach*, Chicago: University of Chicago Press, 1972.

106. The best summary and discussion of the research available on the 1960s riots is Joe R. Feagin and Harlan Hahn, *Ghetto Revolts: The Politics of Violence in American Cities*, New York: Macmillan, 1973. For an excellent case study of the black movement in Detroit, see Marvin Surkin, *I Do Mind Dying: A Study on Urban Revolution*, New York: St. Martin's Press, 1975.

107. "The Causes of Radical Disturbances: A Comparison of Alternative Explanations," *American Sociological Review*, Aug. 1970; "The Causes of Racial Disturbances: Tests of an Explanation," *American Sociological Review*, June 1971.

108. The connection between the black movement as a social-protest movement and the open housing movement as a service-reform movement has been shown in detail by a case study in Milwaukee carried on by a working group from my seminar on urban politics. Ron Blascoe, Kim Burns, David Gillespie, Greg Martin, and Linda Wills, "Milwaukee: Open Housing and the Grassroots," Department of Sociology, University of Wisconsin, Madison, Aug. 1975.

109. In addition to my own observations and data, I have used two excellent papers on the urban crisis, which present a concrete analysis of urban contradictions within a broad Marxist perspective. They are Richard Child Hill, "Black Struggle and the Urban Fiscal Crisis," mimeographed, Conference on Urban Political Economy, New York, Feb. 1975; and Roger Friedland, "Big Apple and the Urban Orchard," typescript, Aug. 1975.

110. See William J. Baumol, "Macroeconomics of Unbalanced Growth: The

Anatomy of the Urban Crisis," *American Economic Review*, June 1967; George Sternlieb, "The City as Sandbox," *The Public Interest*, Fall 1971; Alexander Ganz, "The City-Sandbox, Reservation or Dynamo?" *Public Policy* 21, Winter 1973; and the careful statistical analysis of the determinants of central-city decay by Franklin D. Wilson, "The Organizational Components of Expanding Metropolitan Systems," mimeographed, Center for Demography and Ecology, University of Wisconsin, Madison, July 1975.

NOTES TO CHAPTER 4

1. Thad W. Mirer, "The Distributional Impact of the 1970 Recession," mimeographed, Institute for Research on Poverty, University of Wisconsin, Madison, 1972, p. 24.
2. R. G. Hollister and J. L. Palmer, "The Impact of Inflation on the Poor," mimeographed, Institute for Research on Poverty, University of Wisconsin, Madison, 1969, p. 46.
3. Aronowitz, *False Promises*, p. 266.
4. See Irving Bernstein, *The Lean Years*, Boston: Houghton-Mifflin, 1972; and Richard O. Boyer and Herbert M. Morais, *Labor's Untold Story: United Electrical Radio and Machine Workers of America*, San Francisco: United Front Press, 1972.
5. The AFL-CIO are being increasingly challenged by powerful unions outside the federation, particularly the United Auto Workers and the public workers' unions. Little more than 20 percent of American workers are members of unions.
6. See Frances Piven and Richard Cloward, *Poor People's Movements: Studies from the Contemporary United States*, New York: Pantheon Books, 1977.
7. See Joseph R. Starobin, *American Communism in Crisis, 1943-1957*, Cambridge, Mass.: Harvard University Press, 1972.
8. Hamilton, *Class and Politics in the United States*, chap. 5; Levison, *The Working-Class Majority*, chap. 4.
9. Greenstone, *Labor in American Politics*, pp. 206-208.
10. See Richard Cloward and Frances Piven, *The Politics of Turmoil: Essays on Poverty, Race, and the Urban Crisis*, New York: Pantheon, 1974.
11. See Richard J. Barnet, *Roots of War, The Men and Institutions Behind U.S. Foreign Policy*, New York: Atheneum, 1972.
12. See Peter Marris and Martin Rein, *Dilemmas of Social Reform*, London: Routledge and Kegan Paul, 1972.
13. See Michael W. Miles, *The Radical Probe: The Logic of Student Rebellion*, New York: Atheneum, 1973; and John Searle, *The Campus War*, London: Penguin, 1972.
14. See Cloward and Piven, *The Politics of Turmoil*.
15. See the excellent synthesis of available research by Joe R. Feagin and Harlan Hahn, *Ghetto Revolts*, New York: Macmillan, 1973.
16. See Piven and Cloward, *Poor People's Movements*.
17. See Michael Lipsky, *Protest in City Politics*, Chicago: Rand McNally, 1970.
18. See Alford, *Health Care Politics*.
19. We have followed very closely the excellent analysis of the Watergate crisis in San Francisco Bay Area Kapitalistate Group, "Watergate or the 18th Brumaire of Richard Nixon," *Kapitalistate*, no. 3, Spring 1975.
20. O'Connor, *Fiscal Crisis*, pp. 51-58.

21. See the analysis of the "state of emergency" of the bourgeoisie in Nicos Poulantzas, *Fascism and Dictatorship*, London: New Left Books, 1974.
22. See Arthur M. Schlesinger, Jr., *The Imperial Presidency*, Boston: Houghton Mifflin, 1973.
23. See William K. Tabb, "The Real Ford Strategy," *The Nation*, March 22, 1975.
24. *New York Times*, July 25, 1975. ©1975 by The New York Times Company. Reprinted by permission.
25. William Tabb, "We are All Socialists Now: Corporate Planning in America," *Social Policy*, forthcoming.
26. Chicago Council on Foreign Relations, *U.S. Foreign Policy and American Public Opinion*, Chicago, June 1975.
27. United States military aid to other countries has become a major outlet for the military-industrial complex. From 1950 to 1974, $53.5 billion was spent *officially* in direct military aid. Of the money spent on weaponry, South Vietnam received 28.4 percent or $15.2 billion. Other recipients of more than $1 billion, according to a list declassified by the Defense Department, are Laos, with $4.61 billion; France, $4.15 billion; South Korea, $3.67 billion; Turkey, $3.21 billion; Taiwan, $2.64 billion; Italy, $2.29 billion; Greece, $1.59 billion; Belgium, $1.24 billion; the Netherlands, $1.22 billion; Thailand, $1.16 billion; Cambodia, $1.14 billion; and Britain, $1.03 billion. Information concerning Iran, Israel, Jordan, Kuwait, Lebanon, and Saudi Arabia is "classfied." Actually, Iran, Israel, and Saudi Arabia were the main recipients of American military supplies in the late seventies.
28. *New York Times*, Aug. 5, 1975. ©1975 by The New York Times Company. Reprinted by permission.
29. Quoted by Eileen Shanahan, "The Mystery of the Great Calm of the Un-employed," *New York Times*, Aug. 3, 1975. ©1975 by The New York Times Company. Reprinted by permission.
30. Data from several reports by Manny Topol and Ernest Volkman on inner-city gangs in the United States published in *The Nation*, July 1975.

NOTES TO CONCLUSION

1. James Petras, "Le Mythe du declin américain," *Le Monde diplomatique*, Feb. 1976.
2. Various works by Jacques Attali have shown the possible relationship between the new development of collective services and an increase of social productivity; see *La parole et l'outil*, Paris: Presses Universitaires de France, 1975.

INDEX

■■■

Library of Congress Cataloging in Publication Data

Castells, Manuel.
  The economic crisis and American society.

  Includes bibliographical references and index.
    1.   United States—Economic conditions—1971-
2.   United States—Social conditions—1960-
3.   Economic history—1945-   I.   Title.
HC106.7.C3613   330.9′73′092   79-3194
ISBN 0-691-04220-9
ISBN 0-691-00361-0 Pbk.